A Bearer of Tradition

A Bearer of Tradition

Dwight Stump, Basketmaker

By Rosemary O. Joyce

FOREWORD BY ARCHIE GREEN

The University of Georgia Press   Athens and London

© 1989 by the University of Georgia Press
Athens, Georgia 30602

Designed by Kathi L. Dailey
Set in Mergenthaler Century Schoolbook and Cheltenham
Typeset by The Composing Room of Michigan, Inc.
Printed and bound by Thomson-Shore, Inc.
The paper in this book meets the guidelines for
permanence and durability of the Committee on
Production Guidelines for Book Longevity of the Council
on Library Resources.

Printed in the United States of America

93 92 91 90 89   5 4 3 2 1

Library of Congress Cataloging in Publication Data

Stump, Dwight, 1900–
  A bearer of tradition.

  Bibliography: p.
  Includes index.
   1. Stump, Dwight, 1900–   —Interviews.
  2. Basketmakers—Ohio—Hocking County—Interviews.
  3. Basket making—Ohio—Hocking County. 4. Hocking
  County (Ohio)—Biography.
  I. Joyce, Rosemary O. II. Title.
  TT879.B3S787   1989   746.41′2′0924 [B] 88-29644
  ISBN 0-8203-1148-0 (alk. paper)

British Library Cataloging in Publication Data available

Contents

For Dwight Stump

craftsman, gentleman, and friend

And for all the traditional artists
who offer us their skill, their knowledge, and their history
in the gifts of love they shape

Foreword

For many decades, Dwight Stump of Toad Hollow toiled as a farm hand, timber cutter, field tiler, well digger, and carpenter. Like many of his fellow rural dwellers, he also once worked in a factory. Had his energies been confined to field and factory alone, Dwight would have been remembered in the Ohio Hocking Hills as a hard worker—conscientious, careful, quiet. His proudest claim, "I never had to hunt for a job," might well have served as his motto. Yet it is the craft of basketry, not a job in carpentry or paper production, that marks his life. Dwight took great pleasure in making baskets, and he continued this work long after he had given up his other trades.

For most of his life Dwight sold baskets (for prices far too modest) to neighbors. But in the mid-seventies an "urban woman" named Rosemary Joyce—a trained folklorist from Ohio State University—became his neighbor and inadvertently enlarged the market for his baskets. Recognizing the quality and rareness of his work, Rosemary placed a few of Dwight's baskets in private collections and public museums, and eventually she wrote a book about Dwight's life and craft. Through her work, Dwight Stump will be known for decades, wherever Americans ponder the meaning of the term *craft* in modern society.

In our demarcation of village from metropolis, marginal society from mainstream society, and folk art from fine art, we have conveniently ascribed anonymity to villager, handcraftsman, and folk artist. Clearly, the publication of a university-press book about Dwight Stump will help to lift him from obscurity. Rosemary Joyce's book plays many roles, not the least of which is introducing a particular basketweaver to curators, archivists, public-sector folklorists, and a host of other interpreters of vernacular culture.

Several years ago I had the good fortune to visit the Joyce farm in Hocking County, where Rosemary and her husband, John, walked with me into a deeply shaded dell. Climbing out of the glen to an open hilltop, the Joyces pointed to a distant wood: "That's where

Dwight cuts white-oak saplings." In retrospect, I should have hiked over to the basketmaker's woods or even farther, to his Toad Hollow workshop. Like other folklorists, I have at times been close to master artists without pausing to observe their skills or absorb their wisdom.

At a personal level, I welcome the present opportunity to add a few words to Dwight and Rosemary's book. In a sense, the book has given me a second chance to walk to Dwight's workshop and test my experience against his. I speak for those readers who will know him only through the printed page. This book will not only keep Stump's name fresh, but it will add to the body of texts, ethnographic or conceptual, that note the continuing importance of craft in our age of space satellite and computer terminal.

But Dwight's basketmaking is prior to and independent of any text, academic or popular. His craft did not flow from an ethnographer's findings, nor did it depend upon author, editor, commentator, or revivalist. The man from whom Stump, as a youth, learned techniques and norms (by observation and imitation) made and sold his baskets without consciousness of "craft revival," as event or cause. The movement we label "the craft revival" caught up with Dwight Stump in the 1970s. Dwight, born in 1900, plied his craft long enough to be "discovered" by a sensitive scholar, and to be invited to "perform" at the Library of Congress.

Rosemary Joyce served happily as a mediator between Dwight Stump's community and large society, between folk skill and academic analysis. At public events, she has championed him with the same high spirit that informs this book. In the best manner of our formal discipline, she has maintained a sense of responsibility to Dwight while keeping in mind three critical paradigms: contextual framing, cultural relativism, and the place that folk expression holds in the polity.

Joyce has not penned a polemical treatise. By quietly focusing on an "ordinary" worker and his artistry, she has avoided the shrill language of debate. However, readers attracted to object and process are free to pose their own questions: Why do we need biographies of folk artists? Does a single type of basketry merit a university-press book? Beyond Dwight Stump's lifetime, will we continue to cherish his and similar oak baskets? Do *all* Americans wish to store *all* goods in plastic containers? This last question must, of course, be understood both literally and symbolically.

Even in this plastic era, many citizens use handmade objects constantly. An oak basket still holds eggs, or magazines, or yarn. This same basket, on display on the Washington Mall or in a local museum, holds instead a narrative voice. When we see a Stump basket in a glass case, we hear it yarning: telling a tale of pioneers, a story of homespun, a chronicle of paths taken, a homily on present-day values.

Dwight Stump is, above all, a craftsman—a very old word that we today casually apply to modern building-trades or metal-trades workers, contemporary urban hobbyists, and fine artists beyond the bounds of conventional art. Willingly or not, Stump shares the title of craftsman with labor-union hardhats on Manhattan skyscrapers, senior citizens making styrofoam chicks at leisure classes, and avant-garde artists sculpting abstractions with acetylene torches. Dwight's baskets are intrinsically neither inferior nor superior to high-rise sheath, styrofoam toy, or abstract assemblage. The word *craft* flows from scene to scene, covers a complex of forms, rolls from antiquity to modernity. The tag stretches widely precisely because it remains durable, time-tested, eclectic. In short, *craft* is as useful and attractive as a Stump basket.

I close these introductory remarks with one of Dwight Stump's vernacular coinages, "Ordenas color." When he was a little boy, his grandmother encouraged him "to look for Indian arraheads," by following the plow in cornfields reclaimed from Ohio forests. When he was old enough to plow, Dwight began to explore nearby caves for other artifacts. In time, Dwight began to sell his finds to archaeologists, who not only gave him a few coins in exchange but also added to his knowledge. He began to see flint arrowheads and skeletal remains as more than clues to the past: a field or cave finding became a building block in Dwight's enlarged cosmos.

From a university scientist Dwight learned about the cave-dwelling Adenas, who lived in Ohio well "before the Indians." Fascinated by this glimpse into time, Dwight described his own baskets, when they aged and darkened, as "Ordenas color." Social scientists and campus humanists are not the only beings who conceptualize prehistory or fashion neologisms. Practicing the ancient craft of basketry, Stump turned archaeological nomenclature into a key marking continuity in his own handiwork. Magically, Dwight's baskets became older and finer than anything else he had built in formal employment.

To touch antiquity's cloak, to respect the historical record, to weld beauty to utility, to teach skills at the Library of Congress, to fill a book with folk wisdom, to see "Ordenas color"—these are Dwight

Stump's measure. We thank Rosemary Joyce for sensitivity and patience in telling his story, and in bringing his baskets into our parlors and offices.

We can use this book variously to learn how a basket is made, or to extract meaning from the basket's message. We can also use it to bring fresh appreciation to countless craft workers who have practiced traditional skills and treasured native beliefs as they have cut timber or plowed fields—altering the national landscape, amplifying the American voice. We praise Rosemary Joyce and Dwight Stump, together, for adding another welcome metaphor to our working vocabularies, to our daily lives.

Archie Green

Acknowledgments

One wishes there were far more than a few lines in which to pay the debts incurred in writing a book. For me, such a small space must convey enormous feelings of appreciation, joy, and love for the tutelage and encouragement that flowed into this book and made it a reality.

My first acknowledgment is, of course, to Dwight Stump, for his kind, patient collaboration. Knowing him has been an enriching part of my life, and I trust the book itself will constitute my sincerest form of thanks.

Professor Archie Green's contribution as author of the Foreword is visible. Less obvious, but even more valuable, have been his years of encouragement and educating—he was my first folklore professor—in the finest sense of the word. No matter how many times my resolve flagged, he was there gently to demand persistence and perseverance and scholarship.

Professor Dan Barnes of the Ohio State University, scholarly tutor and fine friend, has helped me with several quandaries on this particular book. Anything I have written or will write bears testimony to his strong guidance and brilliant teaching, so that his influence on my work will always be of major importance.

Professor Pat Mullen of the Ohio State University, another of my fine teachers, was the first to encourage me to work with Dwight those many years ago. He has continued to support my efforts ever since, reading successive papers and then the manuscript of this book, offering excellent ideas, constructive criticism and bibliographic suggestions.

Professor Claire Farrer, California State University, Chico, has long been one of my most valued teachers and friends, my mentor in more areas than I could possibly list; she also gave me entirely new ways of looking at the potential for study with Dwight.

Malcolm Call of the University of Georgia Press made this book possible by his interest, trust, and hard work, as did Debra Winter with her excellent managing of the project. Kathi Dailey designed the book and artistically incorporated the large portfolio of photographs. And Ellen Harris, the skillfull, sensitive editor of the manuscript, became a friend long-distance, much admired for her firm but thoughtful guidance. Together they have honored me by this association with the University of Georgia Press.

Ann Joyce, beloved friend and daughter, contributed the clear basketweaving drawings in figures 1 and 2, and made her usual concise, knowledgeable suggestions after reading the manuscript. Michael Houghton taught me to see a new world through the lens of the camera, and also painstakingly and beautifully printed my photographs with professional skill.

Several of Dwight's children, Mary, Gladys, Bobby, and Harold; his former son-in-law, Bob Mansberger; and his grandsons Jeff and James and Tommy were all extremely helpful during the years of research. The members of his family are devoted to Dwight, and were always supportive of my efforts, always patient about being interviewed, explaining some facet of their lives, or searching for photographs or clippings or books or herb trays.

My sincerest thanks to my assistant, Cerena Miele, who guided me through the complexities of word processing and database retrieval systems and volunteered her own time to work on the difficulties of the National Survey of Traditional Basketmakers; to Marcia Preston, who kept my household in Hocking County together so I could write, then offered excellent suggestions upon reading the manuscript; to Mary Zeisler, friend and neighbor in Hocking County, who continues to broaden my own understanding of and feeling for this land, these people; to Anne Castle, who spurred me on to completing this volume, then read the manuscript carefully and offered different kinds of insights; to Cynthia Peck, whose editorial abilities added immeasurably to the book's total organization; to Michael Rosen, my collaborator on another work, for his precise, perceptive suggestions for the manuscript; to Cindy Taylor and Rachel Nash Law, for educating me in areas of basketry and basketmaking that were new to me, and for sharing important information from their own exhaustive research on white-oak basketry; to Judy Kahrl, for expert technical advice on many areas of the complex field of photography; to Liz Harzoff, folklife in education coordinator for the Ohio Arts Council, for generously lending me her xeroxed material on basketmakers in the Mammoth Cave area of Kentucky (from a class with Lynwood Montell at Western Kentucky

University); to Tim Lloyd, traditional and ethnic arts coordinator for the Ohio Arts Council, for sharing comments on his long association with Dwight and relevant ideas from his book with Pat Mullen; to Amy Shuman for offering invaluable bibliographic help; to Ted Kessel at the Center of Science and Industry and Douglas White and Ellice Ronsheim at the Ohio Historical Society, for giving me their expertise and an opportunity to study and photograph their respective basket collections.

My thanks also for the specialized kinds of information from Dr. Martha Otto, curator of the Ohio Historical Society, on Indian artifacts; Don Hutslar, curator of the Ohio Historical Society, on nineteenth-century archival and bibliographic sources; Professor Emmanuel Rudolph, the Ohio State University, on botany; Fred Ruland, Ohio State University statistician, on analyzing survey results; Martha Clutter and Tim Gathers, pupils of Dwight's, on basketmaking; artists Nancy Crow and Dorothy Barnes, on their personal knowledge of Dwight and other basketmakers; Judy Lanning and the Logan Historical Society, on old basketmakers in the area.

My heartfelt thanks go to those who gave so much of their time and energy answering my earnest plea for information for the survey of traditional basketmakers (Appendix A). Several called long-distance to philosophize and sympathize and edify, or sent long letters and books and clippings in a heartwarming display of generosity: very special appreciation, first to Roby Cogswell, Tennessee (whose support for a stranger defied description), as well as to Lynn Martin, Hawaii; Dan Overly, Mississippi; Nancy Perdue, Virginia; Suzi Jones, Alaska; Betty Belanus, Indiana. Thanks also to Robert Teske and Bess Hawes, whose encouragement—and whose willingness to supply the addresses of the state folklorists from the National Endowment for the Arts—made the survey possible, and to the other contributors, whose names are listed with their reports in Appendix A.

I am indebted also to the many scholarly teachers and colleagues whose work preceded and informed mine. Many of them are recognized later by being cited in a note or bibliographic entry, but several deserve special mention for their years of supportive friendship and professorial help: Erika Bourguignon and John Vlach, as well as Raye Virginia Allen, Richard Bauman, Robert Bremner, Peggy Bulger, Ricky Clark, Kurt Dewhurst, Susan Dwyer-Shick, Henry Glassie, Gay Hadley, Alan Jabbour, Gerri Johnson, Michael Owen Jones, Yvonne Lange, Marsha MacDowell, Eugene Metcalf, Judy

McCulloh, Yvonne Milspaw, Patricia Moots, Ellen Stekert, Beverly Stoeltje, Bob Teske, Madeleine Trichel.

I am most appreciative of my sister, Suzanne Furlong, who gave her usual full measure of support to yet another of my projects; of Lennie and Bill Copeland for their continuing encouragement and generosity; of Mim Chenfeld, teacher, writer, and performer, who inspires and instructs simply by being; of Larrilyn Edwards, who is a stalwart helper by believing in me privately and publicly; of the many people in Hocking County—amorphous a descriptive title as that is—who have helped me in numerous ways, with information, with physical help, by sharing their homes and their country, by just being themselves.

My children, Jay, Ann, Lucy, and Mary, are always founts of love and friendship and succor, sustaining me in any way I'd want (and in ways I don't even think to ask for). They make me inordinately proud to have been their mother, to be their friend.

Most important of all—hoping that the "last but certainly not least" category mirrors that importance—my deepest thanks to my husband, John Joyce, who gave me incredible support in my work with Dwight (and heaven knows with how many others), accompanying me on interviews to pick up information I might miss (such as how to cold-punch metal dies), tramping the woods to find more oak for Dwight, saving him used baler twine, combing botany books to find correct Latin names for the plants Dwight uses, explaining technicalities such as the properties of forged metal, dropping off and picking up contact sheets (even though he hates such errands), picking up tons of pizza or Chinese or Stouffers, and, finally, reading and making valuable comments on the manuscript itself.

Introduction: Of Springtime and Values

Today I visit my friend Dwight Stump again. But before descending into Toad Hollow, I inhale the glory of this magic season, when even the ugly patches of lumberers' scars are softened by smoky haze and dogwood blossoms. The panorama of wildflowers and warblers and the profusion of beauty is instant renewal for me, a respite from proverbial city cares. Entering the woods, I find dozens of miniature greens pushing through the brown leaf floor, exuding a moldy perfume. In my euphoria, the hemlocks seem a darker hue than ever before, especially juxtaposed with the unfolding chartreuse of delicate fiddlehead ferns.

But as I trace my way farther downward toward Dwight's workshop, I am plagued again by familiar, unsettling questions: Is it this same beauty—the sights and sounds and smells of this place—that also draws Dwight here? Or, rather, do I impose my own values on him, seeking the comfort of a common denominator in the human experience? Is the sustenance Dwight gains from these hills purely economic, not at all matching my personal aesthetic? And his work: Is it, after all, necessitated only by material want? Or does it answer deeper cravings for him than merely the satisfaction of hunger pangs and the need for shelter?

No matter how many seasons pass, my questions are never definitively answered. As a folklorist and an oral historian I have questioned Dwight repeatedly, trying to come to some understanding of his craft, his choices, his life. Yet he speaks a language to which, since I am not a native, I am never completely privy.[1] As an urban woman I must realize that my culture and language will always be different from his, as will many of my reasons for returning again and again to these hills.

Nonetheless, my goal in studying these cultural and language differences is, first, to gain an awareness and an understanding of the thinking and learning of others, and then, through various media for varied audiences, to share the knowledge gained. Without such studying and sharing of cultures, most of us will continue to assume we are on the same life journey, nodding affably across the highway divider strip but actually gathering speed as we race headlong toward quite different destinations.

Numerous books treat the subject of basketry, but most of them deal with technique; maintenance; baskets of particular cultures, historical periods, and geographic areas; or basketry as a contemporary craft. Few, if any, have featured an aspect of prime importance: the individual maker of those baskets, the person who marries material with process and achieves the basket.[2] Therefore, when I first began my own research pilgrimage in preparation for this book, I planned to describe the single craft of basketmaking, while featuring Dwight Stump as a basketmaker.

But during these years of interviews, research, and introspection, the book has moved in a different direction. Like a novel, it has "taken on a life of its own." Dwight's basketmaking remains the important element, but it has become only the frame around which his whole life story is woven. The book has become instead what I think of as a folk biography, one narrated in Dwight's own words and one mirroring a life of work: hard, difficult, physical, menial. It has evolved, in fact, into a paean to the labor that is the *raison d'être* of one man's long and satisfying existence.

The book is not a history of basketmaking. Actually, part of the original manuscript had included just such a section, detailing the origins, the developments, and the status of the craft of basketmaking. Subsequently it became clear that the tail was in danger of wagging the dog, and the history chapters were dropped (albeit not without much gnashing of teeth on my part). Nonetheless, Appendixes A and B provide summary material.

Neither is the book a historic-geographic or a sociocultural study of the area. It does not incorporate a social-scientific profile of Dwight's and his family's backgrounds, their economic and educational status, their dependence on or independence of government support, their inner family workings or closet skeletons. Nor is it a survivalist treatise. If the craft is in danger of being lost, the book will provide important historical materials. If there is no such danger, better yet for the health of the tradition.

Instead, the book focuses on Dwight's crafts, their processes, and his aesthetics, exploring his evolving traditional process and at the same time documenting the nearly vanished craft of round-rod basketmaking. The book also speaks eloquently of the potential value of continued work—broadly defined—to forestall the problems endemic to aging. But, most important, it contributes to the corpus of common-person biography through Dwight's own narrative of his life as a hardworking man.

While the book draws upon scholarly research, it is nonetheless meant for academic and general reader alike, for specialists in or students of folklore, anthropology, history, sociology, American studies, art, art history, or aging, but also for those interested simply in reading about basketry, about folk art, or about another human being in a different time or place, one who has approached life in another way. Background information is included for other researchers, but notes are kept to a minimum and do not present more than the citations, except when the text interferes with Dwight's own narrative flow.

Analytical Approach

Building upon my own belief in the value of the individual, the book's primary purpose is to answer some of the great need for common-person biography—thus its format. Our literature, indeed literature in general, has always concentrated on "famous man, significant event" life-recording.[3] Except for the fortuitous publishing of a relatively small number of diaries and journals, we have little information on our forebears, recent or ancient, unless they were men—and famous men at that, usually heads of state or armies.

We need then a larger body of the life histories of common persons, that is, the *un*famous rich or poor, old or young, male or female, and the "insignificant" events of their lives. We also need new paradigms by which to assess those texts,[4] models based on broader definitions of rightness and goodness and wealth. For common-person biography seeks the universal humanness beneath the skin of cultural differences, the need for both education and wisdom, the value of both material and spiritual riches.

Presented in that specific biographical format, the book is grounded in several aspects of theoretical analysis, a body of research (a) described contextually, (b) based on the principle of cultural relativism, and (c) acknowledging the political significance of defining culture and culture's manifestations—the particular one here, traditional art. I use the term *culture* to include the full range of attitudes, beliefs, practices, customs, and lifeways of a group. Although the book is based on these theories, it is not a battleground for their explication or defense, since that has already been brilliantly accomplished elsewhere.

I believe that folklore texts—the biography here—should set a specific life or event in its own time and space, that is, describe it *contextually*. Accordingly, I elaborate on the historical, social, and cultural contexts of Dwight Stump's narrative, indicating the many ways in which they influence his personal context.[5] Those contexts will dramatically influence the life of every person, ultimately imposing many of the differences found from culture to culture, individual to individual.

Cultural relativism refers to the practice of interpreting others' behaviors and beliefs only in terms of their own ethical standards,[6] all of which have derived from a specific context. All persons—all cultures—are different, in large part because of their differing contexts. But they are only that: different. The difference implies neither superiority nor inferiority. Dwight Stump's life, influenced by his particular set of contexts, has importance in and of itself, as does every individual's. His art, similarly influenced by and a product of that set of contexts, has importance because of its creativity, even though his artifacts may not be found in the galleries of the elite.

The *political significance* of cultural studies and the politics of culture may seem to have little to do with Dwight Stump, or even with folk art in Appalachian Ohio. But political values and subsequent actions obtain in all the manifestations of a culture, for example, in language, foodways, costume, architecture, art;[7] judging, dealing in, and collecting folk art are all politically influenced actions. In fact, simply defining art can become a political matter, for a people said to be without "art" reputedly show themselves lacking in the qualities that dignify human experience.[8]

I use the term *folk art* here to mean an expression of community norms, a visual depiction of a tradition within family or community groups; since it is handed down by word of mouth or by example, folk art is not idiosyncratic. While individual expression can and does exist within those communal forms, it is informed and extended by the underlying influences of tradition. Such emphasis on community does not preclude my personal recognition and admiration of any other forms or levels of art and craft, be they academic, contemporary, or revival. However, in this particular book I am dealing with only folk, that is, *traditional,* art.

The term *folk art* often connotes reference to a medium that is "unsophisticated," "naïve," or "charming," to employ favorite euphemisms of art criticism. This use of the term intimates, first, that such art should be judged differently from elite art, since it originates at a "lower" level of culture—a stance I completely reject. Second, it often covertly implies an intent to pay artists much less than the value of their works. As folk art becomes "collectible," and the going market rate for select pieces rises accordingly, some sophisticated buyers or brokers take advantage of the naïveté of local traditional artist-suppliers. This may sound exaggerated. But folklorists working in the field report increasingly disturbing evidence of such practices. Some are only distasteful, others actually border on theft—stealing both product and recognition from the artist.[9]

This is not a polemical book. Dwight himself is philosophical about his negative experiences, which fortunately have been few. Still, as we shall see, the whole subject of pricing and marketing is one which ultimately affects folk-art process and production, sometimes in very negative ways.[10] Dwight's story underscores a need to alert folk-art enthusiasts to the dark side of the seemingly benign production of functional and beautiful traditional objects. Buyers and sellers alike must recognize that the exchange of a quilt or a basket or a music performance involves as well "an artist's history, identity, and human worth."[11]

Background of the Research

I subscribe to recent academic opinion regarding reference within a book to its own author: first, that the pronoun *I*—along with the researcher's personal opinions—should be used overtly, underscoring the importance of showing the biographer as the other person in a biography, one who necessarily filters the life of the subject through his or her own screen; and second, that the stance of "detachment and objectivity" has very limited practicality, since it so often obscures necessary information about the researcher.[12]

Interviewing and editing are the principal tools of the trade in the complex pursuit of biographical information, but since I have detailed the methods used in that pursuit elsewhere, I will only encapsulate them here.[13]

My interviews with Dwight continued from 1977 through 1985, as my interest increased in him as a bearer of tradition and the practitioner of a nearly lost art.[14] Except for a few trips to look at his biographical landmarks, all our interviews took place in his shop, while Dwight worked on a basket or a rug or, occasionally, a cane.

His hands were almost never still, and it was soon apparent that his thoughts flowed most freely when he was working. Usually there were just the two of us, though several times either my husband accompanied me or Dwight's son or a customer dropped in for a short time.

The interviews were primarily informal and unstructured. I am most comfortable with the "blank screen" posture of a nondirected interview, since the results are far more autobiographical in content, and tend to elicit what the consultant—not the researcher—thinks is most important. Formality was imposed only by use of the tape recorder for most of our discussions, and structure by the list of questions I had accumulated since our last session.

I believe, along with many researchers, that tape recording is the only way I can know—not *think* I know—what has actually been said to me. I can also return, aurally, to the "scene of the investigation" to recheck voice inflections and, consequently, meanings. Further, it releases me from the tyranny of that most unreliable of assistants: memory.

The basketmaking process itself was quite difficult for me to document in detail. Finally, in a moment of frustration and desperation, I grasped the three protruding splints in a half-finished basket and attempted to duplicate Dwight's weaving on the near-top edge. How upset I was not to have remembered sooner the byword of teaching days: "We learn by doing"! But then (I comfort myself), had I learned more quickly this would have been a book on basketmaking only. Had I been a fast learner rather than a ridiculously slow one, I would not have garnered Dwight's hours of serendipitous biographical comment.

Often, in addition to tape recording Dwight, I photographed him as well, building a full set of color slides and black-and-white prints: of him, his geographical and physical environments, his products, and the steps in each of his traditional crafts or occupations. To illustrate all facets of the book, I searched, with little success, for old photographs of Dwight and his family (his daughter Gladys had a few, but they were too dark for reprinting), for the houses he had lived in (they were no longer standing), the places he'd worked (they too were gone). It was a striking illustration of how ephemeral the lives of most of us are.

Cooperative as Dwight always was—for example, about my using the tape recorder, about my continued and continuous questions, about demonstrating any part of a process over and over, about holding an awkward pose while I laboriously focused—he could not be considered loquacious. In fact, he is a very taciturn man, talking at any length only when drawn out. Neither rich autobiographical nor any other kind of detail poured forth at the click of the recorder's "on" button. It took many hours, days, years of interviewing to glean the answers to a laundry list of questions, or to get Dwight comfortable and in a mood for recollecting new material. I asked him to jot down notes or "key words" of anything he remembered between our visits, such as the names of some of the old basketmakers, but he never did. Reconstructing a chronology of life events was problematic: "several years ago" ranged anywhere from 1920 to 1980. The more interviews we accumulated, the more time was needed for transcribing.[15] Fortunately, I was able during that particular period of my life to continue our visits over many years.

As with all extended interviewing schedules, there were the goods and the bads, the fun times and the not-so. Dwight has no telephone, so any careful scheduling I did from Columbus was for naught if Dwight had happened to leave home for his own set of appointments. The visits were not in any way social. They were strictly professional work. There was no fresh pie and coffee served in an immaculate house, as was often the case in my years of interviewing others. In fact, until a day in 1986 when I visited Dwight because he was ill, I had never been invited into his house. All our sessions took place instead in his cluttered, excessively hot—in both summer and winter—shop, complete with tobacco-encrusted spittoon, buzzing flies, threatening wasps, and smells of ancient dirt and stale perspiration. (True, the ideal of cultural relativism is difficult to sustain in the reality of everyday experience, the clash of habits and attitudes and aesthetics between an "objective" fieldworker and his or her consultant.)[16]

The editing of the voluminous transcriptions of the tapes posed two major problems: first, the method of collating, and second, the handling of the dialect. Controversy about methods and rationale has always attended the presentation of oral historical materials, of interviews taped and faithfully transcribed into hundreds and hundreds of pages and then edited into a viable form for printing.[17] With Dwight's life story, I have chosen to collate the interviews we shared over a period of nine years, so that portions of one paragraph may have been pulled from several different conversations. This lessens the number of editorial "voice-overs" from me; it illustrates the reliability of his testimonies, since Dwight always tells the *same* story at these differing intervals, even when the tellings are years apart; and it spares the reader deadly repetition.

This construct posed difficult choices for me, since collation creates as well as solves problems. For example, though I describe Dwight as quiet and nontalkative, compressing nine years' interviews creates the impression that Dwight is quite voluble. He is not. And two of my goals—presenting myself as the other person in the life-story process and presenting the whole of Dwight's life in context—were certainly diluted when I omitted my questions or conversational comments during the dialogue chapters.

Further, the chronological coherence, both in the biographical and the craft-process chapters, is misleading. Life stories just do not flow in that kind of detailed, chronological narration. Neither do serial steps of process, such as in basket- and rugmaking, pour forth in sequential order. Almost no one speaks in such careful chronology. I imposed form where no form existed in order to better translate for the reader. This is, then, the cut-and-paste result of interweaving hundreds of pages of my conversations and interviews with Dwight over nine years' time.

Many scholars fiercely oppose such tampering with the natural progression of the spoken word, as I did myself. But after poring over numerous oral histories, querying dozens of avid readers, and engaging in intensive soul-searching, I evolved this particular method for this particular life history. Both aesthetically and academically, *not* overshadowing the important flow of natural speech with editorial intrusion became the most viable method for presenting Dwight's life and his artistic accomplishments.

The second controversial element here is the handling of the dialect. Presenting aural material in visual form introduces numerous problems, especially because the material is already at one remove from the original speech. Further, it loses those important adjuncts of vocal tone, gesture, facial expression, and body language.

Nonetheless, because language is such a vital element of every person's heritage, I have represented Dwight's dialogue in the form of his own native speech patterns, including grammar, syntax, vocabulary, and pronunciation, in as nearly a representative form as possible. (Some of the texts sound inconsistent, because Dwight uses different pronunciations at different times, such as *-ing* endings both with and without the final *g*.) Certain scholars criticize this practice: since we never, their argument goes, quote bank presidents with any kind of provincial accent, we should utilize Etonian English in transcribing everyone's speech.[18]

I consider that argument another example of "melting-pot thinking," which is embodied by a desire to "melt" all ethnic and racial groups into one cohesive sameness. Thus it denigrates the principle of cultural diversity by attempting to obliterate all traditions except the standard: white Anglo-Saxon Protestant. It assumes that only educated middle-class speech is "right and proper." Further, a long history of changing conventions in English writing and spelling ultimately makes following "correct rules" an impossible task.[19]

Any faithful reproduction of linguistic features takes us one step closer to the actual data, and any deviation becomes actually an error. An interesting fact recurs in the history of science: another generation of scholars can have a quite different emphasis, so that exact speech reproduction may be of crucial import for linguistic study later.[20]

The phrases "faithful reproduction" and "exact speech reproduction" signify the optimum goal, however difficult it is to achieve. Yet this technique of duplicating ethnic speech patterns has been and continues to be used by many folklorists. One of them observed that any attempts on his part to "correct" his consultant's ethnic speech patterns would be "pompous and presumptuous." Still others noted that they "intended to retain . . . as much of the language and perspective of the craftsmen as possible; this, with a view toward capturing the spirit of the people, their humor and values, as well as their attitude towards their product, their technology, themselves"; and, later, "a transcription cannot convey the meaning and savor carried by inflection and regional speech styles—important communicative devices."[21]

Granted, in the case of speech it is difficult to represent the vernacular accurately, with exactly the right spellings or misspellings. But that is *not* a good reason not to try. Better to have some inaccuracies in depicting dialogue than to manipulate, for example, Dwight Stump's speech into sounding—ye gods!—like the bank president's.

Here, then, is Dwight's story. The first chapter explains the beginnings of the research and places Dwight in social context. From there, Dwight himself, with as little explication as possible from the biographer, becomes the teller of the tale.

1. Gathering Materials

It is difficult now to remember exactly when and how I met Dwight. In 1969, after years of poring over county maps and classified ads, my husband John and I bought a small farm in southeastern Ohio. That purchase was the culmination of a long-held dream: having a place to stay in the country to extend hiking and camping adventures with our five children. Several years later I entered graduate school at the Ohio State University, as an interdisciplinary student in American folklore. Neighbors in Hocking County, recognizing my professional interest in traditional crafts, introduced me to a local basketmaker, Dwight Stump.

The circumstances of our first meeting blur into a composite memory of my dozens of visits there over the years, trudging from the muddy driveway up a worn grass path and bypassing the small white house where Dwight lived with his wife and youngest son. To the right, the path led past a deep gully—which Dwight had nearly filled over the years with oak shavings from basketmaking—to his weathered log-and-clapboard shop. In winter, smoke floating from the rusty chimney, or in summer an open door, indicated that Dwight was present. And he usually was sitting there unobtrusively and contentedly, often weaving round baskets out of the white-oak withes he had worked into smooth rods. I soon discovered this was the same process he had learned as a teenager from one of the numerous weavers in that community.

Dwight was quiet and courteous, just as he remains today. But because he was exceptionally nontalkative, my only memory of that initial meeting is of being discouraged from hauling recording equipment there for further work. Nonetheless I did pursue the research, because as a student then I was aware of the need to report on such technology. For example, in 1967 Henry Glassie had opened his article on a basketmaker in New York with these words: "When the scholar—whether he be folklorist, culturogeographer, anthropologist, or historian—finally turns to the study of American mate-

Dwight Stump's "Hocking Hills Basket Shop"

rial folk culture, he will find a great abundance of material awaiting him by the roadside, in attics and museums. He will find, however, the few—and daily fewer—who know well how that material came into being. He will also find that the majority of the American reports of folk technology are unfortunately superficial, and that of even superficial ones there are not many."[1]

Dwight's baskets are special for two reasons: first, the process for making round rods is so time-consuming that it has become a nearly lost art (it was reported extinct by a well-known researcher in 1977);[2] second, although a few people have learned how to make round-rod baskets recently, Dwight was one of the last in the country who came directly out of an actual family or community tradition—community in his case. His baskets are simple, with no ornamentation or coloring or carved notchings.[3] Nonetheless, Dwight was an interesting bearer of tradition in his own right.

During the period I first knew him, Dwight was receiving more and more attention from the public; he had been "discovered" after almost seventy years of pursuing his craft. Surprisingly enough, his physical seclusion—far from the main highway with no signs to lead the way—had deterred few buyers. Visitors began streaming to his isolated shop in the mid- to late 1970s, eager to purchase their own piece of Americana.

Many, expecting a well-stocked shop with a range of choices, were disappointed in that quest. They found instead a cluttered workshop and a solemn old man who punctuated monosyllabic answers by relieving himself of a large wad of "chew" into the encrusted pail at his left side. If they were lucky there would be two or three baskets from which to choose, or—if their star was hovering in the exact spot in the heavens—four or five. More often there would be a selection, instead, of rugs braided out of discarded baler twine, or strange-looking canes.

But even though his round-rod baskets were a nearly extinct species by then, few of his customers recognized that uniqueness. Instead, his popularity was, and probably is still, an outgrowth of a larger trend nationally: an explosion of interest in anything "folk," that is, anything which at least seems to reflect our American heritage (pointing up the economic and political significance of defining folk art). Even his neighbors had gained new respect both for Dwight himself and for the utilitarian objects they purchased from

Dwight's white-oak egg baskets, before and after wrapping and handling

Dwight in his workshop

him: market baskets, egg baskets, sewing baskets. Local art groups invited Dwight to join and found him a principal drawing card at their annual shows.

Eager photographers, amateur and professional, snapped hundreds of shots, as Dwight posed with patient aplomb. "I don't know how many have been here. Every few days they's somebody coming and taking pictures. Most go out and don't never come back and bring me one. I've had more pictures taken than anybody in the state of Ohio, pretty near. I tell them, some of the old fellas want them to back off, but I don't care. They like something to look at." Dwight is clearly proud of these outward manifestations of success, happy to display clippings and photographs of himself (a few people are thoughtful enough to send him a copy).

The trek to Toad Hollow continued. Eager reporters discovered Dwight, and articles appeared in the *Logan Daily News,* the *Talespinner,* the *Athens Messenger,* the *Columbus Dispatch,* and the *Columbus Citizen-Journal.* Television crews, not to be outdone, arrived as well. In December 1983, WBNS-TV of Columbus included Dwight in a series on Ohio craftspeople.

He was also invited to teach: the fifth grade at the East Elementary School in Athens, the eighth grade in Laurelville, the campers at Camp Akita, the students at Nelsonville Tri-County Vocational School, the senior citizens at the Hocking Hills Gallery in Logan; and he was included in the Artist-in-the-Schools Program of the Ohio Arts Council. More invitations followed, to demonstrate at Ohio festivals: in Adelphi, Middletown, Worthington, Athens, Portsmouth, Columbus, and at Old Man's Cave State Park. Often I acted as interpreter.

Dwight's work has been included in various folk-arts exhibits, such as the 1980 Ohio State Fair. He was featured in an exhibit of my black-and-white photographs at the Cultural Arts Center in Columbus in 1983. In addition, his baskets are in the collections at the Museum of American Folk Art in New York City and the Museum of International Folk Art in Santa Fe.[4]

On a hot August afternoon in 1985, the governor of Ohio dropped in to buy a basket. Dwight reported it with obvious delight: "I don't know how he knew about me, but he found out some way. He was at a camp somewhere out on the ridge, and he seen one of my grand-

Demonstrating at "Middfest," Middletown, Ohio, October 1982; Dwight's son-in-law Bob Mansberger assisting

**Answering questions
at the "White Oak
Basketry" presentation,
American Folklife
Center, Library of
Congress, April 1982**

sons out there. He asked him if he was any relation to me, and Tommy said, 'Why, that's my grandpaw!' Then he come down here, him and his wife and his mother. He come in the door—I was standing right there—shook hands with me, said, 'I'll bet this is the first time you ever shook hands with the governor.' I looked at him—he was dressed just as common as anybody else, had shorts on—and I started to laugh and said, 'You're just a-kidding me.' But he finally convinced me that's who he was. Got a kick outa me not recognizing him. They took some pictures, bought one of them baskets and a rug and one of Tommy's macramé hangers. We got a letter from him there in the house. My boy, Bobby, said, 'I'll bet Rosemary would like to see that.' I'll go and get it, I never even read it yet."

Soon he proudly displayed it, complete with the seal of the State of Ohio, for my husband John and me: "Dear Dwight: It was a pleasure to meet you and see some of your beautiful basketwork at first hand. I hope we will have a chance to see you in Columbus one of these days. With best regards, Richard F. Celeste, Governor."

But Dwight's finest moment by far was in 1982 when he was invited by the American Folklife Center to demonstrate at the Library of Congress. When I arrived with news of our invitation, he chuckled, "If we go to Washington, I'll be quite a celebrity!" And, laughing heartily, "Funny, making a celebrity out of an old hillbilly—just an old hillbilly, out of the hills!" It was his first trip in an airplane and his first visit to a large city. But he handled the three-day experience with poise and serenity, answering questions during the all-day workshop with equanimity, enjoying every minute of "being a celebrity" to the fullest.

To look at Dwight with more perspective, we must place his life in context: geographical, historical, cultural, and personal. How and why did he begin making baskets? What kind of geographic area supported such a craft? What was its history? Its economic base?

Dwight's home lies at the edge of one of Ohio's most scenic and popular areas, near the western edge of the Appalachian Plateau, with a topographical relief of three hundred to four hundred feet. Known as the Hocking Hills, the region includes six state parks: Cantwell Cliffs, Rock House, Conkle's Hollow, Old Man's Cave, Cedar Falls, and Ash Cave.[5] The rugged beauty of steep-walled gorges, sandstone cliffs, waterfalls plunging from projecting ledges, with rock shelters and caves below, has long added to the fascination of exploring for hikers, environmentalists, and natural scientists. Unfortunately, it also adds to an old man's difficulty in finding the natural materials for his varied traditional pursuits.

The woods in that area are thick, second and third growth now. Maple, oak, walnut, and sycamore abound on the south-facing slopes of the rugged hills and hemlock on the north-facing ones, except for the scarred, barren hillsides at the head of the hollow where a paper company "clear cut," a controversial practice which disfigures the land for years.

The small towns that dot the region are shoved between or perched on hills or—even more likely—planted by a creek or a river in one of the narrow, gentle valleys. The landscape is not really mountainous; still, the topography accounts for double yellow lines on most of the roads, as well as the nickname "foothills of the Appalachians." The whole southeastern region of Ohio is, in fact, an unglaciated part of the Allegheny Plateau, its steep valleys and narrow ridges spliced by meandering streams.

Historically, this geographic heritage has been more curse than

**Woods in Hocking
County, Ohio**

blessing. In earlier days those handsome ridges automatically meant poor communication, and they still mean difficult transportation. Further, the unglaciated soil lacks complexity and richness, so that hardscrabble farms are the rule, not the exception.[6]

In the early years of the nineteenth century, eager settlers organized counties in the southeastern sections of the state first, since the Ohio River on the south and Zanes' Trace in the middle of the state made that area most accessible. Those first settlers, pouring in from Germany, Great Britain, and the older states, especially Pennsylvania and Virginia,[7] had already been primarily farmers before their emigration to Ohio. And most of them continued as farmers, adding part-time jobs for needed cash.

Even though Ohio was admitted to the Union in 1803, it remained essentially a pioneer settlement until well after the War of 1812. As was typical of frontier areas, family was the significant force underlying all social and cultural activities—and it remains so today. Although the pioneers soon founded schools and churches, funds were limited in this spare countryside; forced to be practical, the settlers prized work more than education (for example, in the 1840s the average length of the school term was only three months).[8]

Southeastern Ohio's economic history has not been happy. Entrepreneurs, excited by the discovery of rich deposits there, opened coal mines and iron furnaces, and by mid-century both industries had developed; they expanded still further after the opening of the Hocking branch of the Ohio Canal and several railroad lines. Still, because of the hilly terrain, no good highway system developed, and consequently no towns grew to cities.[9]

By the 1880s the better quality of the Mahoning District iron in the northern part of the state forced southern Ohio's iron production sharply downward. Agricultural output declined as well, and population figures soon increased by only small increments. And, while coal mining did continue, prices were often so low and the industry so plagued by strikes that it was chronically "sick." After 1900 it, too, declined steadily. In circular fashion, lack of industry precluded industrial development, as the gap between city and country widened perceptibly.[10] Possibly because of those worsening economic conditions during that late nineteenth and early twentieth century period, a large—surprisingly large—colony of basketmakers hewed out a marginal living from the poor countryside near Dwight's home.

The fact that there are so few existing sources pertaining to eastern and southeastern Ohio in the twentieth century continues by inference the story of a troubled land, since most of the references are negative ones. Farmers abandoned large areas of hilly land because of erosion and poor cropping systems. Population figures did not climb in the 1930s as they did in the rest of the state, and they actually declined in the 1940s.[11] Fierce competition from agribusiness in more fertile regions, beginning after World War II and accelerating now, pushed farming into the category of part-time work.

In the 1970s Ohio's Appalachian population had a lower median income than did any other Ohioans: twice as many people there were classifed as living below the poverty level. By 1980, however, the gap between Ohio Appalachians and the state as a whole had narrowed. Similarly, the percentage of families with incomes below poverty level was reduced from thirteen to ten. And, although the population had been decreasing steadily for decades, by 1980 a reversal of outmigration had been achieved.[12]

The revived coal industry had not yet resolved problems caused by the poor mining practices of the past when it ran into new problems, stemming from the coal's high sulphur content. And bad cutting practices have damaged a potentially valuable timber resource. Nonetheless, the outstanding natural features, the "blessing" part of the rugged topography—the deep valleys and woods and waterfalls—are being further expanded as recreation attractions; slowly state and private developers are overcoming the obstacles imposed by the topography, and the area is beginning to show the usual aspects of "progress," such as a transportation network.[13]

An entirely different group of people, urbanites, now visit for weekend and leisure-time activities. This brings rural residents into further contact with different customs and viewpoints and lifestyles, and, not incidentally, brings area artists into contact with new customers and viewpoints and aesthetics—as it has done for Dwight.

Today, with farms still going out of production, and most of the remaining ones marginal, farmers continue to expand a pattern begun during World War II: commuting twenty and even fifty miles away to town and city jobs. Men, and now women as well, are so firmly committed to the difficult lifestyle of residing in a beloved rural area that they are willing to drive great distances for income. Another recent group of commuters, an expanding number of exurbanites, live in mobile homes on one- or two-acre plots. Indeed, trailers sprout everywhere; as local children marry, they place them next to their parents' traditional houses, renewing the pattern of an extended family in the same location.

In this social and historical background that colony of early craftsmen made their baskets. One cold evening in 1917, a mild, impressionable teenager intently watched one of those basketmakers weaving in his small general store in Buena Vista. The boy, whose name was Dwight Stump, thus began to learn from an older craftsman how to make the white-oak round-rod baskets for which he later became known.

Eighty-eight years old in 1988, Dwight is a bearer of tradition, tradition pervasive in every aspect of his life: the patterns of daily living; the folk-architectural layout of his three and a half acres; his skills of herb gathering, collecting Indian artifacts, and "water smelling" (dowsing); his expertise in crafting sisal rugs, canes, and—most important—white-oak round-rod baskets. He has produced those baskets since that night in the general store seventy years ago. And he is still hard at work.

An even-featured, handsome, short man of slender build, Dwight has a shock of white hair. Brown-stained teeth and a slightly protruding lower lip signal that omnipresent chew of tobacco tucked in one cheek. A short white stubble often covers his ruddy complexion. His dress is much the same summer and winter: loose-fitting twill trousers; a tee shirt and a long-sleeved patterned shirt, flannel or wool for very cold weather; heavy boots; and almost always—inside or outside, rain or shine—a hat or billed cap.

Even though Dwight is not a talkative man, he will converse when directly questioned, especially about his favorite topic, his work. Most of the rest of his unfolding biography has been the result of plain hard work on both our parts. When not working or when posing for a photograph, he sits or stands with arms locked awkwardly across his chest.

During all the years of our acquaintance, Dwight has been ever the gentleman, literally a gentle man, smiling a happy welcome when I arrive, expected or not. He is always anxious to please, always patient. No question—or more appropriately, no series of repetitive questions—seems to be bothersome or silly to him. He has taken all phases of our work together seriously and considers each of my queries carefully, pondering several seconds, or sometimes minutes, before answering. I used to worry: "Did he hear me?"

**Dwight as interview
subject**

"Does that seem so silly it doesn't merit response?" Finally I realized how involved he actually was with our joint venture.

Dwight speaks slowly, very slowly, thinking long and carefully
before replying to questions. His conversational modes are to me
quite interesting, especially his stylistic device of using direct
quotes from the past. It's as if he owned a marvelous trunk of lively
memories, one which he can painstakingly unpack and enjoy at any
time. His recollections have a joyful immediacy for him, a reality
which he succeeds in communicating to me as well. He obviously
enjoys the company and the attention, too: "See, we're a-sitting here
a-talking and weaving and going right up" (the sides of a basket).
His good humor held even through all my constant lens switching or
film changing or calling on him to "Hold!" some yet unrecorded part
of a process. If I arrived late for a planned meeting, he was never put
out or upset. In fact, I have never seen him openly agitated or angry.

Dwight was "born and raised," as the local people would say, in
Hocking County. His attachment to the rural environment has obviously been a major influence, affecting where he lived, where and
with what he worked. Although he has moved and changed jobs
many times in his life, he has with one exception chosen rural home-

sites, and—except for his stints of working in Alabama—he has always lived in Hocking County. All of his jobs, with the one exception of factory worker, have involved working either on the land itself or with organic materials.

While Dwight is more than content in his rural surroundings, he still retains a lively interest in the outside world, kept up mainly through the family "grapevine," customers, and watching the evening news on television (he loves to tease my stockbroker husband about the market's ups and downs). And his grapevine is an efficient one: on many of my visits there, he has—to my surprise and his delight—informed me of my own recent whereabouts.

Although Dwight has relatively few memories of his youth, he has still recalled more than many of us can. However little he remembers about those early days, it does become obvious that the effects of being poor bound the family's spare existence. Less obviously— one must read between these lines—emotional deprivation laced young Dwight's personal existence, because of the paucity of affectionate guidance and response in his family and his culture.

One wonders what indeed might have been for Dwight, obviously intelligent and inventive, had he been able to receive the education he so earnestly desired. Unable to continue his schooling, Dwight began working at age fifteen, for the work ethic was (and is) strong both in Dwight's family and in Hocking County. Dwight was taught to work, and work hard. And so he did—and always has—at an astounding variety of jobs in addition to farming: as a carpenter, timber cutter, sawmiller, candy vendor, cook and waiter, layer of field tile, well-digger, dog trainer, road worker, store manager, bookkeeper, constable, Sunday school superintendent, factory worker, and plumber. And, of course, there are all of his part-time traditional arts and occupations.

He has always taken pride, not only in the quality of his work, but also in the fact that he "never had to hunt for a job." He has always been able to provide for his family, however modestly. And that was no small task, for in 1922 he married his childhood sweetheart, Maisie Pinkstalk, and they had nine children: Junior, Gladys, Mary, Homer, Dolly, Harold, Opal, Robert, and Grace (who died when ten hours old).

I have never been able to ascertain how many grandchildren and great-grandchildren there are; my best approximation is fifteen grandchildren and fifteen great-grandchildren. Dwight never talked about his family, and for a while I assumed he was quite distanced from them, physically or emotionally, or both. But as I interviewed Mary and Gladys and Harold, a totally different picture emerged, one of Dwight as a dedicated family man, devoted to his wife and his children. Evidently he is simply a very private person, and I had no justifiable reason to invade that privacy.

In 1970 Dwight "retired" to his youngest son's three and a half acres in remote Toad Hollow. He and Bobby built a house, then a workshop, and later a garage, all out of reclaimed building materials. Large trees dwarf the house, which looks west toward a tangled field across the gravel road below; the shop sits behind the house in a clearing, an unmowed field to the north. Woods begin at the back end of the property, where they shade a trailer, a doghouse, and a hound dog.

Despite progressively declining health, Dwight has continued to work full-time on gathering herbs and making braided sisal rugs, canes from odd-shaped vines and tree trunks, and, of course, baskets.

But this is, after all, Dwight's story. And he will tell it.

2. Growing Up

Pupils and teacher at
the Hemphill School,
6 November 1912;
Dwight standing behind
girl with big white bow
in her hair

My great-grandparents on my father's side, the Stumps, came from somewhere in Pennsylvaney—where I don't know. One of my boys, Harold, sent for a book—do you remember here a few years ago you could write and get the history of differnt ones? It told in there where they derived, where they come from originally, but I don't know what country that was any more. They settled for a while in Pennsylvaney—they was Pennsylvaney Dutch—and then they scattered out. That was way back in the early 1800s. It was 18-and-12 one of them came back here to Ohio, then some more of them came afterwards.

My father's parents, Joseph and Mary Stump (her name was Lindsay), lived down toward Laurelville in Perry Township, there in Laurel Valley where Moccasin Creek crosses 180. There's a lane turns off to the left, goes back down in there and goes across Laurel. Just one house standin' back there.

Grandfather was a thrasherman. He had a farm, but he operated a thrashin' [threshing] machine. All that generation of Stumps was all some kind of a mechanic—engineers, sawmillers. I never cared much about that, but yet I could operate a steam engine too. I could, but I never cared too much about it. My father was a steam engineer too, and I had one uncle, he was the engineer of the whole Stump family. He had 'em all beat when it come to handlin' and operatin' an engine. See, they had what they called a separator operator on the thrashin' machine. He took care of the separator, see it run all right. He was good at that. And the rest of 'em was farmers.

My father, Edward, and m' mother lived there with his parents, on the homeplace where he was raised. After my grandfather died, they stayed with grandmother, and mother took care of her. But, do y' know, m' grandmother outlived m' mother.

My mother was Maude Hibbard, born and raised in South Bloomingville. I wouldn't have the least idee where her parents were from. But her mother died with TB, and her father left and went clean over to Colorado, back in the late 1800s, someplace along there. An old

lady by the name of Holby took my mother to raise. I never saw m'
grandfather, he never come back.

I was born in either 1898 or 1900. I'm the only man ever born that
had two birthdays! My mother wrote down 1898 in her Bible, but my
dad put down 1900 on m' birth certificate. That was a curious bunch,
the Stumps, the whole bunch was curious. Don't make any differnce t'
me, though.

My mother at that time worked for the superintendent of the Old
Folks Home Infirmary, and there's where I was born, down below
Logan. They didn't live there. She stayed down there with the super-
intendent, worked for him. Then when she quit there, she come out to
where m' grandmother lived 'n stayed out there. [Dwight searched for
a tool as he talked.] *Father was out in Illanoys, had him a job out*
there, probably steam thrashing. He wasn't gone too long; they said I
was about six months old when he concluded he'd come back.

My mother, you never seen any woman as partic'lar as she was.
Neat and very clean person. She didn't want us kids t' have a BIT of
dirt on us. We got dirty or somep'n and did it a-purpose, we knew
what we'd git! We tried t' keep clean, too. Oooh, I'll never fergit one
time when I was just a kid, I walked up to the windows—those old
houses was low, y' know—'n she'd just washed the windows inside. I
thought I'd lick my tongue up there on the window glass. She had the
paddle layin' there, and as soon as she seen me lick my tongue up
across there, she got that paddle 'n said, "I'll show you, don't you ever
lick that window glass again!" Oh, I'll never fergit that, it sure did
burn! [laughing] *Yeah, she sure was partic'lar; she had a broom in*
her hand the biggest part of the time. That's why I like t' keep my shop
cleaned up; I got that from her.

I think makin' these baskets and rugs 'n stuff, I got that from her,
too. She was the only one did any handcraft work. I used to set and
watch her, watch her sew. She was neat with a needle, yeah, very neat.
She quilted, braided rugs, made doilies, crocheted. She was quite an
embroiderer; she'd even print 'n things. You've seen these covers you
put down over a stand, a cloth about that big square? I never will
fergit, she took one of those and took a plate, marked around on that
cloth, then she sewed around it. I fergit how, sewed around it some
way, and right in the center of it, with needle and thread, she wrote
my name. She followed that out and wrote it. She told me to always
keep that.

And I kept it till dad got married the second time and my step-
mother done away with it. I don't know where it ever got to. She
wouldn't tell me. I said to her, "I wouldn't a' took a pretty thing for

**Dwight, about sixteen
years old, circa 1916**

*that. Where is it?" I looked for it, but it had disappeared. I really
wanted to keep it. My mother, for a woman, she could write prett' near
perfect. She sewed my name right down on that stand cover. I never
will fergit how I stood and watched her make that. I intended to keep
it the rest of my life.*

*Now my stepmother, I can't complain about her kindness. But she
didn't want nothing around of my mother's. But dad had a trunk—
you've seen 'em, these old-timey trunks—had two of 'em, one was my
mother's and one his. His was round on top and mother's was flat.
And my dad had all my mother's stuff in hers. First thing I knowed,
there was nothing in it. Everything was gone, out! Prett' near full of
stuff she'd told me to keep and save. Gone. I did keep the trunk, and*

my mother's Bible that was in it. Them's the only two things I've got to remember my mother by.

I ain't got no old letters, not even m' mother's picture. Couldn't say she ever had her picture taken. I don't have my grandmother's picture, none of 'em. No one in the family has any as I know of. What ones there was, my brother got hold of some way. He kept all a' them old pictures. He's dead now, died in a rest home somewhere down South. So I hain't got an old picture on the place. I don't have any of any of the children even. As the fella says, I had a funny bunch for pictures, they didn't go much fer 'em. Oh say, there's one of me taken back in '16 or '17. Gladys has it. A man by the name of Charlie Hedge took that picture. He made two of 'em, 'n I paid him fer it.

I don't know how my mother died, she just got sick. I was only seven. Three sisters died in infancy, so there was just my brother, Wallace, and me. He was about three—I know he wore dresses yet when mother died. She's buried in the Green Summit Cemetery in Adelphi, but I don't know where, there's no tombstone. My father's buried beside her, no stone there either. The caretaker doesn't know where anything is any more.

My grandmother took care of us—we already lived with her on her forty-acre farm, there the other side of Laurelville. She was gettin' up in years, but yet she could take care of herself pretty good. Grandmaw was what you'd call good to me fer bein' as old as she was. But strict? I'll say she was strict! My mother was strict too! When I was just a little fella she whipped the dickens out of me. Grandmaw too. Had two of 'em thrashin' on me then. They tell me to do somep'n, the chores—get water or wood—I knowed that's what they meant fer me t' do and I done it! I was old enough to know not to contrare Grandmaw, not to aggravate her or anythin', do mostly what she wanted me to do; mostly I listened to her pretty good. I was big enough then I could carry in the wood, and the water had to be pumped out in the well, and things like that. She had chickens and I'd feed the chickens. We got along just fine.

Grandmother was white-headed, wore glasses, 'n was fair-complected. She was a little woman, crippled. Had a crippled back. She was very religious, went to the Baptist church down below Laurelville. Whenever she could, she'd go to that church, and take me along with her too. I really liked goin' to church and Sunday school, learn all I could. She always told me to behave, never cross nobody up, 'n be honest!

Grandmother was friendly with everbody—more friendly than any of her children was. I don't know why they didn't seem t' be, some cause or other. But SHE was. My father was friendly, but as the old sayin' goes, he was "set in his ways." He had his ways, 'n he wanted us kids t' listen to him in those ways too. We'd do somep'n he didn't want us t' do, he'd say, "Now that ain't the way I want that done!"

We had a little wagon, one of them little red wagons, you've seen many of 'em no doubt. That's what we had to play with. Hauled wood in that. My grandmother, she'd put me to haulin' wood to the house in it. After I got up to any size, my grandmother didn't want me to play very much; she wanted me t' work and do chores, pull weeds outa the garden and outa the yard, hoe. She had potatoes, nice big cabbages, onions, pickles, tomatoes, all that kind of stuff. Blackberries and raspberries, I picked a lot of those. Got plenty of jiggers! No strawberries though.

I had an uncle that was a sawmiller and a thrasher. They used t' thrash clover seed with what they called a clover-huller. And m' grandmother had a clover field there, wanted the clover seed off of it. Well, they got ready t' thrash out in a separate clover huller (they run that in a steam engine), 'n my uncle he thrashed it.

And I and my grandmother and a hired woman that was there— my grandmother had a hired woman at that time—we pitched the clover in the huller. Hauled it on an old sled, piled all we could on that sled. I led the old horse—he wasn't afraid of anything—led him right up side the huller and then pitched the clover in the huller and hauled out the seed. I remember goin' around by the spout where the clover seed come out into a bushel measure, and I'd go around there, look at that clover seed comin' down out of there, down inta that. Let that clover seed run acrost m' hands. I was between ten, eleven years old, along there. I was little, but I could handle a pitchfork pretty good, pitch the clover.

Sometimes Grandmother'd want somep'n or other—after I got up t' any size I could go—she'd send me up to m' uncle's, doin' chores or gettin' differnt things she'd want. He raised a lot of potatoes, she'd send me up fer a basket of potatoes to bring down. He lived up on the ridge right above us, 'bout a quarter of a mile, somep'n like that.

Grandmother always had a basket to carry stuff in, groceries. I got t' studyin' about it 'n I think it was a man by the name of White, Johnny White, made it. It was a homemade one, an egg basket. I tried t' get ahold of that basket, I s'pose I was about ten. My grandmother had a sale, and I wanted that old thing the worst way. I tried t' slip it away at the sale, but they watched it a little bit too close. My aunt kept her eye on me, 'n said, "I seen what you was up to, you're after that basket!" I told her I didn't want that basket t' sell, I wanted to keep it.

But she carried it out there and put it on the table and the auctioneer sold it.

That was back in the horse and buggy days. Grandmother had a horse she drove, a black horse, 'n she'd go to the grocery store oncet a week. She'd go sometimes t' Laurelville, sometimes South Perry. See we lived 'bout halfway between each town, down here on Laurel. She had a son-in-law that run the store there at South Perry; then the place at Laurelville was Metler's store. I was just a boy when I went there. Then after I growed up and got married I still dealt there. Tom Metler. He was a young fella yet and I was just a boy.

I'll never fergit one time—see, I remember when automobiles first come out—Doc Hemenger from Adelphi run the first automobile that ever I seen. And that automobile had them two lights on the front. My grandmother was drivin' her buggy, started to go past Doc's automobile, and that old horse thought that was a big guy lookin' at him. He just give a great big jump! Old Doc said, "He won't run off with you, he won't run off with you." He was a nice gentle horse, too, but he was afraid. No, that horse wasn't scared of anything—'cept an automobile. He wouldn't have been afraid of that if it hadn't been fer them two lights. M' grandmother said he thought them was two big eyes 'n was afraid they'd git him! He leaped *away from that automobile! That was over seventy-five years ago.*

I was along that time. Sometimes she'd take me along and sometimes she didn't. Sometimes she'd want someone t' stay at the house. I had an uncle stayed with us part of the time, 'n I'd stay home with him. She drove the buggy herself. And she could hitch the horse up to the buggy same as anyone else. At that time 'bout all the women learned to hitch their horse to a buggy. I never got to drive, but I never cared too much about it. They wouldn't trust me, 'fraid he'd get away from me. I never had no pony; they only had that one buggy horse around.

Do you remember back years ago, did you ever hear 'em talk about Halley's Comet? I saw it! When I was only ten years old. I still recollect seein' it. Now there'll be another Halley's Comet in December. I don't know whether I'll ever get t' see that or not. But that other one, it was right in that direction, 'n I seen it two differnt nights. Looked like a star with a long tail. Oh, dozens of people saw it, my grandmother even saw it.

It was about eight, nine o'clock, somep'n like that. Us kids always went t' bed pretty early, 'n it was 'fore we went t' bed. Our dad took us out. He told us—he wouldn't let us go t' bed—he said, "You kids wait.

I'll watch, and if I see the comet, I'll call you out." He was outside, 'n told us t' come out when it was right the brightest, told us t' come out and take a look at it. Next night was the same thing. We didn't watch it any more after that, but we watched it two nights in succession. I never forgot that. I thought mebbe I'd mention that to ya, so you'd know there is a few things I remember back when I was a kid. Not very many, but I can remember that.

Now that was onusual, 'cause it's funny, but no one ever tried to show me or tell me anythin' when I was a kid. My grandmother always told me what I learned I'd have t' learn in school; said that was what it was fer. My father wouldn't show me anything. He wouldn't try t' show us boys nothing. *He wanted us t' learn the hard way. Biggest influence on me when I was a kid was an uncle, my granddad's brother, took more of an interest in me than the whole Stump family. Uncle Eli. He'd come there and I wanted t' know anything, I'd ask him. He'd tell me not t' get in no trouble of no kind, told me t' go t' school all I could, learn all I could there. Them old fellas, all they knowed at that time was WORK, 'n he told me, "You'll learn that if you want to have anything, you'll hafta work t' git it."*

No, there wa'nt much play time. When I was twelve years old I got t' go down in the fall of the year to the Punkin Show at Circleville. First time I went to Lancaster Fair, a neighbor boy by the name of Earl Kane took me up there. Logan Fair, I been t' that, but it's just about like goin' to the carnival. I never went t' Columbus t' do any shopping or anything. But when I was about fourteen, I went up there first time to the state fair, went with m' dad two differnt years. We viewed the machinery, the horses, cattle, watched the races, rode the merry-go-round and the ferris wheel.

Do you remember that great big log they had made into a house, made outa redwood from California, on a big truck? They had that one year at the Lancaster Fair, and I been through it. That was somep'n! A tree growin' big enough—they had three pretty good size rooms hewed out of the length of it! Then they had a basket (basket stuff was pretty plentiful at that time) big enough t' have a door in it, had baskets inside sellin 'em. It was a great big outfit, you could see in there, see him sellin' 'em. I think that was in '18, along in there somewhere.

I started school the next year after my mother died, to Union Special, just across the crik. They was a few of them special schools around the country at that time, and it was the only one I could go to—we happened t' live right there by it, right across the crik. You had to be eight years old t' start. I can remember my first teacher was Pearl Armstrong for two years, and the second teacher was Albert Archer. I went there for three years; but then my grandmother died, and I and my brother and my father went up on to Pleasant Ridge with my uncle.

Father kept us together, but we moved around a good bit. I went to Drum School up there for three months (it was called Drums Ridge [Dumm] at that time, but it's called Pleasant Ridge now, goes by Sky-line Drive, so many differnt names). Then I went t' Whitesel Number One for the rest of the winter. That prett' near slipped my mind. The teacher there was a woman, Mabel DeHaven, first woman teacher I ever went to. We moved over to Salt Crik Township then. My father was an engineer, a steam engineer on a thrasher. He thrashed all summer, and that winter he worked on a sawmill. We moved to Adel-phi for a while, but not long enough for me to go to school, then went up on Long Run. That's where he got his second wife, Alice Clark. Her father lived right below us there, and m' dad had been goin' with her for quite a while, finally got married that winter. There I went to the Hemphill School for three years, and passed two grades in one year. Supposed only to make one grade, but I made two in one year. Sam Everett taught the first year, then Hazel Hardsell, Charlie Frazier, and Max Steele. After that I went to Dry Tavern School for about three months, to Jimmy Hufford. (That school's not there any more. None of those schools I went to are left, not a one. Ever one of 'em 's tore down.)

And then I was out. Through. (There was eight grades, but at that time they called the eighth grade the tenth, high school.) I got all I could in the common school that way. So that's where I wound it all up. I passed the Boxwell Examination and that ended that. That's the examination to teach school; but I was only fifteen and I couldn't teach no school at that age. The county superintendent said it beat anything he ever seen! He come out to see me and said, "You passed the Boxwell Examination; you're supposed—you can teach school any place in the county." "Oh no, no," I said, "I can't." "Why not?" he said, "Here you passed the Boxwell Examination, and you can't go back to school any more—no high school for you to go to." I said, "Well, I'm up agin it there, I'm too young t' teach! I'll just go work on a farm some-place." And I did.

I went over here to Bewney Visty and started workin' for a man by the name of Carroll, Claude Carroll. He owned two big farms, lived on one, worked the other, and I helped farm 'em. But that fella played a trick on me. After he found out I was pretty well educated, he said, "I'll tell you what I'll do. You work for me this summer, then this fall when college starts, fall term, I'll put you through college four years." And I worked for him. Fall come, he said, "Go home, I don't need you any longer." He paid me for the work, 'n then told me, "Go home," he wasn't gonna send me to college. He found out it was gonna cost him too much. That ended m' college career!

But after that I stayed there with Carroll, 'n him and me together we farmed both those two big farms, had two team of horses. That's the period when I learned to make baskets. See, in the winter we didn't have mucha anything t' do on the farm 'cept feed. Bad weather I'd go down to Bewney Visty, to the store we dealt at.

The owner, name of Mart Hines, had to tend the store, but he made baskets in between times in the back of the store. He was a basket-maker from Tar Ridge, just a young fella then. I'd heard 'em talk about baskets and I'd saw baskets before that, 'n I'd always inquire and want to know how they was made. When I was a kid, we lived over on Long Run on the Lindsay place—no, lived on the Krafthaver place—'n my father raised a crop of corn. Old man King brought him a coupla baskets to pick up corn in. I got t' lookin' at 'em, 'n I told him, "Them don't look like they're hard t' make." He says, "You try t' make one and you'll find out it's hard enough." I said, "The time'll come I'll be a-makin' 'em." And it did!

Fact is, I was only about twelve when I said, "Time'll come when I'll make a basket." "Oh," he said, "you'll never make one!" And I said, "I will make a basket, and you'll live to see me make one." And sure enough he did. He seen me make many a basket. And, he told me, all the Stumps he ever knowed or knowed of had all kinda trades but baskets. Never was a one learned the basket trade but me. Hines always said, "This is a trade that someday won't be many doin'." And he was right! Lots of 'em said men was too pernickety t' make baskets and rugs. I used t' say, "You wait and see where this'll get me some day."

They's been other ones told me they never thought there'd be a Stump ever make baskets, worked everything else. Wanted t' know how I got on to it. I said I got it into m' head I wanted to, and after while I was makin' 'em. But Mart Hines was the first one I ever got a chance to watch.

So I watched Mart, watched him while he was makin'. Then I helped him pull through the holes—I was just a boy then and it was fun fer me. And that way I picked it up. Just watched him real careful, watched how that was done, but didn't say nothin'. I just knew I could do that too, so I studied on it, then went back to Carroll's and worked it out step by step.[1] I'd make a few once in awhile, practice up so I wouldn't lose out.

Where I lived at that time there was a bunch of white oak to make 'em out of. (At that time they was still a good bit of white oak around.) We had plenty of stuff there on the place where we lived. Everyone told me, said, "You won't get no basket timber off that place you live on, that old man won't let ya have it." And I said, "Well, I don't know about that, he just might. But I won't cut any till I see him, 'n he says so." Man owned the place, Carroll, I asked him about cuttin' it—I knowed he was pretty partic'lar. I said, "I wanta learn t' make baskets." He was a pretty nice old fella at that, 'n he said, "Well, boy, if you want to learn the basket trade, you go up there to the woods 'n get all the white oak you want to make with. It'll never do me no good anyhow. That way you can learn a trade." 'N he let me get all I wanted!

I stayed and worked for Carroll about five years. Oh, in between there, I was drafted into the army, First World War. They caught me on the eighteen-year-old list, and I was the second eighteen-year-old draftee in Hocking County. I had told 'em I was gonna join the army and make it my life career. And they said, Oh . . . that, don't do a thing like that. I was gonna stay right on in. Carroll talked me out of it, had quite a little talk with me about it. The day I reported was November eleventh, Armistice Day, and I was mustered out right then! I was in the army one day and out the next. So I didn't never have t' go. I was willin' to go; I said I'd go and serve my country. If I'd a had to went, I wouldn't have thought nothing about it. But I wasn't a bit sorry that I didn't have to.

I really made my first baskets down in Alabama, made a whole bunch when I got started in, on a plantation, the Rittenour Stock Farm. This Charlie Rittenour run a thrashing machine over here at Kingston, and he formed a company of ten to buy a stock farm down there. Ten of 'em bought stock and Rittenour was the president of it. He went down to Montgomery County and got twenty-eight hundred acres, 'n hired my father as a machine operator—tractors, trucks—for this stock farm. They had a lot of hay to make for all them cattle.

My father sent for us to come down, so we went, my stepmother and brother and I, all down on the train. Boy, goin' around them mountains, that big old train—it had two locomotives on it—and settin' there, you'd look over across at that round side of the mountain there, 'n you could see the train goin', pullin' the same coach that I was on! Funny how they wind around them mountains like that, just wind their way, way out around.

That first time I went down in the fall and stayed down till spring, I suppose it was someplace between 1918 and '20, someplace along there. But I didn't like it. We moved back into a place worse even than back in here yet. I didn't like it back in there. Boys, I wanted out where I could get out and around and see things, get things done, do things. Move back in a doggone—I thought when he said about goin' down there, I thought, "That'll be just the thing," so I went along down.

A lot of people wondered how I got back. Well, when I left Carroll's farm in Ohio, I left enough money there with him to buy me a ticket back. When I got down there and got to workin' and sharin' what I made—tried to help keep the family together—I had all my money gone. But I got pretty homesick, so I wrote back up there and Carroll fixed it, he had bought me a through ticket, down there and back up. That way I got back.

3. A Hard-Working Man

**Dwight, in a photograph
on the back of an
unmailed postcard,
circa 1919**

The first girl I ever went with was a schoolteacher, from over at Atlanta City, other side of Circleville. But after I started goin' with Maisie Pinkstalk, I didn't go with anyone else. I went to school with her at Dry Tavern, childhood sweethearts. A couple of years after I come back from Alabama I got married.

I got to carpenterin', helpin' Paul Hilliards build houses. And I made some baskets along then—I got a timber cuttin' contract up here on the Fetheroff place right close to where you'uns live. My daddy-in-law cut that timber out, and I don't know how many other pieces we cut out around here, some over by the Boys' Industrial School. I don't know just how many years I cut timber in the summertime, then I'd make baskets in the winter when it was bad.

I worked some for Carroll then, farming, and I drove a team, logged some on a sawmill for him, then on McDonald's sawmill, and I helped at the Hilliards boy's sawmill, Harley Hilliards'. I got to workin' first one job and then another. I've worked so many places, so many differnt jobs I can't keep track!

I worked for Jimmy Wacker in his restaurant for a while. How I happened t' get started workin' there, he used to have a candy stand—candy he made himself—'n took around to differnt concessions. Chester Morris was livin', and the first time I ever helped him was when Chester had a store up here, and they had a little doins' goin' on up there. (That was the first place I ever heard Reverend Williams. He had a choir with him—he was the chaplain at the Boys' Industrial School at that time and he had their choir with him. The choir sang first, then he preached. Oh, and he had a ventriloquist who could mock a whippoorwill 'n a quail. He could imitate a lot of people, too.) It was right up there on 180, where that road comes out where my daughter Gladys lives, first house this way.

We'd been over to the Circleville Punkin Show twice. And next I sold the candy for him out at the Lancaster Fairgrounds. Then when fall *come he wanted me to work in his restaurant in Lancaster. I tended bar when the bartender wasn't there, waited on table, did the biggest part of the cookin'. That was work I didn't like very good, 'n I didn't work there too long.*

And I've worked tilin' out a field. I tiled one out for that man over here at Bewney Visty, Claude Carroll. It was swampy and low, and I tiled it out t' Middle Fork Crik. Mebbe you knowed Dan Seesholtz, I tiled some for him; and some fer Ray Kastner, down by Laurelville, and fer Harley Glenn too.

You take a reglar ditchin' spade, cut a ditch. Take a long twine, mostly start back at the foot of a bank, or a hill with a spring, that's what they usually tile out. Draw a line to the crik or ravine, wherever you want it t' drain, then set that line and go back up t' the end. Start in and spade on that line, get a grade so 'at the water from the spring—or wherever you're tilin' from—will foller right on down through. Spade that all out, anywhere from a foot and a half to two foot under the ground, so when they plow they'll go over the top. Sometimes y' have t' go clear across the field. That's a job all right!

And then y' gotta clean the bottom out of the ditch an' lay the tile in there, one right agin the other'n, right down end ways. Lay them in there and lay them clear up through the ditch. What I used was these clay tile, about sixteen inches long. And I've laid cement tile, too, but it didn't prove out as good as the clay. I don't know why. The clay tile, they're burnt and that sets 'em hard. But the cement tile, they only get just so hard, 'n when they're in the ground so long, they get soft and break.

Then spade 'n cover 'em all back up agin. Just put the dirt back on, no gravel. Y' fit the tile up close together—but not real tight—then what water come along there would seep right down inta the tile and right on outa the field. Rosemary, that's the hardest work there is on earth! Nowadays they got a ditchin' machine, they can tile out in just a little bit. Y' jist have t' lay the tile by hand. It was a job all right! Didn't seem t' bother me much, I could work right along. But that was back when I was younger, 'fore I was married and some after.

Oh, and I've dug water wells by hand, too. That one up by Snuffy's, dug that by hand. It was about twelve, fifteen feet deep. Then I dug one over there where Jim Lunsford lived, over there on 180, O'Neal owns it now. They used tile, those great big sewer tiles in, and that's what Lunsford used too. Dig the hole first, clean down as fer as they wanted the well, then started there and come right on up with the sewer tile. Never had no trouble with no cave-ins. When you're diggin' a well it's round, and that braces itself back. Unless it's a soft place— that might leave go, but you hardly ever get one of them places, diggin' a water well.

I bailed the dirt out with a bucket, had a winch up on top, someone up on top t' draw it up. Had a ladder down in there t' get out myself. Keep movin' it around out of my road as I dug. Herman mostly was there pullin' it up. If he wasn't there, I'd take m' time myself, go up the ladder 'n pull it up. I didn't worry about it fallin' in on me. Never worried much about anything. Ain't nothin' to worry about.[1] No, I never was much t' worry about anythin'. Yup, I've done a lot of work other people wouldn't do. I didn't mind. Just got used to it and kept right on goin'. Same way with the basket stuff, just got used to it, keep right on tryin' t' make out on it.

I used t' train coon dogs back years ago, along in 1927, '28. Used to take 'em out and hunt, train 'em. I'd have a regular huntin' dog along in the beginning; it'd run onto the track 'n track 'em. I'd jist take 'em out to the woods where I knowed they was coon, long about nine, ten o'clock at night, take 'em out t' get the track. Sometimes I'd train the dog fer other people, or sometimes I'd get a young dog and train him, then sell him maybe, or use him t' hunt with. I sold the coon hides. They'd bring a pretty good price at that time, two, three dollars apiece. (Now you get maybe twenty, twenty-five dollars fer 'em.) I did that fer about three winters, and then I quit on it, didn't bother with it anymore. It was after night and I needed m' rest, so I didn't like the idee. That was back when I was just young yet, right after I was married. I didn't do it very long, 'cause my wife didn't like it, bein' out at night, blunderin' and stumblin' around. I used to keep a coon dog, but don't any more.

I worked on WPA for awhile, from the time it started here in Hocking County up prett' near to the time they quit off. That road work wasn't s' bad in the summertime, but when the ground was froze, 'n bad weather, I didn't like that! Cold! Mostly some of us close together'd go in a truck belonged to one fella. Sometimes you had a good piece t' go t' get there.

But I got other work: that was the bargain when I took the WPA job, I told 'em I'd work on it till I got a better-payin' job, 'n I got a job cuttin' timber. Used to cut a good bit of it. Fella over here on Coley named Dan Seesholtz, he knowed I'd cut timber for Prendergast before, so he asked him about me. "If you want somebody t' cut timber fer you, you'd better get that Stump fella." "I thought he was on WPA." "You see him, you get him." So he come on down t' see me, 'n I said,

"Yeah, I'll quit WPA and go to cuttin' timber, that's a little differnt job." I liked it, and I cut a lot of timber.

Then them Alabama people wanted me t' come back down there. The family told me, "Now bring your wife and come back down here." I don't know what year that was, but she didn't like *it, she was dissatisfied. We went back and forth so many times, I couldn't begin to tell you. I rode thousands and thousands of miles on the train and bus, that's where it come in. I spent prett' near a young fortune ridin' back and forth in trains and buses, 'cause m' wife wanted her children born up in Ohio, there at the home where her parents lived (where that pond is goin' up Jack Run, right up on the hill). But they wasn't all born there; two were, but the other seven in differnt places, all in Ohio though. The oldest was born in 1924; the youngest—she lived only ten hours—in 1944.*

I made some more trips down to Alabama, along in the '40s. I liked it a little better this time than the first, but I said, "I ain't gonna be in no hurry about goin' down." Fella that I worked fer down there then, he had a proposition for me, wrote me to come down. When I got there, he'd died, but I wrote back and told my wife, "I've got things arranged."

His boys took over and they said as long as they's any of the three of 'em livin', I had a home down there. I worked on a dairy farm right there beside the Rittenours, and whenever I wasn't working at anything else, I'd go back to m' baskets. They was plenty of white oak in just about all them swamps, just go in there and get most any kind you want.

Then I began makin' baskets nearly full time, for Dallas Rittenour (old man Charlie was his father, the one my father went down to work for). And Roger Kingston went down from here; he knew I made baskets and he discovered he had a bunch of white oak on the place he owned. They've got the same kind of oak in Alabama, only they got one—it looked like a white oak, but it's called swamp oak. And it won't work out!

I made a basket there a lotta people up here never saw, and that's a cotton basket, about thirty inches high. The colored people down there made 'em. Them were flat splits. And I made a vegetable basket, big as a bushel basket. They raised a lotta vegetables in that part, 'n they wanted big *baskets. I made a few, and lots of 'em came back and wanted more. But I said they'd hafta get somebody else t' make 'em. I*

Dwight chopping firewood, 1947

A Bearer of Tradition

Dwight's wife, Maisie, with their first grandchild

didn't like *doin' those flat splints! I went right back t' makin' the round kind I always had done up here. And I think they's probly some other people down there started copyin' my kind, they liked 'em s' much.*

I sold baskets out in front of my house, had a table back off the road, about like that one settin' there, about four by eight, put 'em out there in the daytime. I made 'em for about a year or more, got the market pretty well filled up with 'em. Then the fella that owned the super-market store across the way come down and said, "How'd you like to come at night and manage the store for me?" I said, "I can't do that, I make baskets." He said, "Manage at night." Well, I took him up. Mostly I kept the man's books, but when I couldn't get enough help, I'd help out in the store. It was on the Troy Highway, about twenty miles south of Montgomery.

See, that Carroll I worked for 'n stayed with on the farm, he had a store in Bewney Visty, 'n there's where I got started in the bookkeepin' business. He had a pretty good-sized store at that time, and he said, "You're pretty well educated, I'm gonna turn the book work over to you, managin' that one." And that's where I got started. I got to likin' it pretty good. Old as I am, I could still keep books! Oh yeah, I could keep right up to the penny, right up to scratch!

I was makin' a few baskets in Alabama while I worked there at the store, sold 'em there. I worked there for about two years, and right at two years he sold the store out. People he sold to in Montgomery, they just took all the groceries and everything out of the store, left it set; so I went 'n started right back in makin' baskets.

Went back down to Alabama once more, late forties mebbe, wrote back and told my wife to come down. I was pretty well satisfied and had things so we might make out, and she come down there and said, "I don't want no part of it." And when I got the malaria fever down there, the doctor told me, "You'll have to leave this part of the country, you've got the malaria fever." And he said if I didn't leave I'd get it again. You see, it was pretty much swampy down in there where we were, lot of swamp land. Talk about mosquitoes! You never seen any mosquitoes till you got there! They claim they's the ones, that's what carries the malaria. So I left, and never got it any more.

We wrote the oldest daughter, Gladys, told 'em to come down and get us, her mother wanted to come back; and Gladys and her man and the other girl's man, they come down. We come back to Ohio and I've been here ever since. But my brother married and stayed down South all the rest of his life. And my father and stepmother stayed until the '50s, right around 1956, then come back up here and lived with me, over on the Williams place.

I came back up here and worked on a housing project, helped build houses for National Homes in Lancaster. We lived out on Dry Tavern Ridge—I owned property up there, lived there about four, five years. A farmer bought me out, wanted to build a bigger house on my land—I had about five acres. I moved then to Bewney Visty, and had a regular basket "factory" there. It was a big outfit, building was twelve by twenty-four (this one's about fourteen by eighteen). I worked alone there, only m' girls helped put the strips through the holes, the dies.

I was a township sheriff, constable, for about four years: in Perry Township for two years, and then in Laurel Township for two years. After I moved over in here, they got after me right away, said, "We're gonna put you in fer constable." I said, "Oh, don't do anything like that." "Yes, we are." First thing I knew they'd voted me in fer constable of the township. It's about the same kind of work as the sheriff, "peace officer" is what it is. That was back in, let's see. . . . I lived down here below Butch Barnes, 'n Bobby was just a little fella. So that was about forty years ago.

I didn't mind it too bad, didn't have too much t' do. Y' didn't get paid. Only time I got any money out of it or anything was when I served a warrant or things like that. And y' didn't get much out of a warrant, unless they got fined, then I got a percent of the fine fer m' pay. (Now the constable gets a salary. But Laurel Township or Perry, neither one's got a constable either: they don't have the money to pay the salary. Good Hope Township said they'd take care of Laurel fer us if we'd pay 'em.)

Yeah, I wore a gun and badge both, same as any other officer. Had t' buy all that myself, too. Had a big shoulder holster I wore. Yeah, I had t' carry a gun, it was a .32 Special, no a .38 Special. Had a badge, handcuffs, had it pretty well equipped. After m' time was up—I was only elected fer two years—m' cousin, John Stump, down here at Perry got it, and I gave him the badge. I says, "Now I'm gonna give you this badge, and I don't ever want t' see it again." Last count I had, he's still got it, but he ain't constable any more, fer they done away with a constable in Perry Township. The gun and holster, I sold that t' someone, I don't know any more who.

I was death on moonshiners. I didn't believe in moonshinin'; I didn't go fer that, because it was Prohibition days, and it was highly agin the law, that moonshinin' business. That come under the jurisdiction of the township at that time—when I was constable.

And the sheriff tried t' make me a lackey boy fer him. Every time they'd hear about moonshinin' out here someplace, they'd find me to look the place over at oncet, look it over and get a warrant. The sheriff'd have me go, 'cause he knowed they'd spot him. They wouldn't spot me s' good, by bein' amongst 'em here. If he'd happen t' come in, they'd spot him. I'd look it over all right, but they'd know I was a comin' and get everything in the clear. I never catched 'em. I could see where they'd been, 'n had their outfit—you could easy tell what'd been there. But I didn't have t' go after too many.

Over here at Sherman Floyd's place, the moonshiners had their barrel set over there. I didn't see it, or anything of the kind, but I was told afterwards that the moonshiners had a bunch of barrels over there and had mash in it. Minnie Floyd had some cows turned there in that field; the mash was in the woods—kind of concealed like—and the cows got in it. They got in it and drank it down, drank it down as fer as they could reach in the barrel. And that night when she went t' get 'em, she said them old cows was staggerin' all over the field [chuckling]. *She said them old cows was* all *drunk, staggerin' around all over the field.*

She said somebody told her if the cows got into anyone's moonshine, it'd make 'em drunk, so she suspicioned somep'n like that around there. She got t' lookin' 'n she found it, found the barrels, said each one of 'em was just about half full. The old cows drank it down half way. She called the sheriff right away, he come out there, upset the rest of 'em, mashed 'em all up!

They had a lookout a watchin' fer 'em, and he was up in a big tall tree, just covered with grapevine, thick, nobody could see him up in there. 'N he sat up there and watched the whole procedure of everything and they didn't even know he was up there [still laughing]. *I found out afterwards about it. It was George Notestone, he was the lookout. He said he coulda shot the whole bunch of 'em and they wouldn't a knowed where it was comin' from; but he wouldn't do that, said he wasn't up in there t' shoot anybody, just t' watch t' see what was goin' on.*

They played a dirty trick on George Notestone, right over here at Eddie Floyd's place. Eddie was an old bachelor, stayed by himself, and for a while George'd stay with him fer four or five nights. And George was over there one night, and Eddie said, "George, m' water bucket's got t' leakin', 'n I've got some solder and stuff, how about you settin' down there on the floor and solderin' it fer me?" George said, "Well, get it and get me the solder, and put the iron in the fire 'n get it hot." While he was sittin' there on the floor talkin' t' Eddie, somebody rapped *on the door, 'n ol Eddie come 'n opened the door, seen it was the sheriff right away. 'N the sheriff says, "We're after George Notestone," and said, "We caught him now! Here he is, sittin' on the floor solderin' a still."*

And he was solderin' Eddie Floyd's water bucket. Eddie Floyd showed me the water bucket afterwards, where he'd soldered it. Says "Here's what they got George Notestone up at the penitentiary fer, fer solderin' my water bucket." "Now," he says, "ya sure got a nice sheriff in this county!" He said, "That water bucket don't look like a still." George Notestone died, right up there in the penitentiary. Right up there's where he died.

I could never catch any of 'em, though. But I'd see where they'd been, when somebody told me where t' go t' look. No, I never found any moonshiners. They'd always find out I was a-comin', and I took m' time and let 'em get away. A lot of 'em, that was the only way they had t' make a livin,' couldn't get a job of no kind. I didn't want t' deprive 'em of a livin', didn't wanta run on to 'em unless I had to.[2] *I wasn't a bit scared about anything like that, because them moonshiners was afraid t' shoot anybody. One thing about, they put up a big ruckus, but they wouldn't do no shootin'. Down South they'd shoot 'em, but not around here.*

Now I heard here a while back that down in here—I don't know what the name of the place is now, Bobby knows—where Butch Barnes went t' hunt that wildcat, down there about every day last winter. And Bobby said there was some fellas down in there makes whiskey, 'n if he gets too close t' their still, they'll *shoot him! But lucky enough he was, when he was huntin' that wildcat, he didn't get very close t' anybody's still. "That's the kinda fellas down in that part," he said. I can't think of the name of that place back over in here, kind of a wild country, and a lot of them moonshiners from Kentucky and West Virginia come up in there and camp. He didn't find no wildcat, hunted four or five days.*

M' daughter Mary told you wrong: I never preached anywhere. I was a Sunday school superintendent. I made announcements and things like that. Then they used t' have Stumps' reunions, and nothing would do but prett' near everyone of 'em I had t' make a speech of some kind. My brother told me, "Now whenever we have a reunion, you get your speech ready, 'cause you'll be called on." We've had Stump reunions at Rock House, Old Man's Cave, Cedar Falls, down t' the park at Laurelville. Wasn't hardly enough t' make it go at first, invited several other families, had a pretty fair crowd. I talked mostly on our generation, and the old people.

And I made a few speeches at some of the basket outfits, too, they'd want me t' give a little talk. Over at 'Delphi on the fourth of July, I had t' make a little talk fer 'em over there, five, six, mebbe seven years ago.

I worked in Lancaster for three years, in two differnt factories, Anchor Hocking Glass and Loroco Paper Mill. I lived in Lancaster, and Bobby went to school there. (I can't think just when it was.) I worked in the glass factory first but had to take some kind of examination, and they said they'd have t' leave me go. Said I couldn't take that work in the factory. I went down to Loroco and worked there two of the years. I didn't like it very good, but they paid good money at

A Hard-Working Man

Dwight advising a friend, 1962

that time, so I stayed with it.[3] *They bought used paper, baled paper, newspaper, and stuff like that, then made it back into paper again. I picked up the trade there of what they call "paper cutter." I got to be the main one; they said I could cut the paper nearer to exact size than anyone they ever had in there. I'd cut by day one week and next week by night, day and night shift.*

It wasn't so bad. I'll tell you why I got out of there. They was gonna go on strike and I knowed it. I told the timekeeper, "You count up my time, I'm leavin' here. They's somep'n gonna happen here and you'll find out what it is in just a few days." Three days after I quit they went on strike, 'n he didn't know it. I didn't want no part of that. I don't go for strikes. That just hurts everything when they go out: it hurts the company and it hurts the workers. The workers that strike are out of work, and the worst of it, in there after the strike was over, all that was on strike didn't get back. There was only four out of the whole bunch that got back. The rest never did. So, you see, they lost out.

I lived on the Stahr farm, farming for Vernie Stahr's father, Louis,

Dwight's house, built from reclaimed materials

fer a while. Then I worked for a plumber, name of Williams. He lived over here on Coley [Little Cola Ridge]. Then I worked for Harley Glenn, carpentering, and got Williams a job plumbing for Harley too. I worked a long time for Harley. He bought the old county home to make into apartments, 'n I started up with him the first day. He started cleaning up the yard and remodeling—old tree stuff out of the yard first—and I wound up starting the carpentry then after I got it cleaned up around the inside. We were still working on it when he died, twelve years later.

After I quit workin' for Harley (when he died), that ended m' workin' days. I didn't get no job of no kind no place else. I'd started t' build my house here even before he died. I lived over there on Harley's land, stayed there about a year after he died. His wife wanted me to stay longer.

But I had this place by then, m' boy bought it, and we saved up building material. I'd salvage an old building or an old house some- place and tear it down. It took the best of it t' do these buildings here with. I got one old house up to Gibetown [Gibisonville], *and I got I don't know how many in Logan. I bought me old barns in Logan and tore 'em down. Part of that house o' mine is the old superintendent's house down on the infirmary farm, down below Logan. The one Harley Glenn and those Denton sisters bought. That was a big old house. I got enough virgin poplar siding to side my whole house there with. That's all virgin timber outside there, poplar. I don't think there's a knot in the whole business. It's all worked out nice. After the house, I built the shop out of it, and then I built the garage out there too.*

About a year from the time we started to build the house—started in August, . . . about a year from then—we was livin' here. Just my brother-in-law up by Fairborn and Bobby and me built it. Junior, my oldest son, worked on it some too. He helped me build the chimney. Oh yes, I've carpentered pretty much in m' time. I learned this basket-making and still carpentered too when I was a young man. So after we finished the house, then we built the shop, and then that there garage. And then *I went to makin' baskets full time. I worked right on. I sure didn't retire!*

Funny, I can remember things that happened when I was a boy better'n I can things today. Somebody ask me things that happened back years ago, I can tell them exactly, but the last four or five years kind of got away from me. I couldn't begin to tell you all the jobs I've done, 'n make baskets too. I guess I've been everywhere and everyplace, 'n hain't been no place either.

4. Making a Round-Rod Basket

Laboring in many different traditional pursuits, Dwight has received probably the most enjoyment, and certainly the most attention, from making baskets. His baskets are different, not only because they are handsome but also because they possess unusual strength from the material and the process he uses.

Astounding variety is possible with basketmaking. Think of the dozens—hundreds, even—of baskets with which you're familiar from photographs, paintings, houses, shops, museums, or restorations. Yet that marvelous diversity in shape and size and function is the result of just three methods: coiling, plaiting, and weaving (fig. 1).[1]

Those three have been and still are being used by weavers around the world to achieve an astonishingly wide variety of sizes and shapes and textures. *Coiling* consists of winding a bundle of tightly gathered material—usually a type of grass or straw—into a spiral, then sewing it together at regular intervals with a binder (which is either a long strand of the same material used in the bundle or a different material altogether). *Plaiting* involves working materials in two opposite directions, in an over one–under one pattern, or over two–under two. In *weaving,* warps or stakes are held together by wefts (that is, weavers); in one type, wickerwork, wefts are moved round through the stakes; in twining, two or more wefts are twisted and locked around the stakes. Weavers use either flat or round splints, depending on the preference of the maker.

I am describing Dwight's basketry by using the term *white-oak round-rod wickerwork* to denote material, shape, and technique, although I have often shortened that to *oak-rod* or *round-rod* to lessen repetition. But I must point out that in any discussions of basketry, especially basket types and materials, the terminology is complex and sometimes ambiguous. The terms *flat-split* and *flat-splint* basketry are interchangeable in general usage, depending on preference and reflecting the similar definitions of *split* and *splint* (*split:*

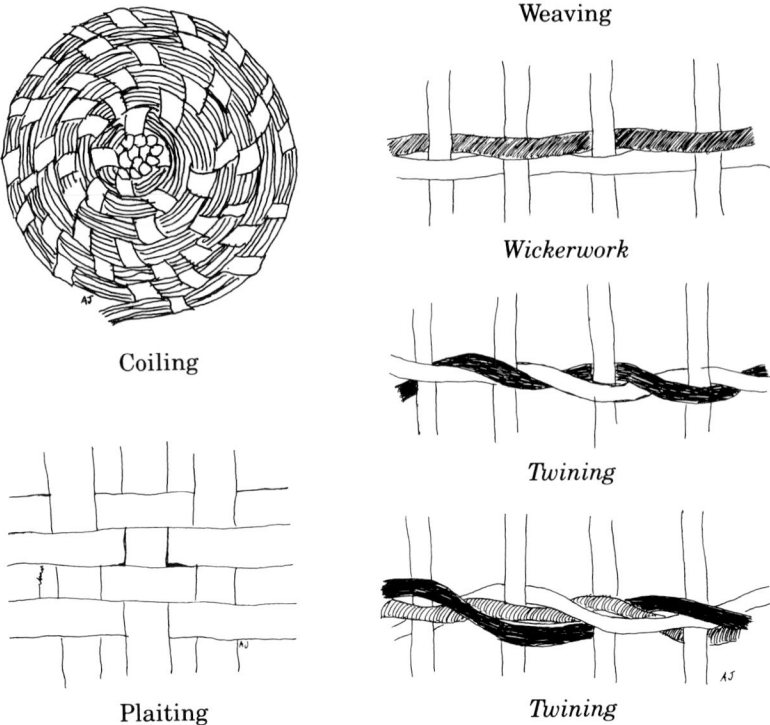

Coiling

Weaving

Wickerwork

Twining

Plaiting

Twining

**Figure 1.
Basketry Weaving
Patterns**

a lengthwise separation of wood caused by the tearing apart of the wood cells; *splint:* a piece split off; splinter). A *reed* is defined as a material: "any of various tall grasses with slender often jointed stems"; or "a stem of such grass." However, *rod* is also defined as a material, a "straight, slender stick growing upon or cut from a tree or bush," as well as a shape. *Wickerwork* is a "texture of osiers, twigs, or rods."[2]

Jeannette Lasansky, in researching basketry in Pennsylvania, used "round oak *spoked* basket," adding reference to technique—since she considered *reed* only a material and *rod* only a shape; (however, she also used *spoked* to describe a flat-splint technique, which is essentially different from the round-rod one). Sue Stephenson, working in the Appalachian Mountains, referred to these as "oak-rod wickerwork baskets," to wickerwork as "round rod weaving over a firm framework," and to spokes as "the vertical members of the framework of a basket." In England, Dorothy Wright referred to rods as "young shoots, especially of willow, used in basketmaking, and any single length of material which has not been split."[3]

Needless to say, ambiguity in terminology is of no concern to Dwight. He refers to his baskets sometimes as "round-splint," sometimes "round-split," sometimes "round-reed," and occasionally as "round-rod." Yet in answer to my question, he stated that "round-rod basket is the right name."

Interested now in all methods of basketry, as a teenager Dwight was exposed only to weaving with flat and round splints (although probably at some point he observed the use of plaiting on chair seats); but he always preferred the round-rod weaving. Using a combination of twining and wickerwork, he continued throughout the years to weave with round rods or splints (fig. 2).

I was about seventeen when I first started on handcrafts, and the very first thing I did was make baskets. And I've kept in practice ever since. Wherever I worked at, I still made baskets on the sideline.[4] I haven't any idee how many I've made, but it'd be way up in the thousands!

Here's m' book I filled out, set that down myself. I got all the measurements of basket sizes from the old basketmakers in there. This here's the book I kept tab on how I made differnt baskets fer 1944 and '45. See, I was workin' pulpwood and baskets too, both of 'em. That pulpwood, I cut them along Mill Fork; there's willa and ash—not ash, but cottonwood—*willa and cottonwood. Blamed ole cat! Get outa that basket!*

Let's see, the smallest one I make is the sewing basket, then the egg

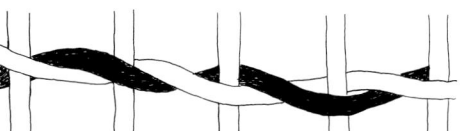

A. "Lock weave," used on the bottom frame

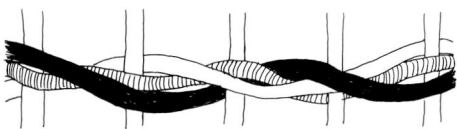

B. "Triple weave," used on the bottom band
and top band of the side

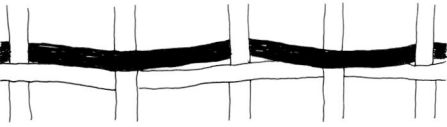

C. "Straight weave" or "single weave," used on
center section of side

**Figure 2.
Dwight Stump's Weaving
Patterns**

basket, then the peck, half bushel, two-thirds bushel, and bushel. Ummm, what else? I'll have t' consult m' book. Apple bushel! And clothes basket [see table 1].

The bottom diameter and height are the same on all of 'em: whatever size the bottom is, say it's a magazine basket with a ten-inch bottom, then that'd be ten inches high (and that one's fourteen inches wide across the top). You kin go higher, but if you go too far, they get too heavy, topple over.

There's two sizes to an Easter egg basket, a little one and a big one. Used t' call that bigger one the sewing basket. The Easter egg basket's a newer one. People wanted 'em—wanted t' see if I could make 'em more 'n anything else, I have an idee. And of late years they call the peck basket a "magazine basket." The half bushel is a general purpose basket: used for the garden, or a lawn basket, or a feed basket, carry

Table 1. Names and Sizes of Dwight Stump's Baskets

Traditional Name	Popular Name	Height	Diameter	
			Bottom	Top
	Easter Egg Basket	5″	5″	8″
Sewing Basket	Sewing Basket	6″	6″	9″
Egg Basket	Egg Basket	7″	7″	10″
Peck Basket	Magazine Basket	9″	9″	15″
Half Bushel Farm Basket	Half Bushel	10″	10″	18″
Two-thirds Bushel Corn Basket Farm Basket	Two-thirds Bushel	12″	12″	19″
Bushel Farm Basket	Bushel	12″	12″	23″
Apple Bushel	Apple Bushel	12″	13″	18″
Clothes Basket	Clothes Basket	14″	14″	24″
		15″	12″	22″
Hamper	Hamper with Lid	20″	14″	16″
	Apple Basket or Tray	5″	12″	12″
		5″	14″	14″
		5″	16″	16″
		5″	18″	18″

corn to the chickens, hogs, stuff like dig potatoes, gather beans. Some of 'em had handles across the top.

A two-thirds bushel basket, they call that a corn basket; that's what the old timers all made. It's made out of heavier splinters than the clothes basket. Now the little clothes basket, it's made the same size as a two-third bushel basket, only it's a clothes basket.

I just started makin' these apple baskets lately. I don't know where the name "apple basket" come from; sometimes I call 'em trays, but some say, "That's a pie basket!" I said, "You kin call 'em a pie basket if y' want to." That one's only a ten-inch, but I make 'em bigger yet than that. There's a preacher over at Circleville had me make one with a fourteen-inch bottom; that's a big one. But the sides are the same height on all of 'em.

They was somebody here and had bought one, told me what it was like, wanted me t' make 'em one; they told me how it was done and said that's just what they wanted. I been makin' 'em ever since. I can't make 'em fast enough. I forgit who that was. Differnt people come and suggest things and I pick up and go on with it.

I've made a good many clothes hampers, but only as they order 'em. I have orders now for at least six, but I haven't got none made. It takes as much wood to make a lid on the hamper as a whole big basket. I got a whole buncha orders on that nail there over m' workbench. Lots of 'em wants these picnic baskets, twenty, twenty-four inches long, four-teen inches wide about. Oblongs. People talked me into makin' some. But not very many of 'em. I've made square ones, too, but the round one is the easiest made. I like t' make the peck basket best. I've made pie baskets, square ones; but what happens, they break. No, they don't break, they snap. *I don't want that!*

To help clarify each of the separate procedures in Dwight's basket-making process, I first divided them into four categories: I. Finding and Splitting the Wood; II. Preparing the Splits for Pulling; III. Pulling the Rods; IV. Weaving the Basket. Then I numbered the steps in each category. While such categorizing and numbering are arbitrary at best, this system does illustrate the large number of steps—at least forty—involved in the process. Some are easy, some difficult. Some are quick, and some time-consuming. (The best example of the latter is chopping down a tree by hand in the middle of a woods *and* hauling the wood out by hand!) The measurements used in this description of the process will be, unless otherwise designated, for an egg basket.

I. Finding and Splitting the Wood

(1) *A' course, first you gotta get y' some wood. M' neighbor was tradin' me trees for baskets—anyways he did till he thought he had enough containers. I tell people if they want baskets, then leave me have some wood. Like a woman 'chere day before yesterday, she wanted one. I said, "You bring me up four or five little trees and that one won't cost y' anything. What extry I have left over, well, that won't 'upset the basket,' see." So they come up and got me and we selected them trees right there in the woods. A man brought me this piece down from New Plymouth, about thirty miles from here. He wants a clothes basket and an egg basket. If they bring me a nice pickup truck load of wood, why I make them one or two baskets and then the rest are mine. I use the best of it t' get their baskets first. So that way I have the wood and they have their baskets.*

Lots of good oak in Athens County. I saw advertised a hundred-some acres, all white oak.[5] Boy! If I had that I wouldn't need to worry. The fella runs the bait store at Lake Logan, Jerry Hutchinson, he's got a farm on Big Pine, told the boys to tell me he'd take me down 'n I could have all the white oak I wanted, if there's any there. The farm next door, I can use that, but I'm savin' them for reserve. He has seventy-five acres there, plus another big farm adjoinin' it. He owns all this land up through here. And we got some off Ikey Kuhn, Clayton, and some off Moyer, lives right here back of us. And we got some up off your place up here. A fella here the other day, he has a lot of white oak, said, "Next time I come back, I'll bring you a pickup truck load." I hain't seen him since. Bobby sees t' gettin' it now, he gets some wood fer me.

(2) *Now not any tree'll do. Yeah, it's got to be white oak. You can use honeysuckle, for tiny baskets. But a big one, that's the highest price basket there is. Last summer I got a book, I fergit what company it was, they had baskets in it not much bigger'n a peck size, fer $184! Bittersweet breaks real easy. Lots of people say willow, but it can not. It won't bend. The old makers all used white oak.[6]*

Now I'll tell you about a bur oak. It looks like a white oak. It'll make just as good a basket as another, but on the outside, about a quarter of an inch, or prett' near that, you take that off. If you don't, boy! talk about a fuzzy-looking basket! You got a fuzzy one then, if you don't take that off. That'll break, snap off like a piece of glass! Now a bur oak will work, but there's so much to workin' and gettin' it out. A lot of work. You got to take all the outside of that sap out. Anyone'd look at

Searching for a good tree

that and say, "Looks like that'll work; what's wrong with it?" Hmph! Just catch it like this and turn it and snap! [Laughing.] You cut 'em open and there's knots in there. Oh yeah, knots all over the place! I found one here a while back, the bark on that was white, purt' near white as snow! Real white, and the center, it was white clear through! I made two of the purtiest magazine baskets you ever wanted t' see outa that. Boy, that was purty! White as snow!

I've made 'em out of hickory, but not in this country. Down in Alabama. The hickory here won't split out like that down there does. That makes a pretty good basket. That hickory down there is a white hickory. It's white clear through: you needn't worry about brown in them, and I made as pretty a round basket out of hickory as you ever saw. They make good ones, but you better—you gotta work that up right quick; if you don't you can't bend it or work it.

You know, differnt ones have told me about ash, and I have tried it—with flat splints. I'll tell you about ash. Ash will make baskets, but you gotta have a bandsaw and saw them out and gauge them, saw them out real fine. They's a certain one, a white ash, after it gets six, eight inches across, they pound that and it'll leave loose in strips, 'n use them strips t' weave up. It looks like a dogwood, only it's real white lookin'. They use that t' make hammer handles, too, or if it's long enough, mattock handles. Now maple: maple will make baskets, they'll make a nice flat-split basket, but you got to keep it wet. And a lot of this stuff, even this white oak I make and use, I got to keep it moist. But. Don't weave it up wet! Let it get just so it feels a little bit damp.

White oak is a funny piece of timber. You can't use just any old white oak. I've seen the old fellas try it and couldn't get no place! Y' gotta git one clear of knots and bulges. Has to be clear of knots, straight grain: the bark runs straight up and down. Cut 'em when they're gettin' in size from teacup, up to six, eight inches dimension. I have made 'em up to fourteen inches, but they get old when they're like that, 'n they ain't so good. Once in a while I can get two lengths out of a tree, but very seldom; mostly just one. The first length is best anyhow, 'cuz the top end gets brash [brushy, brittle]. I kin git three to five baskets out of an ordinary-size tree, one about six inches across, eight-foot lengths. I'd only git another one or two out of a top length—it's got a lot of limbs 'n knots, a lot of waste. When they get old, they get brash too. They break, snap, they break off. See when they're young like that, they are more, a young tree is more—stout. The young oak tree is mostly what I love!

Pointing out a knot that makes the tree unsuitable for basketmaking

I watch when I'm cuttin 'em, 'n aim to get 'em all as straight as I can, no big knots. Now I have cut trees where one side of the tree may be a knot or limb that big around, 'n still made awful good baskets. But the other side of the tree was all—looked like the very best. Well, I cut up that tree, 'n got strips up to the knot on that side, where it wouldn't break off or cut loose; now the whole side of that tree up the one side was clear—'n make baskets like that. I have split 'em where that limb come out, split right along beside where that big limb was. Oh, there's all differnt ways to work things like that!

You can use the brown wood in the center as long as there ain't—see, you take a little tree about that big around, they got peth [pith] right in the center; well, you can't use that, that peth will break off. There's just a wee little streak right up through the center of the white oak. That's the peth in there and you can see it when you split the tree. That part won't work in a basket. Try to put that in there, it'll break. I always cut that out: split that out and work from there t' the outside, work back on it. See, the peth is right square in the center of the tree;

it's the center of the stick. Then comes the heartwood; *that's what I discard, 'cause that's brash too. Sometimes I use it to make handles.*

Then comes the outside, the sapwood, the white part. Mostly I use that. [Later he was forced to add:] *The old basketmakers always used just the sapwood; they wouldn't bother with the brown atall. But with wood gettin' so scarce, you have t' use the heart, the whole thing. An old basketmaker told me once, "You'll find someday you have t' use the heart too." It splits okay, but it's harder to pull through the die the first two times.*

The grain any more in the timber in this country don't run like it used to. Used to, you could cut a log about that big around and split it and run just as straight through as if it 'uz sawed. Now these little second-growth white oaks, you go out about halfway, and if you find one that runs straight, why you get up about halfway and it breaks off. You wanta get down fine; but get much smaller 'n your little finger, and you go to bend it, it'll snap right off, just like that!

And you won't get 'em just any *time. Summer time is the best, is the season t' get 'em, when the sap is up. On account in the winter, you're just taking chances in the winter time when the temperature freezes up. I kin usually get it as late as Christmas. I store up some, but if that happens t' freeze, it's just as bad as if it was standin' out in the woods. There is still a little bit of sap in it, 'n that freezes 'n keeps that from bein' workable. I can get back into the woods t' get it again around mid-March or April. Years ago I would cover the wood up outside in the winter, dig out a place and put dirt over it. And it'll keep in a basement, but I can't find a place to put it.*

This year I want t' try buryin' it, if I kin find that much. If it ain't frozen too much, I git it inside by the stove here, 'n thaw it out. But the bark's harder t' git off then. Now if it freezes hard, it's done. It won't split. It freezes up, and they say *it'll split, but you can't make; it won't work out. Trouble is, if y' leave 'em in the woods, cut, even in summer, they get bugs, or they dry out. You kin only leave 'em two, three days. Bill Riddle gave me four logs up there where the Mead Paper Company timbered. I never was able t' get 'em.*

(3) I use an ax 'stead of a saw t' cut 'em down, 'cause they don't split good that way. The boy's been cuttin' 'em with a saw, but I like t' do it with an ax, unless they get caught up. 'Bout a foot above the ground. Don't cut none of 'em close t' the ground, even the best won't split right down there. I most generally cut 'em anywhere from six inches to knee high. My boy, he cuts 'em off sometimes twelve, fourteen inches above the ground. I have t' have him get 'em now, 'cause

Felling a small tree

I go out in the woods and tumble around and fall down. So I stay in here and work.

The size basket I make depends on what size tree I was able to find. When I go t' make a big one, I have t' have all long stuff. I don't like t' get 'em over ten feet long; sometimes the way they work out they'll be six to ten feet. Eight's what I like. I use all size trees, but about as big as a stovepipe is big as I want. From then on I don't want to bother anything bigger, 'cause in about twenty years from now they'll make a saw log— takes twenty to twenty-two years to make a log. I kin git a lot of baskets out of one big as a stovepipe, but that size is gettin' very scarce. Usually I get about two out of a decent size tree. I gotta use smaller 'n smaller ones; can't find them big ones, 'n can't carry 'em out.

(4) I got three wedges I made, pound them inta that log; then I split it in half, then quarters, then eighths, 'n end up with eight splits. A bigger tree'd be more pieces, mebbe even up t' sixteen.

(5) Hoisting a split to one shoulder—which he protects with an old quilted pad—Dwight walks slowly home, literally "up hill and down

dale" in this convoluted terrain. A neighbor said he'd seen Dwight carry out logs weighing over a hundred pounds! The burden of gathering the raw materials cannot be overstated, and it is the primary factor in making white-oak baskets which has discouraged or eliminated all of Dwight's would-be apprentices. A supply of the trees is certainly not easily accessible to urban residents, but perhaps not to rural ones either, since the quantity of white oak is apparently reduced sharply—at least in the area surrounding Dwight.

Elmer Knott, a flat-splint basketmaker in Glouster—approximately thirty miles southeast—claimed in 1980 that "there never was more white oak around." Yet nearly every other maker, both in my personal interviews and in the reports from the survey I conducted on traditional basketry today (Appendix A), noted that white oak is indeed becoming very difficult to find. A well-known Kentucky maker, who moved to Indiana, uses maple now instead of oak because of this scarcity. Early in the century, Kentucky peddlers often warned potential customers to hurry and buy, since the "white oak timber is about gone." It was strictly a sales ploy, but in fact they were probably correct.[7]

I find the best on the north hillside—I read that in Foxfire. *But then I've found pretty good on the south side too. I been makin' fer years 'n years 'fore that book come out. 'Fore I read that I'd go around and cut wherever I found a good tree.*

II. Preparing the Splits for Pulling

(1) *Now when I'm ready to work up some baskets, I gather a bunch of them large splits, and I take the bark off each one with a tool I made up m'self: it's a beveled chisel blade set into a handsaw handle.*

That peels, takes the bark off the tree. You see, that's the bevel of that side there. A bevel for a left-handed person. (You put them blades in either way, turn 'em towards the right or left.) And that bevel, that'll only go so deep—it won't go down in the wood. But it'll go down in the bark, right on down through, take the bark right on off. I got two of them, so if I break one, I'll still have another to use. One's got a plastic handle, one a wooden one. That's another one of my inventions.

Then there's a little layer under the bark called the "inside bark," and I have t' take my knife and scrape that off after I get the outside bark off. I've seen old basketmakers never take that off, but it'll turn brown. Mart Hines told me, he says, "You make baskets, don't never

Making a Round-Rod
Basket

*leave that on, fer it'll turn brown and they'll bring their baskets back
to you. You don't want that!" Y' get that wet, it'll turn brown. Dark.
Brown as a brown hat. Ain't so bad to leave on a farm basket, makes
no difference, but it does on a magazine basket, fer the house. That's
the first thing that'll show up. Just scrape it right down t' the wood. I
say I'm so slow now I take the inside bark off and it grows back on
'fore I get the basket made!*

(2) Next, to divide the wood into small splints, Dwight holds the
bark-stripped split by either standing with it in front of him or sitting with it between his legs—depending on the height of the wood.
(Lately he prefers to sit, since he tends to lose his balance when
standing.) Inserting a knife blade into the top end of the split, he
hits the back of the blade with a mallet to start a break in the wood.
Steadying the whole piece under his right arm, he then divides the
wood into sections by pulling them into strips as long as possible. He
repeats this step until the log section is worked down into approx-

**Left: Peeling the bark
Right: Starting the
section split**

imately quarter-inch (or thinner) splints. The grain is not cooperative, and a novice ends up with kindling—obviously another discouragement to would-be pupils! An internationally exhibited weaver and basketmaker, Dorothy Gill Barnes, elaborated: "It is very difficult to divide the long strips along the grain. The way Dwight holds the piece, presses it against his body, and holds the knife, there is a certain body language. It is beautiful because he makes it look so easy."

Look how that there blade's worn! That was a big blade on that. That's called a "Tree Knife." I take that knife and work it down the split, working down from the top end, and take that mallet there and set the blade on it, hit that a lick, and it goes right on down through it. Hit it on the back of the blade. I broke 'em already that way too.

(3) *Now when y' pull each piece off, y' gotta be real careful to lay it on the floor beside y' in the same direction as you was holdin' it while you was workin' it. Because. You have to pull them through the die with the grain the way it runs, so the bottom of the tree—the bottom of the splint—has to go through the die first. That way you're always pulling the "bottom" of the tree through first, just the way the tree grows. Otherwise, if it was turned the other way, against the grain, that die'd cut it off just like a knife.*

(4) *T' pull that "bottom of the tree" through the die there, I whittle one end of each rod to a point 'bout two inches long: sharpen the large end of the splint—that would be the butt of the tree, the bottom. I sharpen that off so it'll start through the die, 'n then I can get ahold with the pliers to pull it on through. Then I lay them down beside me the same way always. That point makes it start through the die and keeps track of the bottom end.*

(5) *I tie 'em up in bundles, 'n lay 'em over here on the floor, so they're all ready fer pullin' through. First though I wet 'em down, so they pull through easier and won't break off. The size of m' bundle depends on the size basket I wanna make.*

III. Pulling the Splints into Rods

(1) In order to pull the readied splints through, Dwight fits a die board into brackets on the frame of the shop's opened east door. The old basketmakers had a different system: they hung a two-by-six vertically, usually in a barn, fastened from the haymow down then to the floor. (Since cold weather soon made it impossible to work

The die board fixed in the doorframe

with the door open, Dwight recently constructed a simulated doorframe holder inside the shop; that cut down still further on precious floor space, however.)

Each board has a series of square metal dies nailed over large round holes in the board itself. Each of the dies has been specially manipulated for its intended task of rounding the square wood splints. Using these dies is the crucial step in round-rod basketmaking, and the one which makes round-rod baskets so different from flat-splint ones. The die is dimpled by placing it over the hole in an anvil and pounding a large bolt against it. (Sometimes, depending on hardness, the die material must be heated in a forge to draw out the temper before the dimple can be formed.) The hole in the dimple is then punched with a pointed instrument. The shelves above Dwight's workbench display a variety of used coffee, paint, and oil cans holding craftwork miscellany, including different size punches.

I drive 'em in there [the punches onto the metal die], *just punch 'em out cold, keep working down and work down. After while they'll bust right on through, and then I file the hole sharp, make sure that it's round. I file it on the outside, 'n that makes an edge on it just about like a knife. Then you got a die, a "reed die." Some fellas call 'em a "stripper." But a* die *is what they are. I've 'sperimented with different metals for the dies: I've tried used sections of old mowin' machine blades, sickle blades—same ones used by the old basketmakers—or iron stripping.*

I'd like t' get some more dies made, they're all gettin' pretty well worn, can't use 'em any more. The mower blades holds out the best. Sometimes you gotta get the holes white hot on a forge, then cool 'em and temper 'em back again. They can be red before you put 'em in the water. Just so they're soft enough, real red; don't take very much t' get a hole through once you get 'em red enough. Just set 'em on there, sock a hole down through in just a little bit. Take a pair of pinchers and dip 'em in the water. Take 'em out right away, don't leave 'em in, just so the red leaves 'em. Throw 'em down, they cool off, 'n have the right temper on 'em. An old-timey blacksmith can make 'em and make good ones, but that's somep'n you ain't gonna find any more, is an old-timey blacksmith. Harold's got my forge, said he'd make me a set whenever he got the time.

I can show you somep'n else; sit still, I'll get it. Now here is a board that one of the old makers, Salem Kinser, used; they had a sale and the guy gave me this. And these here [metal die squares], *that one and that one, I added. Mary Zeisler's man, Harry, made 'em up for me. See, Salem had it so he could change it over, but you had to have a wide place t' use it. We call that the "Kinser board," and I use that once in a while. Yes sir, that's an old basketmaker gave me that. I keep that for a keepsake.*

But this is m' favorite. This here is one of my own inventions. That is a victrola part, an old turntable. It's made out of—it's good steel. How I happened to know the turntable business, I was in Alabama. Couldn't find nobody down there to make them plates for me. One day, when an old man had a junk yard right near me, I seen that turntable up there. I asked him what he wanted for that. "Oh," he said, "you don't want that thing." And I said, "Yeah, I want that." "What you going to do with it?" And I said, "I'm going to make somep'n out of it." "Boy," said, "I don't know what you'd make out of that old thing." And he just give it to me. "Yeah," he said, "I'll just give you that" [laughing delightedly at the memory of his coup].

One turntable is mounted on a board ⅞ inch thick, 5½ inches high, and 41 inches long, with the bottom edge 32 inches from the

75

Making a Round-Rod
Basic

floor. The other board is nearly the same size but is more aesthet-ically pleasing to me because of its curved edge (Dwight made it from a piece of an old dining-room table). Besides "working down" the splits more easily, it has an added advantage. Each rod must be pulled through a series of successively smaller holes, until the desired rod diameter is reached: the smaller the basket, the smaller the rod. Yet the turntable, punched out with a series of different-sized holes, can accommodate more holes than a board for this series of steps. This partially accounts for Dwight's preference.

Yeah, because I got all the size holes that I can turn around to; I got them in a circle so they'll turn around where they come through. I can change, pull the big split through, then the next size, and keep on clear down t' where I want it. When you get down to that little basket, it takes at least five times goin' through. You take a mowing machine blade section, that's only one piece of metal with one hole, and each one has to be fastened on the board. I just worked that victrola idee out. Happened to think about it and finally I tried it out.

Left: Die boards, the "Kinser board" in center Right: Die boards made from a Victrola turntable

(2) The next step, then, is for Dwight to select a splint from a packet of the worked-down wood, insert the sharpened end into the convex side of the dimple (that is, the outside edge of the die board), and then pull the splint toward himself with a pair of pliers. The process looks quite simple, but Dorothy Barnes has assured me it is not; rather, it requires skillful maneuvering with the elbow to exert just the correct amount of pressure for pulling each splint through. (She also noted Dwight's talent for innovating: while teaching a class outdoors in Athens—with no doorframe available, of course— Dwight somehow placed the victrola-turntable die board into the crotch of a tree, perpendicular to the ground, so it was braced and at an easier level to use.)

Cynthia Taylor, also a basketmaker, advised, "It is really hard to do right. And it takes a lot of strength to pull those rods through and get 'em round like that. The first time I tried it I was amazed at the difficulty!" Dwight's neighbor and pupil Mary Zeisler noted that she "could not believe how hard it was to pull through!" Dwight himself remarked, "A little gal from South Bloomingville thought she could do that, 'n she couldn't budge it! My son-in-law called out, 'Pull hard! Pull hard!' But she couldn't do it."

(3) Most of the dies are marked with yellow crayon for easier identification of hole size, though Dwight seems to know by sight which he plans to use next. In fact, the crayon marks are even in mixed categories: *s* refers to "stay rod," a specific basket part, while *m* is for "magazine basket," a specific basket size. Now Dwight pulls each splint through the requisite series of holes, usually two or three times for a large basket, four to five times for a small one, or for handle wrappings, or for the initial weavers. These last ones are so small they are easily broken, so Dwight invented a "reed guide."

That's so they won't break off or cut off when you're pullin' them little ones through. That's another of my inventions. You clamp it on with a small clamp onto that stand outside; that steadies it, and it guides the reeds straight into the die so they don't get cut off, since they're so thin.

(4) Gathering a bunch of finished rods of the same diameter, Dwight ties them with baler twine (always on hand for his braided rugs) and stores them on the table beside the die board until he is ready for the weaving process. If the rods are not full diameter, they are used for a smaller-sized basket or added to the kindling pile. Using yellow crayon marks on the workbench as a guide, he measures the rods for length as well (though he never saws a whole bundle to the same length).

Starting the splint

**Pulling the splint
through the die**

I aim t' get enough in one bundle t' make up one basket. I never did count 'em. I intended to, but never did. I'll tell ya, I could prett' near tell ya, I'd be safe in sayin' it'd take about fifty a' them splints to weave an egg basket, 'cause they're so small. And I 'spect it'd be about seven-rods for a magazine, or peck, basket. I'll have a big bundle to pull through. Look down, here's a big pile, 'n I think: "Two or three baskets there." I cut 'em down, 'n after some break, lucky t' be one basket makin' there!

I keep differnt size reeds pulled through, just keep 'em all together. I know what size basket I'm gonna make and I pull the splinters down to that size. I always have extrys ready, so if one breaks, I kin put an extry one in. Lots of the old basketmakers, they wouldn't get enough of these, then they'd have to throw 'em down and make some more splints. I always aim t' have enough, more 'n enough sometimes.

But I always keep 'em goin' the same way, layin' the same direction. You start splittin' from the top, the top of the tree and the top of the cut, down toward the bottom. I'm always careful to lay them down beside me then, goin' in the same direction—which I can tell from the pointed end after I whittle it on. When I pull 'em through I lay 'em down on the table in the same direction they come out. Then the pointed end is ready to start the weave, helps it go into the weaved part. After I'm through weaving, 'n cut off any leftover pieces, they'd be the top [of the tree] still, and more likely t' be the brash part anyhow.

It is important to note here that the moisture content of the wood (either too much or—more often—too little) is crucial at several junctures. The first is when the tree is still standing: it must be chopped down and used as soon as possible before it dries out. If it cannot be used immediately, Dwight leaves it whole and with the bark on.

That keeps 'em from drying out. As long as that bark is on there. Watch them and if they dry out, take that bark off and those boards out of there to where they get air—air gets in them boards and goes right on through and dries 'em. Especially the outside, the sap part. The best part dries out first on a person that he wants to use. And when I'm ready to pull m' splints through them die boards, that wood's gotta be moist, even wet. Gotta use more water on it in the winter than in the summer, 'cause there's no sap. I've got rubber gloves now, so I won't get my hands in the cold water so much.

I got a trough out there, a long trough, just lay them packets of splints down in. The trough's about eight feet long, and the bundles are seven feet. I just lay 'em down and roll 'em around in that water, then pull 'em out and leave 'em drain off. It's no matter how wet they are before you pull 'em through, the wetter the better, 'cause they pull through easier.[8]

Now, 'fore I weave, them rods gotta be moist again: moist, but not wet. I kin tell by the feel of 'em when they're just right. Don't want no water though. I've had 'em dry and I've calipered 'em and put 'em in water and take 'em back out and they was bigger. And that's the reason I don't weave when they're wet. Now, they'll get bigger like that when they're wet; but when they're just moist, when that moisture leaves 'em, they stay the same size. But put 'em down in that water, caliper 'em, and let 'em lay in there, oh, five minutes, 'n when you take them out the caliper won't go down over 'em again. And that's the reason they always claim not t' weave 'em wet, let 'em dry first. 'Cause instead of drawing up tight like you'd think, as they dry it makes the basket loose. So if they're wet, before I get ready to weave, I pull 'em through that die; it's got friction and that'll dry 'em off pretty quick. That friction takes the moisture right out.

Now if they go to breakin' when I'm a weavin' in the summertime, I've got a sprinkler can here, 'n I just sprinkle 'em. This time of year

Sprinkling splints for the next day

[November] *they don't dry near as fast. You'd think they would. In the summertime, all that sap up in it, you wouldn't think they'd dry out that fast, but your humidity is what does it, leaves 'em dry out.*

[And in April:] *I'm tryin' t' use up some old wood from last fall, but it takes ten barrels o' water t' make it work! If I'm gonna leave 'em lay, I put 'em outside with water sprinkled on 'em. The last ones I pull through a day, I drop off pullin' through the last-sized hole* [that is, postpone the last pull through the die], *'n wet 'em; then when I pull 'em through that last hole next day, it gets that water off. I wet 'em down before I pull 'em through, too, or they dry out s' fast I can't do nothing with 'em atall. Like I told the boys, I don't want to get ahead on gettin' m' rods pulled any more; they dry out on me too fast and that's too much work lost! So I try t' work out and then make up only two baskets at a time.*

If I'm goin' to a demonstration, I wrap the wood in plastic on the way, and then spray 'em with water in an old Windex bottle. That's what I did when we went to Washington, D.C., to the Library of Congress.

That's the work, *gettin' the wood ready. Been people come here, ohhhh, they watch me, 'n they want me to show 'em how. I've had 'em come and sit down and watch a little bit, shake their heads, "Don't want no part of that!" Too much work, they soon see!*

IV. Weaving a Basket

At last Dwight is ready for the weaving itself, the step which generates the most attention and admiration but which is actually the least time-consuming aspect of the process.

(1) The organizing structure is an interlocking cross of up to eight rods depending on basket size. *There's five in a magazine basket (three over two) or on the beginning cross with any basket over ten inches in bottom diameter. That's the reason they stand so good. Never six (though I would if I did something* great *big). The length of each o' them rods is accordin' to the size basket I'm gonna make, from five up to twenty inches. A six-inch bottom, I cut six-inch-long pieces. Two—well, actually it'd be half—of these I slit in the center with m' knife, then slide the other two rods through them slits.*

It's called the cross. The bottom cross. Just set that splinter down on the table, then set that knife 'bout halfway on it, 'n go right down through it. Just work it down, and get that slit right down in there.

A Bearer of Tradition

Beginning the cross

Finishing the cross

(2) *I measure it fer squareness by puttin' m' measurin' tape on each arm of the cross to the center. Sometimes I just use a square piece o' splint t' measure with. Then look at it, 'n y' think, "Well, that's all there is t' that part of it." No. You've got to caliper that out. It's got to be the same, from the center out, all four around, right around there.*

(3) *When I got the cross real even, I pick out two lengths, 'bout four-to nine-foot lengths* [again, depending on the size of the basket] *of m' smallest weaving rods, then I split them. Then sit down and start*

weavin' around the arms of the cross with these two real real thin, split rods.[9] *To split that smallest reed, y' start at the* top end. *If you started on the bottom it would run off. I split them all out, even with the biggest basket, 'n go out, weave about five rounds with that piece of split wood.*

I weave left-handed, *clockwise. And I even put the handle on left-handed. That's how y' kin recanize my baskets. I don't need t' sign 'em. You just look at how that weave goes around. I write right-handed. I first started in weavin' righthanded, but it went so slow—bein' lefthanded come more natural—well, I took a notion I'd change and go clockwise. A schoolteacher, when I went t' school, started me on writin' righthanded, kept right after me. My mother was left-handed. I eat, do everything else but write, with my left hand. But I can weave both ways. I teach both ways.*

(4) Wrapping first one split and then the other around the center of the cross in an X form, he locks these under the inside of the cross, then begins weaving them in a tight "lock weave" or "double weave" pattern (see fig. 2), which is actually twining. (When I was drawing figure 2, Dwight did not happen to be weaving a basket just then. We tried rigging several simulations on which he could demonstrate for me. We were *both* surprised when he could not weave without an actual basket in process in his hands, and I had to return the next day when he had one especially readied.)[10] Weaving four rounds for a small basket, six to eight for the larger ones:

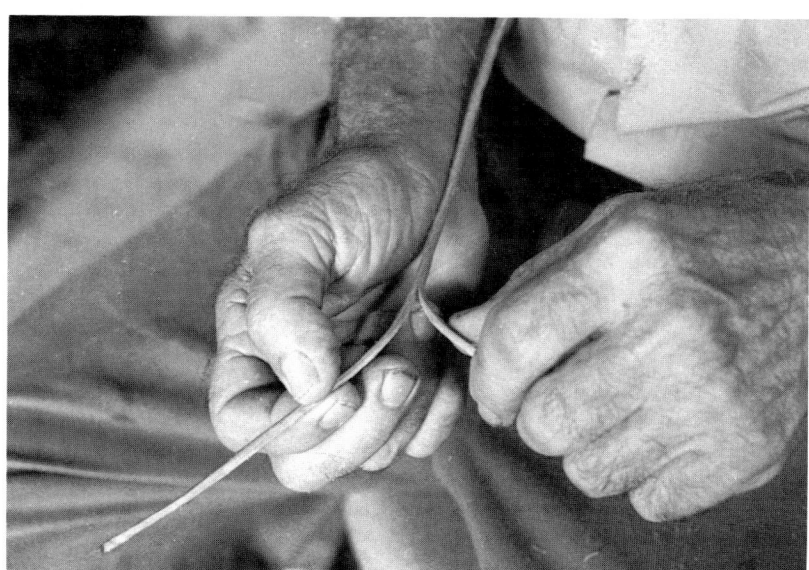

**Beginning the weave
with thin, split withes**

When I get to the end of these, I tamp 'em down there solid [with a miniature "crowbar"]. *It's too narrow there fer my thumb t' push till I git out farther.*

(5) *Now you force them cross rods apart sideways till they look like the spokes of a wheel. Them is called the bottom frame. You have to watch here, some of the time these break off. They'll break, snap, you'll have to pull them out so you kin get a natural bend on 'em.*

(6) Next Dwight inserts two heavier rods and weaves them around in his "lock weave" pattern. While anchoring the ends of the first weavers in this next section, he is watching carefully to make sure—by eye and by feel—that the distance between each spoke remains the same, pulling and forcing any intractable spokes as he weaves: "The lock weave holds the bottom more firm."

(7) When the bottom frame is nearly covered, Dwight bends and pushes the whole flat structure, sometimes with his knee, forcing the bottom into a convex bulge in the center to help brace the basket. The bottom frame will thus pull against the side.

'Sposed t' be dished. I do that a-purpose. That way the weaving can't get out. Put a little bulge in the bottom, braces it up so it won't pull down. When you get sixteen stayrods in there, if you don't have that bulge, it'll pull down. A big basket, that's *when you got fun!*

(8) All the while Dwight is watching carefully to make sure, by eye and by feel, that the distance between each spoke remains the same. When the bottom frame spokes are covered, Dwight pulls the leftover lengths of weaving rods down through the bottom, weaves them in, and trims the raw ends with a pocket knife.

(9) The bottom finished, Dwight selects a packet of measured stayrods to make the framework of the basket's side (with the number depending on the size of the basket). Aided by its sharpened point, he pushes a stayrod as close to the center as possible on both sides of each spoke of the bottom frame.

The stayrods is what the old basketmakers called 'em. They're a little bigger'n the weavers, 'cept in a bushel basket. Then they're the same size. But makin' 'em a little bigger, they weave down real nice, nice and tight, at the top. They're connected into the bottom after it's made. We always called that the web. The web of stays. Some call it the spider or spider web. See, y' put one on each side of the bottom spokes, and then they stick out like it's a spider web.

I bend each of these stayrods into about a ninety-degree angle, 'n that makes the stakes for the side of the basket. You turn them right up, but y' have t' watch, some of the time they break off. They'll break,

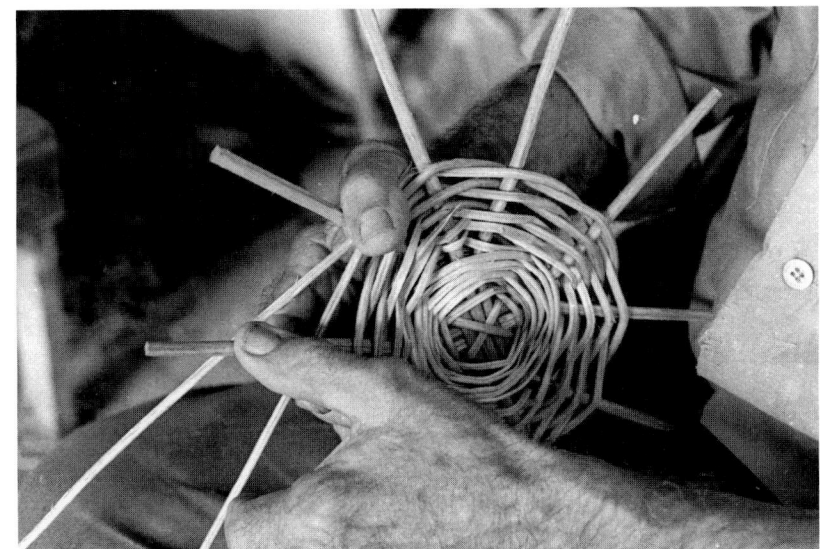

"Lock weaving" the bottom

Forcing the bottom into a convex bulge with the knee

The "web of stays,"
sometimes called the
"spider web"

snap, you'll have to pull them out, 'cause if you happen to have one or two in there broken, and go on *like that, you'll have a sideways basket.*

The number of stays runs from sixteen to twenty-one. Big one, there's twenty-six in a big basket. Sixteen in a little one, and that's the smallest they go down. They're supposed to be about two calipers heavier 'n the ones in the rest of the basket, but the same if they're larger baskets; in large baskets the caliper's always the same.

(10) *Pull the web of stays together a few inches from the top, and tie them rods together. Sometimes I got black twill tape, sometimes an old tie. Oh, you* gotta *tie them up t' get the shape or you can't get nowhere. I loosen them after I get up so far, but I tie them up so they can't get away from me.*

I kin make 'em like that, with that top pulled in [it looks *quite* exotic], *but that's* no *basket! People'd say, "What kind of a crazy thing is that?" They'd like t' look, but wouldn't buy it, and I don't like things settin' around. It's kind of obscurious. Makes people think, "I don't want no part of him!"*

(11) *Now I get me three new weavers, 'n start weavin' up the side. First I make me a pencil mark where I began, so later I kin find those bottom three rows. I go three rows of three reeds, triple rows is what they are, "triple weave." It's a lock weave also (see fig. 2). That holds the basket firm so it stays a uniform shape. That makes a nice basket, a good* stout *basket, when they're triple weave. I like t' make that!*

Then I anchor each one of the three behind two stayrods, cut off the end. I always aim to keep one reed longer. Then I don't run out at the same time. I mostly aim not *to end the joints at the same place.*

I use the three rounds, according to size: I go three rounds on any little-size basket, but then when I get to a big bushel basket I go four or five rounds of three. But I don't use one [weaver]. *If you use one, that would make the basket uneven. That's what makes the basket nice and even, to use three.*

However, as wood has become so much harder for him to get, Dwight often goes only two rounds with the triple weave.

(12) *Now I'll go up the longest part of the side with* two *weavers. Gotta stop after one round t' untie the web of stays. You'd think it'd go in ever direction. And if the stayrods goes out too far, I push 'em back by hand. If they bend in too far, I just fetch 'em out a little bit. No special name fer this part, just called "weavin' up the side, the weavin' part."*

I've made several with the whole basket *triple weave, three instead of two goin' up the side. But it takes so much more wood. They look a*

Tying the web up

**Going up the side with
two weavers**

*little differnt, but it takes a half more splinters. Don't make the basket
any stouter, just the looks. Right down there tight 'n you can't see
through it. Been differnt ones here says, "Y' ever make any triple
weave?" And I say, "I don't unless y' order 'em." That takes more
splinters. I charge about a third more for 'em. I think Mary Zeisler got
the last one I made. I don't know who give me the idee fer those. I kin
make it a whole lots quicker 'n nicer 'n I can the other one* [straight
weave up the main part of the side], *but it takes a third more material. They look a little differnt, but they take too many splinters.*

Later Dwight proudly presented me with a basket made of carefully selected, all *white* white oak, with three weavers up the side—
a rare and beautiful gift indeed!

(13) During this part of the weaving, Dwight stops intermittently
and puts the basket down on floor or grass to ascertain whether it sits
straight. Eyeing it on what I consider uneven ground, he still ad-
judges it fine.

(14) *I use a lock weave on the bottom, then a triple weave on the
bottom part of the side. Now this next part, goin' up the middle of the
side, I mostly always called it straight weave or single weave. Some
call it double and some call it single. But it ain't* doubled over *one
another, you* weave *around them single. But at the bottom, with the
three, it's triple weave. (Then again at the top I do triple weave again:
three rounds at the bottom and two at the top for an egg basket, or*

Measuring an apple basket

four and three for a magazine basket.) I'll go a few more rounds, then measure it. I don't do too awful much measurin', but just to make sure they're right.

Dwight's measuring methods—even when he uses a tape—are casual at best, especially when he uses the ground as a base while weaving outside in good weather. However, he is usually satisfied, obviously as confident in his own sense of balance as in the tape measure's results, and continues weaving:

I have a patent [meaning an original idea, not an official government patent] *the rest of 'em ain't got on: they use one weaver and I go right up with two. Makes it lots stronger and goes faster. Holds 'em even, they ain't got no chance to pull in or out. By using two, then the stayrod holds it; it can't get away, go nowhere. When the old basketmakers used one, and they come to the end, they had to go the other way. Mart Hines always used two. His father only used one and he got 'em sideways. So Mart said to his dad one day, "Why don't you try two?" "Oh, it won't work." "Why don't you just try it?" He did try it, and that learned him. Mart said it took his dad so* long *to run 'em up. The bigger the reed the faster it'll build up. A bushel basket goes twice as fast. This here magazine basket is called "fancy work," 'cause it's considered a fancy basket* [since it takes so much time to make and is not purely functional, especially in agricultural or traditional terms].

(15) *When it's about six inches high* [one and a half inches of the bottom rows of triple weaving plus four and a half inches of the wide section of double weaving], *I go back t' usin' three weavers, and add a band of triple weaving at the top t' match the one on the bottom band.*

(16) *When the basket's the right height, I pull them stayrods down and bend 'em sideways, then weave each one into the last round. That's called "braidin' the top." That's the stayrods braided down in.*

The basket side is now tripartite: (a) the bottom band of the side, triple weave with three weavers, one and a half inches high; (b) the center section, straight or single weave with two weavers, four and a half inches high; and (c) the top band, triple weave with three weavers, one and a half inches high, including the top braid.

(17) *Then I pound that top edge down with this here black-gum mallet I made. That's called "levelin' the top." Sometimes I'll follow around with the mallet and make sure they're all down in there good and tight.*

(18) *Now I have to dehorn it. See, I turn it and cut them weaver ends off with the slope of the basket—them ones pokin' outa the basket there on the outside. I use a huntin' knife sometimes; they're purty handy, but usually I use m' pocket knife. But ooohh, I've cut the dickens outa m' thumb, across there. Of late I hain't been doin' it much, been a little more careful.*

But you can't cut them ends off till it's finished. No, no, you don't want to cut them ends off while you're weaving on it. Next thing you know, first thing you know, you'll have to change your basket one way a little bit—it'll go a little sideways so you'll want to change it back and get it straight. But it'll jerk them ends out if you cut 'em off. Leave them go till you get it wove up and everything; then after they're set and after you're done weaving 'n get it straightened out, it won't come out, nine out of ten. They'll lean a little sideways and you'll have to push 'em back. Now if that's cut off, you'll push it back and the weaver'll just go right out like that! That's where a lot of the old basketmakers made their miscue: they cut 'em off too short, way back here, and they slip right up through and OUT they go! Lets the basket

Braiding the top

Ending the braid

Leveling the top

Dehorning

frazzle out. I don't do that. I watch where I cut 'em. And I've never had a basket t' frazzle yet. Never a one brought a basket back frazzled out. Don't cost any more t' cut 'em off right!

(19) *Now I'm usin' pliers t' nip off them weaver ends poking out of the* inside *of the basket. I follow 'em around one way and then the other, beginnings and end. Have to watch so you cut the right place, though!*

(20) *Handling comes next, but I wait t' do that till I finish weaving all the baskets I've got rods ready for—so they won't dry out. That handle's made of my thickest reed, a special one about twenty-five inches long, split out same as the rest, whittled down, then pulled through just once. They pull hard. 'Cause they're about a half inch thick for a magazine, a quarter inch for the small basket. The handling's not so hard, you just have to bend it in a perfect rainbow shape first. I learned that from Mart Hines too. Yeah, y' call that a hoop handle, on any kind of basket, even the bushel basket where y' put two small ones on each side.*

Whittle both ends of that rod into sharpened points about five inches long. Then y' bend the rod with both hands into a half-round, an arc shape, 'n push each end into opposite sides of the top. That's called the false handle. Once in a while they's a low place on the top edge, 'n I set the handle right in the center of that. When that handle's on there, you'll never see where that's at. If there ain't no low place, I just kinda guess where to set it. No, there's lots of tricks—tricks to all trades—you gotta trick t' know how t' do 'em.

(21) *After you push it down in there, sometimes that handle is pretty stout held in. Pull it out a little bit, then see if it balances: hold it up there in the air on a coupla fingers and look across. I balance them top and bottom. Look across, see if that bottom is straight, then look across the top. If they ain't balanced, somebody pick 'em up, they'll turn over sideways. If it happens t' flop over one way a little bit, I'll have t' change it. I never had t' change any a second time!*

(22) Then Dwight begins wrapping the false handle with a small-diameter splint in a serpentine pattern, looping the splint through the top rows of the basket where the false handle is inserted.

I use the smallest reed I make to wrap the handle, no matter what the size of the basket. I've seen 'em use bigger, but it leaves too many open spaces. I mostly get the handle out of sapwood, fer it bends nicest. Sometimes I get it out of the brown, the heartwood. The old basketmakers always used all white, but now that wood's so scarce, we gotta use in a basket what we got.

Nipping the inside ends

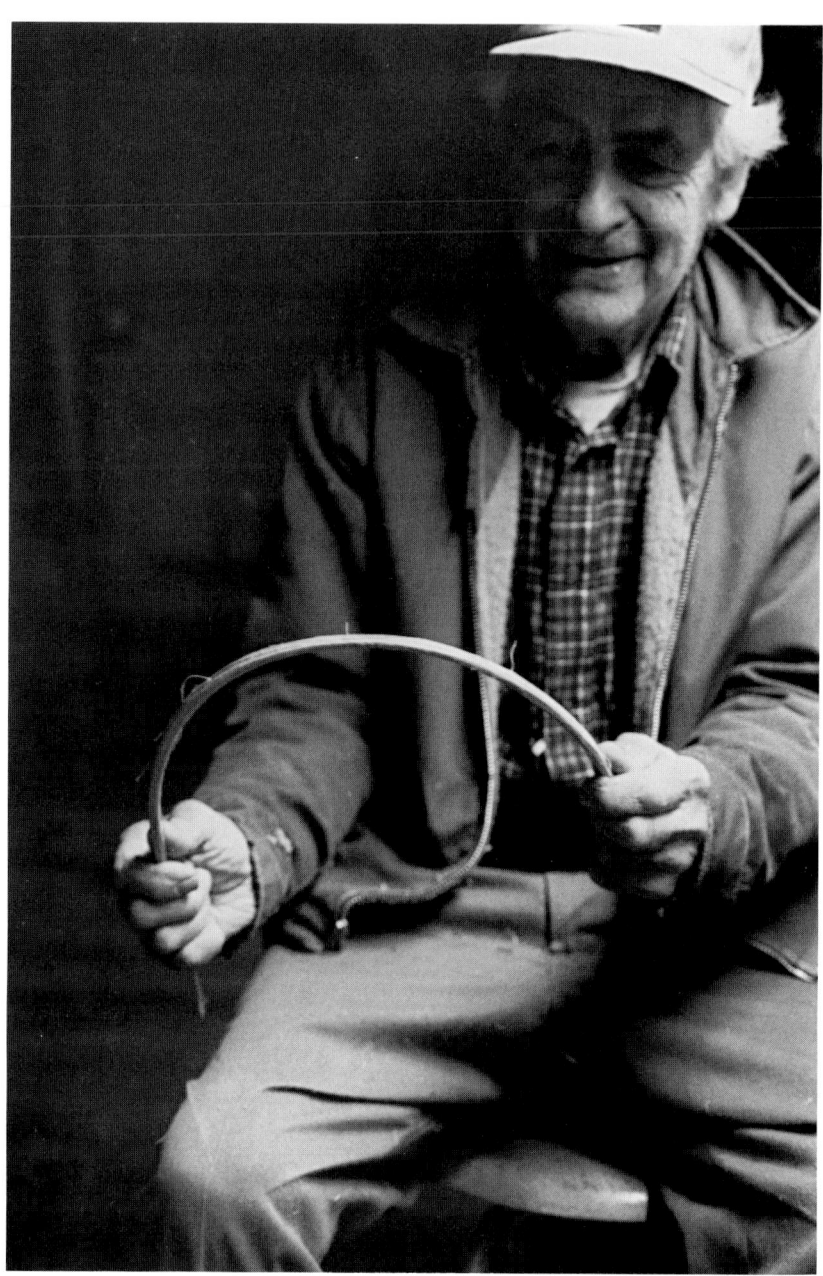

The "hoop handle"

Above: Balancing the handle

Right: Serpentine weave for the handle

Dwight pulls it tight, then reverses and wraps, continuing the serpentine pattern from that direction as well. This wrapping of the handle must not "run out" in the middle of the two traverses back and forth: if he judges the length incorrectly, the rod will have to be replaced. The second wrapping rod is started on the opposite side and also locked around the false handle, so that both sides of the handle will have the strength of these beginning loops.

I go back and forth, one side to the other and back—two rounds. Then trace it through between the reed on the side. I aim t' go down two reeds, back up the two, and back around the length of the handle, do the same looping down two reeds on the other side. That locks it on there tight. Yeah, yer daughter Ann was here watchin' me one day. She seen me wrap the handle on, 'n she said it looked easy. I said, "Yeah, that looks easy, but you start puttin' that on and watch out when you start back through here. That's when they'll break!"

"And there's your egg basket!"

(23) *Keep goin' till the false handle is covered. When I finish the handle, I lock 'em all in the same by weavin' the ends into the side of*

the basket, then cut the reed off inside. That way you can't see no ends where it come out.

(24) Now pound the wrapped handle smooth with the gum mallet.

(25) I almost always sew that top band of triple weave: weave one a' them fine, split *rods up and down the top band, diagonal to the top rim and about one inch deep; continue in that pattern twice around, makes a sort of X pattern. I don't* always *sew 'em. Reason I got to sewin' 'em, the baskets're green and give. I tell people, if they don't like that sewing they can leave it on till the basket dries out, then take it off. They's a lot now comes and they don't like the sewed-top basket very good. Say they'd take the basket, if the top wasn't sewed down on it. But a lot of 'em says they want it on: "That's decoration." See, that holds 'em firm and they won't frazzle out while they're green.*

(26) Pound that top down, make sure it's good and tight. Sometimes I also pound down each end where I cut them ends off. I mostly pound 'em down twice, to make sure it's tight. Not on the inside, unless they'd happen to be a bulge. A basket sometimes 'll bulge in—hardly ever bulge out—but I hardly ever get one in my baskets.

And there's your egg basket!

It's right smart of a trick, that basketweavin' business. I was a long time learnin' it. As a fella says, I don't know too much about it yet, but I can make out at it. It's called a "lost art," basketmaking, differnt ones have told me. I say, "You just think it's lost. T'ain't lost yet!"

Dwight's son Bobby remarked, "It's more complicated than y' think." And indeed it is!

5. The Finished Basket

Even though Dwight explained the basketmaking process carefully, there is still more than just that how-to part. For example, who have his customers been over the years? What has he charged them?

While Dwight has strong personal tastes and preferences, mixed in with these is a decidedly practical awareness of his audience, his customers, who—heaven forbid!—"might think, if I made something obscurious, 'I don't want any part of him.'" His customers had been, over the years, his rural neighbors. Local hardware stores bought a large supply only a few times, back in the 1920s and '30s. He has never had to huckster his wares, as so many other makers did, for "someone just showed up at the door," and bought as he finished them.

Dwight was delighted with the prices he was receiving in 1978, which were far higher than he had ever expected, but geared to his new popularity with a more sophisticated audience. Table 2 illustrates his slightly higher prices in 1980. He raised several of the sizes a few dollars more in 1981, though some were actually less than in 1980, owing no doubt to forgetfulness, but also, perhaps, to a measure of personal distancing. He then doubled many of the prices in 1984 but left them stationary after that.

Even after doubling his prices in 1984, Dwight was still making *very* little on a per-hour basis. Because he does the work in stages, he seems unclear just how long it takes to make a basket from start to finish, from that first step of walking to the woods to the last one of balancing the finished basket on his finger. Several widely varying estimates were all unrealistic. While the large baskets take longer, they do bring more money on a per unit, per hour basis. However, they are not so popular in today's gift-hungry market.

Bob Mansberger, Dwight's former son-in-law, had begun the long process of learning from Dwight to "make." He expounded somewhat heatedly: "Usually one day, you spend the whole day splitting

Table 2. Dwight Stump's Basket Prices

Name of Basket	ca. 1917	1978	1980	1984–85
		Price (in dollars)		
Easter Egg Basket		5	7	15
Sewing Basket			8	20
Egg Basket			10	20
Peck (Magazine) Basket		12	15	35
Half Bushel	.25		20	40
Two-thirds Bushel	.35		25	45
Bushel	.50		30	50
Apple Bushel			30	50
Clothes Basket			50	50
Hamper with Lid			75	
8″ Apple Basket (Tray)				12
10″ Apple Basket				25
12″ Apple Basket			10	30
14″ Apple Basket			12	35
16″ Apple Basket			14	
18″ Apple Basket			16	

them out, next day pulling them through. Him and I went out to the woods and cut down a tree, brought it back and split it up, got enough pulled through to make just one basket. I kept track: we made *one* basket in twenty-two hours, so that's really forty-four hours in one basket. As cheap as he sells them, he's working for *nothing*. And they'll buy them from him, take them around to these other fairs and stuff and sell them for about three times the price. That basket there, I could take that to an arts and crafts place, sell it for eighty, ninety dollars, just like that! People been pulling the wool over his eyes, but I did some checkin'."

And it is true: despite the doubled 1984 price, comparable baskets bring far higher prices in other settings, even relatively unsophisticated rural ones. But Dwight himself seems quite unruffled by any middle person's profits.[1] He asks what he asks, gets what he gets. Happily.

Yet, one of the most important questions which ultimately have bearing on the whole subject of cost is this: Does he have, or even hope to have, successors? In spite of the potential market, Dwight has so far found no apprentices, no successors to carry on the old and revered tradition. The fact that the materials are difficult to find and, worse, time-consuming to prepare is an enormous stumbling block. But even more important, the hours of work and the accomplishment of dexterity are not "cost effective," in modern parlance. After all that arduous work, potential successors realize that either they lack knowledge of how to reach urban markets or the customers they have will not pay for the time and skill (and, yes, tradition) involved: the old story of not putting the money where the mouth is.

Thus in spite of Dwight's sanguine and philosophical approach to the material aspects of his art, the whole subject of folk-art marketing, with its political and economic aspects, is brought to bear on any folk artist's biography, any discussion of the future of folk art. For if the art object does not bring adequate compensation to the artist, or in this case, to subsequent successors, there will soon be no product—as is indeed happening with round-rod oak baskets.

Dwight's own discussion of the basket itself is, not surprisingly, far removed from the sophisticated buy-sell machinations of today's dealers. He talks instead about the shapes and sizes he enjoys making, about decorating the baskets, and, when questioned, about prices and finding successors.

I just mostly make my baskets round, like I learned from the old makers. I've tried different shapes but I didn't like them. When I was in Alabama, I made what they call a veg-atable basket; it was as big as a bushel basket. That's all the kind they wanted, was them great big ones. (They raised a lot of veg-atables there where I was at.) But the colored people made cotton baskets. They was all flat splint. I've made flat splits, made them here in this country, but the white oak got so bad I couldn't split it—not t' make anything.

Oh, I make all kinds. Whatever the customer wants—or I think they want. If they don't want what I think, I still make 'em. My favorite now to make is the ten-inch apple basket, or tray. I make 'em bigger too, up t' fourteen inches across. There's a preacher over at Circleville had me make one o' them, but that's a big one. The sides're the same height on all of 'em, though. I like to make that kind a lot, with handles across the top. Yeah, I try t' make what they want. I made a flower basket here lately, a hangin' basket t' put flowers in, artificial bokays mostly. I sold 'em, as fast as I made 'em. They mostly want 'em plain, then set 'em down inside a macramé hanger that m' grandson Tommy made; or get one at the store. In Logan, Jack's Surplus sells all kinds, but differnt places has 'em. You can put a jar down in for fresh flowers.

A few people colors their baskets. Way they do that, the reed is colored purple. They're colored by leavin' them white splinters in water, soakin' 'em in water till they get to turnin' purple. That color goes clear through the reed and it ain't painted. *Now a lot of people would see them and say, "Oh, them are painted." But they are not. Can't get no other color, though. I believe Leroy Arter was the first one t' tell me about colorin' 'em like that.*

While I was down there in the South, in Alabama, two boys asked me one day, "Did you ever color any?" "What color?" "Well, the natural color, you don't have to put anything in." I knowed all the time what it was, and I said, "Well, I got a trough out there, if I want t' color 'em purple all I need t' do is leave 'em in there three, four days. Maybe you fellas don't know it, but you got to take the sap part of that wood; the brown part, the heartwood, it won't faze that." Which it won't. See, down there they color them flat splits, then use some of them dyed, some not, to make 'em look like a checkerboard.[2]

I can make 'em myself: put one color of reed in the handle and a row of colored reeds middleways, or I can put them in so the tops braid down colored. When y' first color them, they come out a real dark purple; but after a while they'll lighten. But they never get any lighter than a dark blue. They'll stay that. I haven't done that yet, but I might later on if I keep on, I might decorate them, change them up a little.[3]

I'll tell you who brought one here one day and showed me. Nancy Crow's man brought a round split that'd been painted. Nancy bought it at a sale. He come out t' get some baskets fer her, and she told him t' bring it along and see if I'd made it. As soon as I seen it I said no. He said, "What's that on there?" I said, "That's paint somebody decorated and made that." I suppose it was made at least fifty years ago, but whoever made it done a pretty good job of painting it. It'd begin to look old though. I said, "Yeah, that's somebody that's had it a long, long time, and they've had it put away someplace till they got it up and sold it at a sale. I never cared about putting paint on 'em myself.

That would be kinda a tedious job. First thing you know I'd have it all botched—splotched up and spotted.

But I don't paint 'em or color 'em. Seems like everybody that wants 'em, wants 'em plain now. They don't want nothing on them differnt. Don't want differnt color in 'em, just want 'em all the same clear through. I thought lots about makin' 'em differnt, but as long as they'll sell this way—. Differnt ones wanted to know how, I tell them. They say, "Oh, I'd just as soon have them plain as t' have them with anything on them."[4]

Then there's ones with open work. But nobody around here ever made those. Nor nobody around here used differnt widths either, of reeds. Now beginners uses that rat-tan t' learn on, but that don't prove out satisfactory. I use it in m' teachin' though, 'cause it's easier to start on fer beginners.

I can do that open work too. I got books here on it. I'm gonna show you.[5] See, every one of them got wooden bottoms, solid wood bottom. That 'un's a picnic basket. But they hain't none of 'em—I got two books here and there ain't none of 'em that makes them like I do. They don't even start 'em off like I do, or finish them up or nothing. Somebody was telling me a while back you can send off and get all the books you want. But I told 'em, "You won't find the kind I make in 'em," and they said, "That being the case, you can get a patent on 'em." I said, "Oh, I ain't takin' no patent," I said, "I know some fellas around if they wanted to make 'em, they can still make them like that, so I couldn't get no patent right on 'em."

The man got that cabin over there yonder is from Fairborn, Ohio. He goes to a flea market up there, and he happened t' see some baskets there made like mine. A man's making them and selling them at the flea market there. He tried t' find out fer me who it was, but seemed like nobody knows the man's name.

Then down at the fairgrounds when they had that there "Appalatch" festival this summer in Logan—I don't know what date it was any more, I lost track of it—a man named Pierce was down there and demonstrated and showed about making those flat-split *baskets. Nancy Crow was there, she seen him. He done it all with a penknife. She said he done an awful rough job. And Elly Del Matto told me about a woman makes 'em over near Glouster.[6]*

I repair baskets too, put bottoms in 'em, 'n new handles on 'em, repair 'em up. I've always done that. The old guys wouldn't do that. After

**A new handle for an
old basket**

they'd sell a basket you couldn't come back and say nothing. Oh no! They wouldn't repair it. They'd sell *'em one, but they wouldn't try to fix it.* Nobody *wanted to repair 'em. I was the only one'd do it. I started right out from the start repairing. I'd always tell 'em, I'd say, "Now get any good basket that the handle's pulled off, the bottom out, 'n bring it and I'll repair it for you.*

For a while there I got quite a good bit of it t' do. Somebody else had made the baskets, the bottom'd go out of 'em. Bring it t' me, and I'd fix it so the bottom wouldn't go out. The way they was made, the bottom'd bow down *instead of up. They got the bulge on the wrong way. I'd put the bulge the way it was supposed t' go and it stayed.*

Some of them was made over in the old country, not around here. Them two over there on the table are two of the oldest ones that's been brought here. Man by the name of Lader, over at Rockbridge, brought that t' me. It's the postmistress's brother is who it is. He told me that one was over a hundred years old. That dark one, Shaw—down in Bloomingville—brought that one up here. See, I can tell the weave of 'em when they're made in this country around here. I know the weave.

Some man had this *one a long time. I don't know whether I can get it rebuilt or not. Have t' use honeysuckle to repair it back again, 'cause that's what it was made out of. It hasn't been too long ago a woman brought one here the dog chewed the top of it. She thought it couldn't be repaired, 'n I told her when she come back I'd have it. She come back and said, "That don't look like the dog chewed the top off that thing!" I told her to put it up, she couldn't tell it from the rest of 'em.*

Old Isaac Arter used t' make a basket with the top lookin' like it was braided. But if y' didn't watch, they'd slip out. I was told afterwards, a lot of people bought his baskets, but he didn't cut the stays long enough and away they'd go! Just come apart, fly right out. Way I weave 'em, I weave the top down, and I've never had one basket t' come back with a thing wrong with it. Only one I ever had come back, that wasn't my fault. Fella had it fer nine years, 'n he used it t' feed. He told me, "You ain't the fault of this. The other handle is still stayin' good, but I pulled this off myself, jerkin' on it." So I put the handle back on, 'n he said this spring, "That handle'll never come off no more."

Tell you somep'n else I've done: chair bottoms. I done that back when I could see good. I picked up old ones now and then and re-paired' em up, put new bottoms in, with the same stuff I make baskets. You've seen them old-fashioned rockers that the arm on 'em is wove; an' most of 'em's wove in the back too. I got one a' them once—I was a long time findin' it—pretty badly tore up. I repaired it up an' some-

body bought it right away. Then you bought that one offa me fer your daughter Mary. I just picked them up somewheres, bottoms out of 'em.

And trunks, too. Made 'bout like that one you've got. Somep'n like the one my mother had, too, 'cept it was rounded on top instead of flat. I don't know how many of them I've been around sales and bought. I got some for fifty cents that was pretty badly damaged and I'd take 'em home and repair 'em and fix 'em. Shellac, varnish 'em. Pretty soon somebody'd come along and I'd sell 'em. I ain't got a one, I've sold 'em all.

As far as selling, the old makers'd sell their baskets mostly t' stores, general stores, like at Revenge 'n Clearport 'n Lancaster. That store down at the end of Tar Ridge, down at Revenge, man that run that was Ray Buzzard. He used t' buy baskets off the old makers. And Frank Hartman run the Clearport store. In Lancaster, most of 'em sold t' Billy Wacker. Oh yeah, and I mind some o' the old makers tellin' they sold at Dixon's store in Amandy.

Most generally theirs was two-thirds bushel; they didn't like t' make any less than that, 'cause they was easier made. A little basket like I make there, you'd ask them t' make one o' them and they'd back off right quick. They didn't want no part of that. They'd say, "Our time's worth more'n what it'd take t' make one a' them." At that time, a two-thirds basket sold for a quarter, so you know they could hardly afford to make a little 'un. That was right around 19-and-22, right around '22. They'd sell t' hardwares.[7] Now I sold to hardwares 'n stores too. I showed you that little book back there showed where I sold to 'em.

Only times I made 'em full time was in the wintertime. It got so bad, the weather got, so there was no farm work. My wife said I made baskets about six months out of the year down there in Alabama though. Long about '38, I sold 'em to a wholesale house, a big wholesale outfit down there in Montgomery. Name of Hudson and Thompson.

Then when we lived along a big state highway down there, a lot of people stopped in. It was twenty miles south of Montgomery, the capitol—that's as far away as I ever got—along a state highway, Troy Highway. I had a table, about four by eight feet, and I fastened a pole up, one on this side, one on that side, put a big stout wire across, and had m' baskets sittin' there hung on that by the handles, up there on display.[8] They'd show up that way good. Set a bunch of 'em down on the bench too. People drivin' past could see 'em, see 'em hangin' there.

I'd get a few out on m' bench like that, and before night they'd all be gone!

There's more material down there to make 'em out of than there was here. I could keep up down there. I had 'em on display there mebbe a coupla years. I got more for 'em down there than I did here, too. But I was in a section down there that was pretty well-to-do. Let's see, what they call a big feed basket down there, I got five dollars for. It was big around as a bushel basket, but bigger 'n one, deeper.

Back up here, Russell Jones had a store at Tarleton, a hardware and a grocery store both. I sold mostly t' him, mostly two-thirds bushels. There was three storekeepers over there bought baskets, bought a lot of 'em. I sold them a lotta peck baskets, that's really what went. See there in m' book, I sold one fer 75 cents, and twelve for $19.25. I sold dozens 'n dozens at that price. A peck is four quarts or two gallons liquid. Also there was a man by the name of Forest Frazier, down in South Perry. And I sold a lot of 'em over at Stoutsville too. And some up to Amandy.

See here in m' book, here's $1.25 for a two-thirds bushel. There's five for $1.75. They was little ones—a market basket they called it, or

Dwight's 1944 ledger

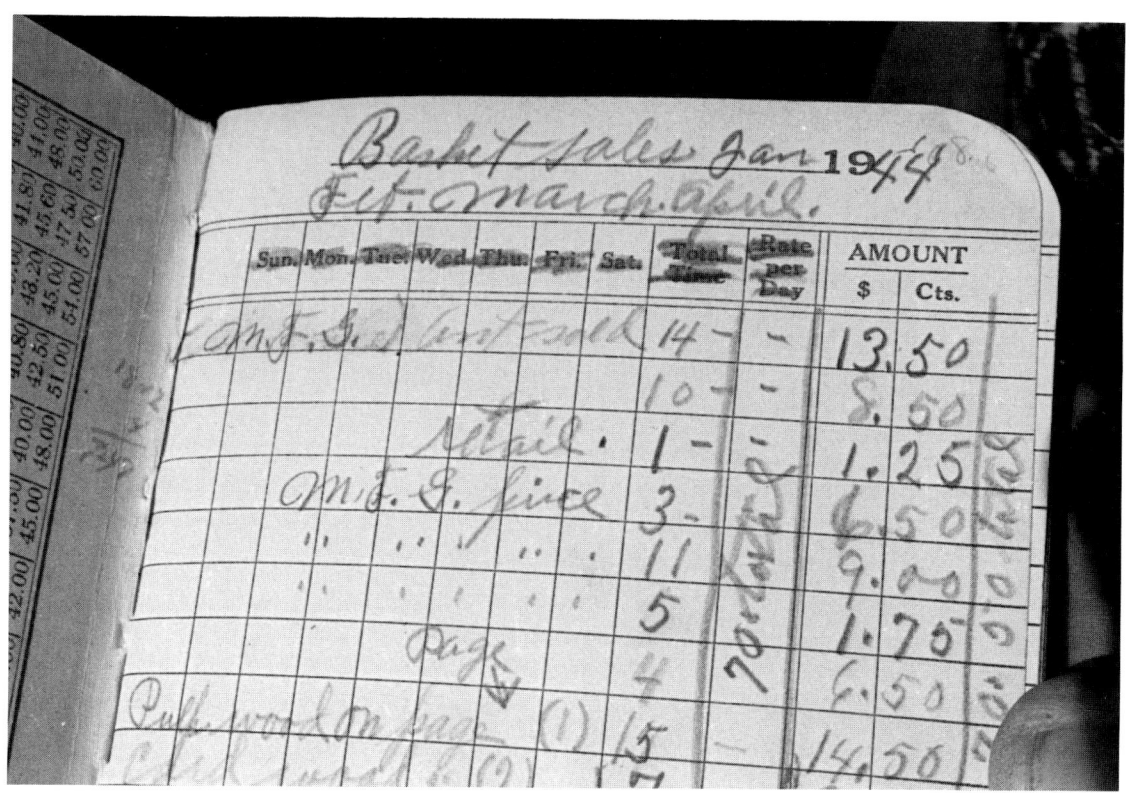

egg basket. Here Armstrong's Feed Store in Laurelville bought four-teen at one time; that come to $13.50.[9] Them was two-thirds bushels. See: I also sold pulpwood by the cord then, got $14.50 a cord. That's when I had a place over on Long Run; it was about all pulpwood. And I used t' sell t' the hardware man in Laurelville, White's Hardware. It goes by the name of White's Hardware yet. Man ut owns it is a Damon Pontious. I'd deliver 'em t' him, take 'em down there, 'bout eight miles west o' here. He'd get me an order of so many he'd want. I could sell a bunch of 'em all together that way. But you know, I'll tell you what I got fer them *then. I got twelve dollars a* dozen! *Made a whole dozen to get twelve dollars. And I think that was just in the '60s. Now I get fifteen dollars fer the one, more'n what I sold him fer a whole dozen!*

The old basketmakers, Hines 'n them, back years ago they made baskets and sold two-thirds bushel baskets for twenty-five or thirty-five cents, back in 19-and-15 and '16. Thirty-five cents fer a two-thirds bushel basket. That's the reason they made that size, they was highest. And they was tickled t' death t' get thirty-five cents! A two-thirds bushel basket back then was the main go. They all made those. And they got a quarter for a half-bushel basket. And fifty cents is all they got for a bushel![10] So you see the price stuff was then. When I started, I got seventy-five cents apiece for a two-thirds bushel. So we weren't gettin' much those days. But [he said, beaming with pride, in 1978] *we know what we're gettin now!*

They got a flea market down in Laurelville. I asked this man ut was there, next day, I asked him was any of my baskets there? And he said yes, there was. I had sold them to a woman that saved them up for that flea market. She had the whole bunch right there. I said, "Did they sell?" And he said, "You ought to 'a seen them things go." Says, "She didn't have them baskets very long." I said, "I bet she got a good price fer 'em," and he said, "I guess she did." But I never said anything about it.

Yeah, you 'n ever' one's been tellin' me I had t' raise m' prices. But I'm one of them kinda fellas, I don't like t' git a thing too high. I've had 'em come here and tell me, "You got kinda 'smart' on your price, didn't you?" I said, "Well, I been a-gettin' that." Differnt ones tell me they don't think that's too high fer 'em. If they want a basket, they'll give the price fer it. I don't know what give 'em all the basket fever all at once, but everybody *wants a basket!*

Oh say, there was a man here yesterday from New York. His sister lives up in Baltimore, and he was up there, come down here and they bought an egg basket. I tried to remember the town that he said he was from, but I can't remember now. But he's from New York. Bobby reminded me I got two sewing baskets over in Germany. That's the farthest away as I've had 'em. Last summer a man from Saint Cloud, Wyoming, took two back with him. Then two families from Vermont bought 'em, also someone from Michigan and from Missouri. Yeah, I'm "gettin' more business than an old settin' hen," as the old people used t' say.

Down here at Chillicothe, people by the name of Garrett, I don't know how many times they've been here wantin' a square basket. But I've never got it made yet. They 'uz here not over a week or two ago t' see if I had it made yet. And they wanted a rectangular fireside basket. Never got neither one of 'em made yet [laughing]. Yeah, guess I got a lotta orders hangin' on that nail there.

No, Rosemary, I haven't kept a one of m' own baskets. I did have one 'round here for a while. No doubt you seen it settin' back there in the corner. But there's a woman in Lancaster got that, by the name of McClelland. She's comin' down here some of these days t' get some little baskets, an' she promised me if I wanted that basket back I could get it back. But last time she was here she said she wouldn't part with it. I don't know whatever possessed me t' sell that basket, but I did. I'd wanted t' keep it, it was old.[11]

It was one I'd made back several years ago, in 1940 when I lived in Bewney; I sold it to a neighbor woman up on a ridge there. When her man died, she broke up housekeeping, and she says t' one of m' boys, "Here's a basket yer daddy made. I'm gonna give it to you and I want you t' keep it." But he brought it t' me t' keep so his kids wouldn't tear it up. It was all turned dark brown, that Ordenas color [Adena]. See, one time in this country, before the Indians come here, the Ordenas lived in these caves, and that's the reason I call it that color. It's historical. I had it stuck back in the corner, 'n I was never gonna sell it! I don't know how many times I've been offered ten dollars fer that darned little thing, but I wouldn't take it. That was what you call an old-timey egg basket!

Guess I always figured I could make another'n if I needed it. And I don't like stuff settin' around. Them two there's s'posed t' both be sold. One of 'em goes to a Hartshorn woman down below Laurelville, and the other, the woman never did come back. I've had 'em here over a month. I told Bobby I was gettin' tired of seein' 'em set there. They're gonna hafta go. I hain't never "signed" m' baskets, though there's been ones told me that'd bring more money. Can't. Reeds is too thin. Mebbe a rubber stamp 'd work. I kept thinkin' I'd get a stamper, but never got

Clockwise from top left: Dwight's old "Ordenas" egg basket, circa 1940; a new egg basket, not yet handled; an oval basket, a rare shape for Dwight

around to it. You kin tell my baskets anyhow. All y' need t' do is pick one up 'n see if it's wove clockwise. Then that's mine [it is a distinction I must admit I cannot make, however]. Another thing, just turn it over and look at the bottom. See that little pencil mark? I put that on when I stop weaving with two and start up weaving with three. Differnt ones wanted me t' put my initials on 'em, or a stencil, but I never got it done yet. I'll do it some of these days.

I don't have any idee how many baskets I've made. I lost the book I had 'ut kept tab on the number. It was an enormous amount. But I just lost it some way. It's in the thousands, though. The boys told me this spring I should keep count, little, big, 'n all of 'em, and see how many I'd made by Christmas, but I didn't do it.

They wonder why I charge such a price fer one of these kinda baskets. If they ever seed one of 'em made, they'd find out why! It is kind of a hobby, and it's quite interestin' in a way, how to make 'em and work 'em out. But come to makin' money, y' don't. No, ain't no money made in makin' baskets. It's just somep'n t' do, just kinda a hobby, y' *don't make no money at it. I like t' see how many I kin get made (but it's not s' many any more). I just like—it's kind of a routine.*

But I try never t' turn out a bad one. I'd take it apart, tear it up and start all over if I had a bad one. But I never had t' do that. Nope, never had a misstart, never tore one up. When I started it, I got a basket out of it someway or other. Lotta people've asked 'bout that, 'n I say, "That's news t' me, I never tore one up yet!"

Yeah, I've done a lot of work other people wouldn't do. I didn't mind. Just got used to it and kept right on goin'. Same way with this basket stuff here, just got used to it, keep right on tryin' t' make out on it. I like t' weave, that's the part I like best, t' weave up. Like t' see 'em get in shape, see what they look like when they're done; see somep'n come up and take form. *That's what I like!*

I've had a lotta students, differnt classes, I've taught. At Athens, at Columbus, over here at Camp Akita, at Laurelville School, the Senior Citizens at Logan. One young man got it pretty quick down there in Athens. But it was all the girls *in the schools wanted t' learn, not a boy in the bunch. Don't that seem funny?*

I weave clockwise, y' know, but when I teach a bunch of children,

Dwight showing his largest "tray" to researchers Rachel Nash Law and Cynthia W. Taylor

why the most of them is right-handed. They wanta weave same as I do, but I tell 'em, "Start off and let's see which way you weave." They start off and weave right-handed, and I say, "Well, that's the way you can learn it." They hain't many clockwise weavers, and I just say to 'em, "Go right on."

I'm sposed t' teach at Nelsonville—they got things arranged—to the vocational school. But they never called me back. They want me t' sponsor [give] a demonstration up here at Gibetown. One of the trustees, Carl Anderson, was here when Elly Del Matto was talkin' about it. All it'd cost me'd be the lights. I could get the community center free. She didn't make it yit, gettin' sponsors. I don't know how many it takes. Opal Wylie might be one. I haven't been to a meetin' for so long, I don't know how they come out on that.

Differnt ones comes here, say *they wanta learn. But I still hain't got one that's goin' on with it. Now that Tim Gathers, that young friend of yours, he looks like he might be. Did you get t' see the basket he learned t' make? He learnt it quick, split it, 'n pulled it through too. He's made two down here, said he's comin' back t' try again; said he wants t' get 'em t' flare out on the top, like I've been doin' lately. I told him I could show him how t' do that pretty easy. (I got a basket set back his mother wanted, too; didn't have a handle on it yet when she was here.)*

But ain't none of the children makes 'em yet. Harold, he just learned but doesn't sell 'em yet. (He's a night watchman for Lancaster Glass.) This summer he set right there and made one. His neighbor wanted t' buy it, but he said, "No, I have t' learn better." "Oh, that's good enough, you kin make me a basket." "No."

Ain't none of the rest of 'em take much interest in it. Bobby learned from me too. He couldn't learn any younger, he's past forty-two. He oughta *be gettin' t' know how t' make a basket. He's seen me make enough, 'n he knows a basket well enough; he can put a handle down on 'em better 'n I can. He could finish one out now if he would. I wanted t' get him started in. I said, "Git you some stuff and start to makin'." "Oh, I don't wanta make now, you do too much* growlin' *at me." I said, "I wouldn't growl at you!"* [Nor is it possible to even imagine his doing so.]

So I never get anybody t' weave with me. Now m' son-in-law's started. He made one one day, 'n I didn't show him very much about it. He had made the bottom over at his home, made a good bottom. I told him, "You make the rest of the basket as good as you did that bottom, you'll do all right. And when he got done, he had a doggoned

The Finished Basket

Log holder made by Dwight's grandson Tommy

nice basket out of it. He said he'd watched me 'n helped me enough he 'bout knowed how it was done. That sort of tickled him. After he made a few, he brought 'em over here and I sold 'em for him. As fast as he brought 'em over they was gone.

On a balmy May day in 1984, Bob Mansberger enthusiastically recounted his plans for the future: "I haven't been makin' lately, haven't had time. But I do the same thing he does now, and I like it. That's what I'm gonna do when I retire. I get m' trees, cut 'em down, do the whole thing. My daughter has m' first basket—she lives in Las Vegas—and she wouldn't take a thousand dollars fer it! My wife's got a couple, the rest are I-don't-know-where. Don't have time t' make 'em now, but I 'spect t' do it when I retire." Unfortunately, after Bob did retire, he and his wife were divorced, and at least for now, his new basketmaking career has aborted.

Now Tommy, m' grandson—Harold's boy—lives out on Wildcat Ridge, he makes a lotta stuff: log holders, macramé hangers. The log holders is made outa the rims of fifty-five-gallon oil drum lids, then covered with baler twine, and a bottom made out of old burlap. I give him the pattern fer those. He puts little old bottles in those hangers; he got the pattern at school fer that macramé. And now he's made a tiny little oak basket. I'm hopin' mebbe I can git him t' start makin' 'em. I'll get a buncha stuff out an' get him started. He is good with his

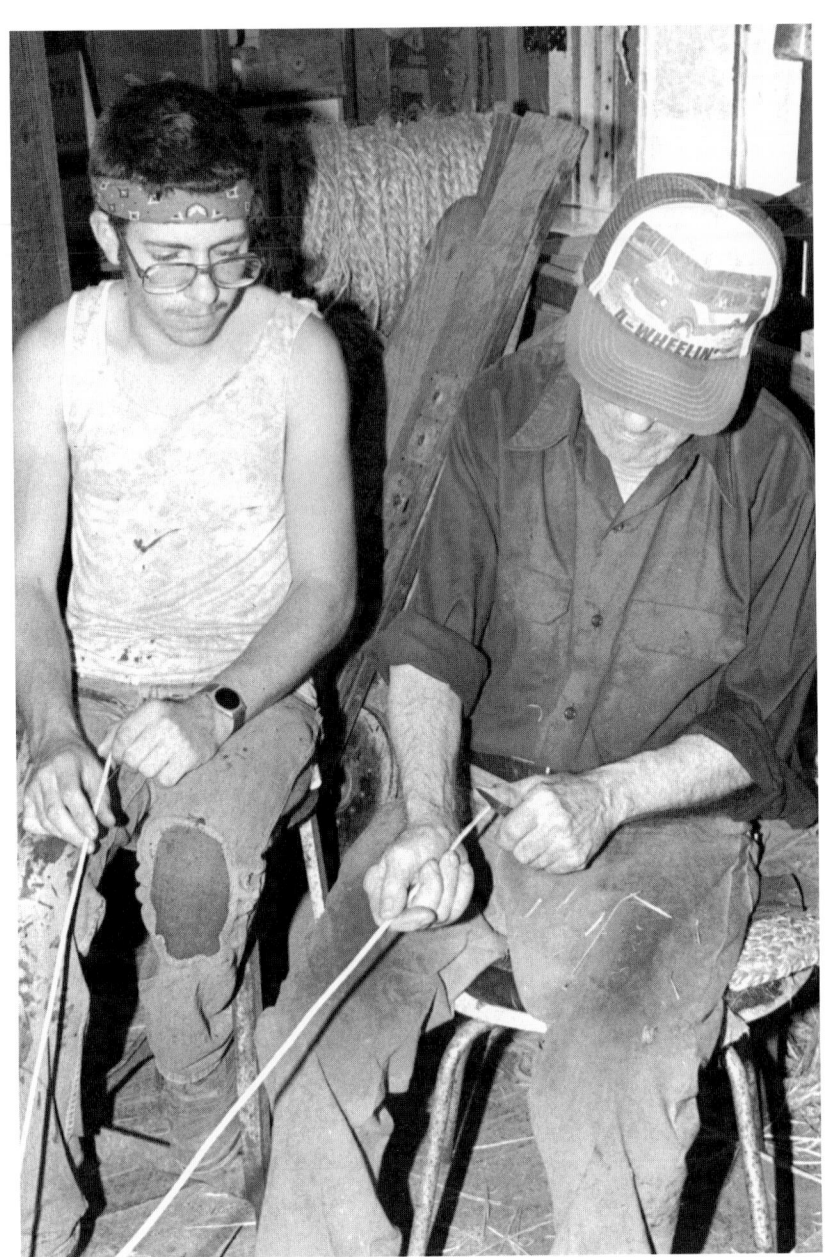

**Tommy as a
basketmaking student**

hands. He made some melon baskets last summer and brought 'em over here, but that's the last. Said he couldn't get the material t' make 'em out of. I sure wish I had some more makers goin' on with it![12]

There may be a chance for that after all. I finally met Dwight's son Harold (Tommy's father), after many years of visiting Dwight. He and two of his four sons arrived at the shop one blistering summer day to cut the four-foot-high weeds in the yard. As they energetically attacked the formidable task with scythes, mowers, and weed whippers (and made transcribing that day's tape a disaster), Harold popped into Dwight's basket shop to file the half-moon sickle blade. It was interesting to hear him echo many of Dwight's expressions and ideas, especially the one inveighing against "settin' around":

> Y' gotta keep them tools sharp, cain't do nothing with dull tools. I think it's hotter in here than it is outside! Those books I had on basketmakin' I brought down here and give to him, but I don't know what happened to 'em. I'll look fer that herb book for you. If I kin find it. It's hard t' find anything over there, them four boys go lookin' fer somep'n, *everything's* messed up! 'N there are so daggone many little kids runnin' up and' down, around, over there. We've got about twenty-five or thirty little kids runnin' up an' down the road. We've got what they call a mobile home outfit up in there; everybody's got a mobile home, and they each one of 'em got about five or six little kids. And they just worry me t' death. See them little kids goin' up 'n down the road with cars goin' up 'n down like on Route 33, just worries me t' death! I'd like t' go down there 'n tell 'em I don't like it, I'm afraid they're gonna get hurt.
>
> I keep m' boys busy, twenty-four hours a day if I can; long as they're not asleep, I keep 'em busy. Kids settin' around not doin' anything, no good t' me. Keep 'em busy. Got 'em all through school, that's one thing I finally got done. That was hard t' do, t' get all four of them boys through, it takes an awful lot. Trouble is, they cain't find no job nowhere now.
>
> I don't like settin' around! I just have t' be doin' somethin' all the time. On my job I walk about thirteen miles a day. I'm a night watchman up to Anchor Glass, all around that whole factory, that's all down underneath an' up top, four differnt stairways, 'bout three floors up. I know I ain't gonna gain any weight, I know that. I got Jeff a job there, but he don't get t' work very much, they're all the time layin' him off.
>
> My job I liked best was blowin' glass. I blowed glass fer twenty years, then had t' quit on accounta I hurt my back; had t' go clear down t' night watchman. That's as low as they can go, they can't find anything lower'n that.

Three generations of Stump men: Dwight (second from right) with (left to right) his grandsons Jeff and Tommy and his sons Harold and Bobby

James, Harold's youngest son—and yet another talker—joined in at that point:

> I just graduated from high school over at Amandy, 'n I'd like t' work in the Automatic or the Slewer department. Somethin' t' keep me busy. I've got my license now, but no car. My brother, Tommy, he's twenty years old an' he can't find no job either. He hain't got no license though. No, I don't make baskets [laughing], I just make trouble fer m' dad.

Harold continued,

> Tommy's the one that makes those melon baskets. He likes t' do that 'cause it's somep'n that's hard t' do. And anything that's hard t' do is what we like t' make. Yeah, I go out in the woods now an' get a piece of small hickory, take an' cut it, an' spread it out t' make the frame of them melon baskets. When you make them with that hickory frame that way, you don't have t' worry about 'em breakin'. We was just messin' around one day, and we had this here book called *Foxfire*. We was lookin' in that an' saw these baskets, an' Tom said, "Hey, we can do that!" So we started in.

We ain't made any melon baskets fer a long time, though. I don't know when we're gonna get around t' makin', the boys always keeps me busy doin' somep'n, workin' on cars an' minibikes an' things like that. We haven't got back into it yet. I'd like to, but I imagine if I get so I cain't work at the factory, I probably will have t' get into it full time, just t' keep myself busy.

Almost a postscript to the story, just before this book went to press, I visited Dwight and discovered that his youngest son, Bobby, had begun to make baskets. A gift-shop owner from a Columbus suburb visited Dwight, hoping for a basketmaking lesson. Dwight was unable to work with her, so Bobby began showing her some of the techniques. Her enthusiasm was apparently infectious, and by the time of my visit he had covered the workshop table with results of his new activity: a whole variety of basket sizes!

His siblings are not completely impressed yet with his proficiency, nor are they comfortable with the fact that he has altered the shapes (the sides are straighter than Dwight's flared ones). One other significant change is his pricing. Acting upon advice from the gift-shop owner, who had agreed to market his baskets, he has nearly doubled the price of each size.

It is just possible that Dwight has found a successor.

6. The Old Makers

**Two white-oak round-rod
baskets by Ocea Steele**

Dwight Stump is one of the few traditional basketmakers still working in Ohio. He is also one of the few in the entire country who are making the round-rod splint baskets, which are, and probably always were, even more rare than flat-splint ones. Most important, Dwight is one of the last round-rod basketmakers who have come out of a family or community tradition.[1] While a historic-geographic treatment of basketry is beyond the scope of this book, a brief look at Dwight's predecessors in his own area places Dwight's basketweaving in a time and space context.

As Dwight has explained, he learned basketmaking from Mart Hines in Mart's Buena Vista general store in 1917. Dwight has an impressive recall of the past, and one of the most fascinating aspects of the research for this book has been his reminiscences about the large concentration of other basketmakers in that area during the late nineteenth and early twentieth centuries. Further, nearly all of them wove round-rod baskets.[2]

The group was scattered over a section approximately fourteen miles long and ten miles wide, primarily in Hocking County with a narrow thrust into Fairfield County. Referring to them often in conversation as "the old basketmakers" or "the old makers" or "the old timers," Dwight has related knowing, or knowing of, at least sixty of them! And Dwight, now eighty-eight years old, is the only one who continues that tradition. (One other—Omen Beavers, a flat-splint maker—is still living but no longer weaves; Bruce Steele, also a contemporary of Dwight's, helped his father weave but never made baskets alone, and he did not continue making them as an adult.)

The annotated list we compiled from Dwight's recollections (Appendix B) has many blank spots.[3] But it still illustrates the astonishing breadth and depth of the basketmaking tradition in that tiny, isolated area—all the more surprising because most of the old weavers made the round-rod type, now rare.

The most interesting of the weavers—possibly because Dwight

remembers them best—were two families, related by marriage, who occasionally wove together. Mr. and Mrs. Hines and their ten children, eight sons and two daughters, were *all* basketmakers! (One of those sons was Dwight's teacher, Martin.) The relationships were complex: Mrs. Hines's brothers, Sam and Noah Cisco, Noah's wife (who was the sister of two more basketmakers), and their four sons were also basketweavers. Both the Hineses' daughters, and one of the Ciscos', married weavers.

Dwight elaborates:

As I told ya, I got interested in this basketmakin' back when I was just a kid. But it seemed like nobody could tell me much about it. I'd ask m' grandmother 'bout her long market basket: "How're them made?" "Oh," she said, "an old man up here at South Perry made this one I've got." Well, he wasn't so old either. Poor. After I got growed up a little more, I got acquainted with him. His name was Johnny White. He made baskets 'n farmed, worked differnt work too. Now he made the first basket that I ever recollect seein' and knowin' who made it. His were oblong market baskets, flat split, with a handle on top. Them's hard t' make. My grandmother she took her eggs in the morning t' sell at market in that basket.

Mart Hines—the one I learnt from, watchin' in his grocery store—he come from a big family of all *makers. His dad and mother before him, they made baskets, and then 'bout all their ten children! Sam was the oldest, then Kate, Jay, the other girl, Charley, Mart, Jury, William, Dewey, and Truby was the youngest. Out of all the makers I knew, mostly all was men. But Mrs. Hines made. I've sat and watched her of an evening many times.*

They's not too many women around the country that made the baskets, just a few. Mrs. Hines and her daughter Kate (I can't remember now for sure if the other girl made or not). Kate made little baskets—then it was mostly the little baskets the women made. Kate wouldn't make no big ones. The two daughters married basketmakers too, Wade Cox and a Smyers.

I don't know where the Hines [the parents] learned, but the whole family knew how t' make when they come out up there on Tar Ridge. I think—I'm tryin' t' study that out—I'm pretty sure they come originally from Pennsylvaney. I think they were basketmakers out there, the Hines and the Ciscos both. I heard 'em talk about relatives there, and 'bout Mrs. Hines goin' to see 'em 'fore she got too old. Don't know if she ever made the trip or not. See, the Hines and Ciscos was all related. Mrs. Hines was sister t' Noah and Sam. And Hedges was mixed in there too, 'cause Noah Cisco's wife was a Hedges.

Two of her brothers, Bert and Reuben, made baskets down on Clear Crik, at Written Rock. Let's see, her name was —funny how that gits away from ya, as well as I knew her, that slipped—humph! Nettie! *Nettie Cisco. (I knowed I'd think of it pretty soon. Fer I was 'round 'em when I was young; you take somebody around when they's young like that, they study a little bit and it'll come back to ya pretty quick.) Oh, and I happened t' think of another woman made 'em, that was Bert Hedges' wife; so her man and her man's brother, Reuben, they made together over there. I've seen her set there and weave.*

And Nettie and Noah had four boys that all made, Arthur, Albert, Ruby, 'n Harry, the youngest. Albert, he cut off three of his fingers with a buzz saw, left only the little finger. That stopped his *makin'! Their one daughter didn't make, but she married a maker, Leroy Arter.*

Yeah, Nettie made a lot! A man I used t' work fer told me he went out there to their log house t' see about somep'n one morning, and he said there Nettie was sittin' there with shavin' stuff piled clear up t' her knees! Just settin' there a-whittlin, the shavins' piled clear up to her knees [laughing].

Sometimes the Hines and Ciscos would congregate together and weave in the winter. Farmed or worked out in the summer, cut corn in the fall, then when it got bad weather in the winter, they'd come back home 'n make baskets. Most of the old makers wove alone, though. Coxes—Wade 'n Phil—mostly made with each other. They all lived out there on Tar Ridge too. Lotta basketmakers out there, whole lot. That was knowed as "basket country." And they all made the round-reed [or rod] *basket.*

But they all made big ones. I never seen *a little one. They all made two-thirds bushel baskets, 'n half bushel, 'n bushel, 'n that's as small as they made 'em. You couldn't have got one of these kind of little baskets, like the Easter egg, fer any kind of money then. And they specialized in the two-thirds bushel. You couldn't get 'em t' make anything less. That's what they started in on and learnt, and that's what they'd make. They was easier made, too, didn't take s' long t' make.*

I'll tell you a good story. One time I hauled a whole wagonload *of two-thirds bushel baskets to the depot over at Adelphi fer the Hines bunch. They was six to a bundle, tied with reeds, handles drawed down tight. I haven't the least idee how many that was, I just fergit how many—so many baskets was considered a train carload—but it was a* bunch of *'em. Fella that sold Hines the store, he had the wagon. Do you remember the big old huckster wagons used t' go around? This was an old huckster wagon with the canvas top taken off of it.*

They're about eight, ten feet long, so they can get lots of stuff in 'em. I tied 'em on this open spring wagon and hauled 'em over. Had 'em piled up there on the seat, 'n tied way up over m' head. The man at the depot had a camera and he said, "Wait! I wanna get a picture of that!" So he took a picture of me on the wagon seat. But I never got to see it. Some big hardware company bought them, they all went to the same place, but I fergit where.

Oh, they was so many of them old makers out there on Tar Ridge (see, now they call it "Snortin' Ridge" on the Fairfield County end, and "Jack Run" when it comes into Hocking County, but it was "Tar Ridge" then). They called it Tar Ridge 'cause they used t' make tar out there. They tapped the pine trees and 'd take the pitch and make tar outa that. They made a lot of it out there on that ridge at one time.

Funny, you wouldn't think they'd have good water wells clear up on that ridge, it's s' high. But they did. Good water up on these hills. Let's see, who else was there? Johnny Glenn started out there 'fore he moved t' that little cabin on 180. I never knew him—he was close t' ninety when he died. But his son, Joshuay, used t' tell me 'bout his father makin' baskets. They'd be workin', Joshuay wouldn't do things right, and his daddy'd gather up a handful o' basket splints and go after him. That tickled me. Joshuay he used t' say, "Pap used many a basket splinter over my back 'fore I learned t' make baskets." Poor old Joshuay, he's been dead and gone a good while now.

John Leisure, he made an awful good basket. At that time they could get nice stuff t' make 'em out of. I saw one of his clothes baskets, and boy! it was a nice one. That thing was prett' near perfect. I tried t' buy it off the woman had it, and she said, "No, you'll never get that basket! I'll never part with it." The Leisures had a different kind of weave, a crossweave: they moved up as they went around. Like that picture we looked at a while ago.[4] I do my bottom like that, in that lock weave [twining], but then I go straight weave up the side.

Hollis Tucker and his son William made up there on Tar Ridge too. Bill had a sale here a few years ago, and he sold one of his baskets there, the last one he had. His intention was of not sellin' it, but I was kind of overseein' it fer him, and some people come along and wanted that basket. The auctioneer asked me 'bout it, and I said, "Well, might as well sell it, sold everything else, might as well sell that too." So I sold it. And Bill told me afterwards, "Why'd ya have t' sell my basket? I wanted t' keep that, it was all I had left outa all the baskets I'd made." Bill made a mighty good basket, too.

But then they all did, always tried t' see who could make the best one. That way they took more time and pains in makin' 'em. Back at that time work was awful scarce t' git, and they was glad t' make baskets and could sell 'em. Most of 'em worked at somep'n else in the summertime. They'd work at it and make baskets in-between time, but most all of 'em had a place they gathered in and made baskets in the wintertime, when they had nothin' else t' do. Mostly they farmed, fer themselves if they had a place, or fer someone else if they didn't.

I bought baskets off of Reuben Hedges and his brother, a clothes basket and a peck basket, when I worked in that part of the country. How it happened, I and my father-in-law cut a set of timber out over there for him, and I told m' father-in-law, "Now them fellas makes awful good baskets. I'm gonna get a couple of 'em." And I got two. I mostly made 'em for myself, but I was busy cuttin' timber, so I didn't stop and take time t' make any. Finally wore those baskets out. I forgit how many years we kept that clothes basket, scootin' around on the floor. Them splinters in the bottom was wore just as flat and thin, they snapped then, they wore so.

Henry Springer made baskets fer several years, but he turned out t' be a preacher, and quit makin' then. I was well acquainted with him. He lived on Dry Tavern Ridge, it was called, and his mother lived over here at Jack Run—he mighta been raised there too. He moved t' Lancaster, died there.

Let's see, there was another one came t' my mind a while back, I hadn't told you about yet. A "new hand at the ballast," as the old saying is. Amos Waters. He made, and Bert, his brother, did too. They lived not too fer from Tar Ridge, over there near where m' boy Harold lives now. Then Link Poling lived on up the ridge in a log house, 'n he made baskets and had a store there too, alongside the building.

Whatever store was closest to 'em is where the makers sold. Most of 'em out here sold their baskets right at the north end of Tar Ridge, at Revenge. Way that place got its name, they said there was two old women tryin' t' get revenge on one another. And when somebody concluded t' build a store there, 'n said, "What'll we name it?" everybody said, "Call it 'Revenge,' because of them two old women." They've called it that ever since. Frank Hartman had the store, lived in the house beside it there. He'd pay the men so much fer the baskets t' buy groceries with, 'n he bought a whole lot of 'em. Then later, about the 1920s, he sold t' Ray Buzzard and bought a store at Clearport.

I happened t' think of a man who used t' buy most all the Ciscos' baskets: Billy Wacker in Lancaster. He bought nearly all the baskets they made. And he told me one winter they made baskets, brought 'em in there, and all they wanted was groceries for 'em. And he said, "Why you have t' have more 'n groceries." (He happened t' run a store, grocery and seed store is what he had, out on North Columbus Street.) "I'll give you groceries and give ya money besides." They insisted, though, all they wanted was t' get their groceries. But he used t' give 'em money besides anyhow.

One time I met a DeLong—can't think of his first name. He lived down on Clear Crik, oh, some years ago, about 1923, '24, someplace along there. Way I happened t' run on t' him, back at that time I was workin' fer a man that bought telephone poles outa the woods. So where I was pullin' them poles, he lived right there, him and his little boy. And he was settin' out in the yard a-weavin' baskets. First clothes hamper I saw, he had sold that t' Wacker, up there in Lancaster. I happened on 'em, settin' out there in front of his store, and I asked him, asked Wacker who made that. It was DeLong. And he made the first ones I ever saw had a lid on. Phil Cox made that kind too.

He used t' take baskets t' Chillicothe, to the stock sale. See, these stock men'd buy all the baskets he'd take down there. I was down there to the sale one day and I ran onto him, sellin' 'em out of his automobile. The funniest thing about them baskets, you can get four or five dozen two-thirds bushel baskets in the back seat of an automobile. They put one right down inside the other, six in a bundle, and tie 'em tight, put 'em in there so they don't take up much room. Get a whole bunch in there, an' when they go someplace like that t' sell 'em, they just set 'em out—ontie 'em and set 'em out. One bundle on display, then sell 'em all, just ontie another bundle.

Just past Revenge, there's a little crik comes down, empties into Clear Crik, called Bold Splinter. That's where Sale Kinser and his father, too, made baskets. I think they were Dutch. I saw his father a few times—I fergit his name just now—I wasn't really acquainted with him like I was Sale. I'd knowed him fer a long time 'fore I ever got t' see his father. First time I did, he had an armload of market baskets on each arm, goin' south (that's when I discovered him) and he told me, "I got a boy called Salem and he makes baskets, too, but he's not so brisk on 'em." 'Tain't been so awful long ago [probably sixty years!].

He made oblong market baskets, with split reeds, flat on one side, then round side out! The old man's the one sent off t' buy some willow, basket willow. I remember I and my father went to the State Fair, and we come back on the BIS [Boys' Industrial School] Road, on that electric line. Walked from there, come down through Revenge. On this side of it we met Salem's father. He had baskets on both arms, made outa them willows, market baskets he was takin' down there to the store in Revenge t' sell. We stopped there and talked to him, looked 'em over, sat in the shade and talked. They made an awful pretty basket! It was pretty near white, that willa, had a yellow bark, but you took that off, and the inside was just as pretty and white. Made the prettiest white basket you ever seen! I'd sure like t' get a start of it. Fella tells me they're still growin' up there, but I never got up t' see. I know where he lived, but I'd have t' find someone out there knowed where it was at.

I saw some of the baskets Sale made down at Savings Hardware at Logan. They had four two-thirds bushel baskets settin' in there. I went back again, made up m' mind I'd better get one of them—I wanted it fer a keepsake. I went back in and I told Saving, "You got any more of those baskets Sale Kinser brought in here?" And he says, "They're all gone. They didn't stay long." I said, "My land, I didn't know! I did want one o' them." But I have that die board of his, he did give me that.

The old makers mostly all had wagons and horses, back when they were in their prime. They'd all go out in the woods and haul in the basket stuff—not carry it like I do. I knowed a man they bought a lotta timber offa, basket timber. They was still makin' there in the '20s and '30s, biggest part of 'em. But 1916 and '17, that's when they was to the height of their glory out on Tar Ridge, a-makin' then, '16 and '17.

They was so many of them by 19-and-20, they had about all the white oak on Tar Ridge that'd make baskets all gathered up. They was that many of 'em. I liked to hear them, used to tell a joke about it. Said in 19-and-20 they couldn't find a white oak out there big enough to make a broom handle. They got 'em down pretty small. Nope, couldn't find enough wood t' make a broom handle!

Mostly on Tar Ridge they made the round ones. But down on Brimstone Creek, some people down there made flat splints. Emer Downs was raised down there, but then later he lived up on Long Run, near Tar Ridge. He lived in Adelphi same time I did, and we got acquainted then, when I was just eleven years old. Then he moved to Bewney Visty, made baskets in the winter, worked on a farm summers till he got too old. Emer was about the only one in this part of the country made the flat splits.

Lot of old makers, flat-splint makers, used t' live down below Laurelville on Brimstone Crik, down towards Bloomingville is where it's at. Two Barkley brothers lived on Ogan's Hill—that's over near Brim-

stone—'n made together, some round, but they mostly made big flat splits, all sizes, little ones, big ones. They had a whole wagonload they peddled, did it right out of their wagon. Fall, it'd get cold, they'd load up and start out, go to Laurelville, Adelphi. When I seed 'em they was headin' fer Tarleton, horse and wagon. Yeah, them two brothers made together, 'n sometimes they made with Leisures. One of 'em gave me a flat-split basket, one of their little sewing baskets, when I was just a kid. Harold's got that from me—I wonder if he's still got that.

After the second World War, seems like they all just dropped out. The baskets weren't sellin' very good then, 'cause prett' near everything went t' plastic. Plastic baskets and plastic hampers and plastic clothes baskets—still have those. No one'd pay much 'tention then t' baskets, thought they could buy plastic cheaper 'n they could baskets. But it's the other way now. 'Cause one of these baskets'll outwear four plastic ones!

Then the makers got older 'n older, and their boys didn't wanta make. Now when you're considered a basketmaker, they say, "You're in the Basket Row"; that's what the old basketmakers always called it. As long as you're considered a basketmaker, you're "in the Basket Row." I used t' torment some of the old basketmakers' boys, have fun with 'em, 'n I'd say, "Why don't you make baskets? Why your dad made baskets!" They'd say, "That don't make any difference. I don't want in the Basketmakers' Row!"

And now Dwight is the last of the old makers in the Row.

7. Using Nature's Bounty

In referring to Dwight as a bearer of tradition, it soon becomes obvious that we are dealing with art, craft, and occupation, at the very least. This is a continuum, however, and thus it is not obvious where one classification blends into another. What was once "occupation" for Dwight—his baskets and several of his other pursuits as well—is now "art." (Receiving wide publicity and coming into contact with numerous buyers of "real folk art" have so expanded the consciousness of most traditional artists that most of them now use that newer term, *art*.)

At one time Dwight thought of these activities simply as "work." That is not a pejorative word. Work is not necessarily either a negative or the opposite of "play," for Dwight or for those in his community—or for many of us. Work is instead a fact of life.

The choice of materials to be used in that work differs, of course, according to the individual's folkloric tradition. In Dwight's case, occupational tradition merges with regional and includes elements of both rural and economic traditions. (For others, ethnicity, race, gender, age, religion—as examples— could affect the choice of product, process, and materials.)

Raw materials are precious to those who have spent most of their lives on the uncomfortable edge of poverty. Consequently the use of natural, organic materials has been a virtual necessity for Dwight. And this was true also for his rural predecessors: it was simply another facet of tradition in a time and place that rewarded the ingenious producer. Still, it is important to note that, for Dwight, such use seems to answer a personal aesthetic as well. Learning to utilize the products of both nature and technology, Dwight has also been an avid recycler of scraps and discards—recent terminology but an ancient practice.[1]

The oak-rod baskets, made solely from natural materials, are Dwight's most important product: They account for the major expenditure of his time and energies, his income (however small), and his fame. Perhaps most significant, they are for him a source of pride. But they are not his only pursuit. In the nearby woods he finds medicinal herbs, the strange tree trunks which become walking canes and "curiosities," and the "tools" used in dowsing and well drilling. Even in the fields and caves he has discovered materials: long-hidden traces of yet another culture, early Ohio Indians. And people—family, friends, neighbors, customers—are the source of still other materials, which become either salable merchandise (braided sisal rugs) or the buildings and tools that make all his ventures possible.

Classifying these activities—that is, breaking them down into some kind of biographical chronology, or order of financial worth, or personal importance for Dwight—was not feasible. Therefore I grouped them around the source of the materials used: traditional occupations employing natural, organic materials in this chapter; those employing recycled organic materials in the next one. Of course, all artificial structuring has its drawbacks. For example, tile locating is a "first cousin" to water witching. Yet these are treated in separate chapters, because Dwight uses natural materials with one, recycled materials with the other. Nonetheless, the important point is not the classifying but rather the detailing of the numerous and varied traditional occupations Dwight has followed over the years.

Herb gathering seems to hold a special appeal for Dwight. The cultural norm in Dwight's region is an inhibition of emotional expression, a singular lack of demonstrativeness, in both speech and action. But when he discusses his herb-gathering activities, Dwight is able—in an unusual departure from that typical reserve—to state openly his love of the products of nature.

The woods, source of many herbs and of the precious white oak for baskets, yield the raw material for yet another of Dwight's handicrafts. Peculiarly shaped tree trunks or saplings about an inch in diameter, with interesting spiraled incisions made by climbing vines, become canes and lampstands or—as Dwight calls them— "curiosities."

Some canes have an L-shaped handle, formed in the wood just below the ground where the root makes a nearly perpendicular turn from the trunk. Dwight particularly likes pieces on which a vine has spiraled around a sapling. On most of the canes he has removed the spiraled vine that had grown *into* the trunk. On a few he has left an invading spiral, giving a different look to the end product. And on still others, he has left a vine which spiraled the *outside* without piercing the bark.

Dwight claims other traditional occupations. One is his ability to "smell water," as he puts it, that is, to be a "water witch" or "dowser," all terms for locating veins of water underground with the help of a homemade tool.[2] After he cut a forked branch of pussy willow and trimmed off its twigs and leaves, Dwight demonstrated for me the time-honored process of walking slowly and carefully over the ground in question. With the magic wand held straight out before him, he moved steadily, waiting for the fork to dip significantly toward the ground and—presumably—the hidden water. Over and over, first in one location, then another, he displayed the skills he had learned as a child, skills which convinced me that Dwight does indeed have the gift.

Herbs: Gathering from a Natural Garden

I've always liked growin' things. Like that little tree in that pot. That's a lemon—no, ain't a lemon, it's a grapefruit tree. They claim you hardly ever see 'em get that big till they die. A woman up here, Miss Morgan, planted it. But she got tired of changing it in and outa the basement and the house. I went up there one day, she said, "Would you take a grapefruit tree if I give it to you?" I said, "I like t' have trees around and get 'em to grow." She said, "Out there sets one, you go home and take it along back down home with ya." So I brought it down—it was in a real old can, rust just about ready to pull it apart—and I took it out and put it in that. Kept right on growin', but m' boy left it sit out there and I think it froze off. Might not 'a froze—might come up again next spring.

I always liked to have a garden every year, too, till we moved here. It's too shady out there, ain't no use to plant stuff fer a garden where there's shade, fer it ain't gonna do no good. My kids, they all got gardens.

Dwight's grandson Jeff added, "We got eight hundred pounds of potatoes this year. Fourteen rows, eight hundred pounds. We had two hundred pounds of just small ones. They're startin' to sprout though. Red Pontiacs. We let the ground go fertile fer about two years, and that really took care of it."

I had a potato patch on the ridge way out there on the old Bainter place one summer, and I had over five hundred pounds out of that patch. I sold potatoes from far and near!

I got me a peach orchard up there on the hill. I got all the old-timey peach seeds I could find and planted up there, and by gollys I found out, I got two trees. I forgit the name of 'em right now—Freestone! They're Freestone, them little white ones about that big around, old-timey hill peaches they called them. Talk about somep'n good! They don't get no more than about that big. They're just little, 'n white, white inside. Boy, they certainly are good.

I got me a book on that herb stuff, too. I can't find it, but I know the biggest part of it.[3] I used t' sell stuff to a man by the name of Leemasters down at Londonderry. Frank Leemasters [Lemaster, a salvage dealer who lives approximately twenty-five miles away in Ross County].

Sometimes you just want t' use the roots. *Burdock [Arctium lappa] is them there cockleburs—no,* not *the cockleburs. (Now the old cockleburs, I don't know what they use them fer. It's a regular nuisance.) But the burdock: dig that, they dig the roots of that out. Now this time of year, winter, them roots are rotten now. But if it's in the fall of the year, they're that big around mebbe, that long, down in the ground like a radish. And dig that, 'n dry 'em. All of that stuff has to dry, dry first, you know.*

Then there's, oh, let's see. Spikenard [Aralia racemosa]. It grows up tall, red stem about that big around, and grows up and grows up fork-ed, has a bloom on it. Leaves on it prett' near the shape of a spike, real slim. And the root of that is hard to dig out of the ground. That's tough. *It grows in the woods. Spiniard, you maybe heard tell it called spiniards, or spignet. Spikenards is the right name of it. I think, one time before you bought that place over there, I think I found some back down in there once up in there. They use the root to make a tea. It's pretty scarce—you don't find much of that.*

And solomon's-seal [Polygonatum biflorum]. They make a tea out of that, the roots of that. That fella down there at Londonderry will buy all he kin get. Frank Leemasters. His boy runs it now, his name is Frank, but the old man died. I sold for years to his dad, and he was in there at the same time. I ain't been down fer a good while now. They had quite a place down there. He buys furs, too, 'n some junk. He buys copper, and metal. Last time I was down there he had quite a junk pile back in the back end.

Herb book

And I'll tell you another one you might not know. Wahoo [Euonymus atropurpureus]. Spindle tree they call them. Wahoo, or spindle tree. The closest I know of any growing around here is down on Moccasin, they're all along there. There was one tree up here on Warner's right back up here. I was up there one fall two or three years ago—late in the fall, and the berries on them is red. And Mrs. Warner was standing there and said to me, said, "See them red berries right up on that bush up there?" and I said, "Yeah." She said, "I'd like t' know what them is." And I was close enough to it I knowed what it was. I said, "You'd be surprised," I said, "if I tell you." She said, "I want to know." I says, "It's spindle tree, and it's got about a half a dozen names. One is wahoo, spindle tree, and fire bush." (At that time I knowed all the names.) Said, "My lands, what a bunch of names fer this one little bush" [laughs]. And don't you know I never seen that bush back up there since. And I didn't get it. Mr. Moore, he wondered what happened to it. He said, "Let's walk up there and see if we can find it." I said, "I know what it is as soon as I see it. Don't have t' have berries on." Well sir, you know I couldn't find that. I happened t' think since what happened to it. The rabbits eat, chewed it, chewed the bark off of it. They'll chew that off as fer as they can get. And that fixes your spindle tree; that's the end of the spindle tree right there.

I got some ginseng [Panax quinquefolius] back there now I never sold yet. My boy, he was going down there the other day to get some new price lists on that stuff, and I never give it a thought to send that ginseng along down with him. I got prett' near $100 worth of it back there. Yeah, it's real dry 'n it's nice. Ginseng is $140 a pound![4] I betcha I got a $100 set back there if I got a dollar. It has to be dried out. It's so hard you can't eat it. Most fellas when they eat it—they'll get it when they're huntin' in the woods, they'll get it and eat it—they like it. They say it's got a good taste to it, 'n that it's good for a person's blood. But I never eat none of it.

But most all the herbs I gathered, all grows yet around here. Lot of people, out when ginseng got such a high price, they got it up that there wouldn't be any more. But there'll always be ginseng here. I studied that out, I studied that pretty close. I always told them, I said, "When you find a stalk of ginseng that has two little prongs on it, you'd better dig it." "Because," I said, "you'll never come back and git it." "Oh, it ain't got a big enough root." "That don't make any differnce. You'll get enough of them roots and it'll count up just the same." Because if you save it, you'll never get it all dug, because it don't come up every year. Ginseng stalk will grow two straight years and the third year it'll still be alive, just stay down in the ground. It won't come up. Then the next year it'll come back up. See, that second or third year it don't come up, but fourth year he'll come back up and grow. That's the reason I claim they'll never get all the ginseng dug up.

There's a root that grows in the woods called bloodroot [San-guinaria canadensis]. You take and make a tea out of it. It's real red. The root of it is real red. And that has one of the prettiest blooms on. Gets just about that high, and that bloom comes out on that just as pretty. I hate t' dig that on account that bloom comes out on 'em. You make a tea out of that, out of the root. For blood. It'll purify your blood, bloodroot.

Ooooh, I have all kinds of roots here. The kind called snake root [Polygala senega], you make tea out of that too. It's got a kind of an oval-shape leaf, only grows about six inches tall. There's one in that book, called Seneca snake root. Then they used t' gather what they call a white snake root.

Then I'll tell you somep'n else, a wild potato [Apios americana]. They only grow about six inches high in the summertime. Got fine leaves on it, and has a little bloom right up there in the center, just a wee little bloom. They grow in pretty soft, loose ground, and you dig down in there, down side of it, get at the tuber. *They're an Indian potato is what they are. Biggest one gets about that big. They claim if you get enough of 'em t' cook and cook 'em, they're just like a potato. Just wash 'em up—they ain't got no rind on 'em—just wash the dirt off of 'em. They'll all cook up just fine. But [laughing], you'll have an awful time finding enough of 'em t' make anything. They're* hard *t' find!*

And then you want just the bark *of some plants. Sassyfras [Sassafras albidum]. Dig the root, take the bark off, then clean it and dry it. Or birch, the white birch, sweet birch [Betula lenta], take the bark off it, take the ends off, keep the white, dry it. I sold 'em both, gathered up a big bunch. They make tea out of them, birch and sassyfras. Oooh, lots of 'em drinks a whole lotta that sassyfras tea. One year that Leemaster bought eight hundred pounds of sassyfras! You can gather it* any *time of the year, not just before the sap starts to run in spring. It gets "ropey" after that, but you can get rid of that by runnin' it under cold water.*

Dogwood [Cornus florida] bark makes a good tea fer a cold, too. I'll tell you what'll cure a bad hackin' cough and a cold quicker'n any-

thing in the world. And if you don't believe it, sometime when you got a bad cold and take medicine and stuff and can't get rid of it, there's just three things you go out and get. One of 'em is dogwood bark, and the other one is wild cherry [Padus virginiana] bark, and—let's see, there's a third one, that's two of 'em, there's three—crab apple [Malus glaucescens]! You take them three and you take the bark—you want to make a bunch—and you boil it. You get as much of one bark as you do the other, put it in a pan and stew it till it looks real brown. And I'll betcha—you'll have t' put a little sugar in it, fer this is so bitter! [laughing]. *Put a little sugar in it—just enough you kin taste it—and you take that, and I betcha you'll get over your cough cold. That beats anything we ever used. I raised my family up on that, they'd get coughs and colds and stuff, got them right over it! The bark off the tree is what I'm talkin' about, off the* tree.

You know what a black haw [Viburnum prunifolium] is, grow in old fields. You can sell the bark off the roots of that tree. Get 'em in the fall of the year, they got a cluster of berries on 'em like a grape. It's just a little tree, with a black haw stickin' on 'em. That haw is good t' eat, but they got a big seed in 'em, ain't nothing much to 'em. They don't get too big, 'bout as big around as your wrist. Don't live too long either—five, six years is about the life of one. Now you take the bark of red alum [Elm, *Ulmus fulva], the* inside *bark, that is; take that outside bark all off on red alum.*

If you're usin' leaves, *they's a plant called century [Centaurea scabiosa?] Old-time century. Take the stem and bloom and the leaves on a century, make a tea out of it. I don't mind now any more what it's fer, but they make a tea out of it.*

And then there's a thing that grows in the woods called pennyroyal [Hedeoma pulegioides], and another 'n called dittany [Cunila origanoides], gits about twelve inches high. A lot of that grows around through this country. That's for colds. Dittany has a little slim leaf, and a little blue bloom. Pennyroyal don't have any bloom on it atall, has real slim leaves on it. About a foot high, both of 'em. Make a tea out of the leaves. Gather it in the fall, cut it off right at the ground, tie it in a bundle 'n hang it up, let it dry; get ready t' use it, just pick the leaves off 'n make the tea. If you don't use it that winter or spring fer colds, whatever you use it for, next fall comes, that old you want to throw that away and gather fresh. 'Cause that old loses strength over summer. It's no good. Now I always gather, take dittany, gather up a bundle about that big around every fall and hang it up in the build-

ing around here someplace. Then I happen around summer see one hangin' up, have t' throw it away.

Let's see, there was a—oh! the leaves off a witch hazel [Hamamelis virginica]! Witch hazel leaves, you can sell them and take the bark off the bottom of the witch hazel, and sell that. Make a soap out of that. I know when the old man Leemaster was livin', I sold him some bark and he says, "Why don't you wait a little while longer, till the leaves gets full grown on it?" and said, "Cut it down and get the leaves and the bark both." He said, "That way you get two crops off of it, the bark and the leaves." So that's the way I worked it from that on, wait till the leaves come out full grown and then cut the bush down, take the leaves off and dry them, peel the bark off at the same time. Up and down this creek is just oodles of it. Some on this place back here, up and down along here. I cut it off a couple of years ago. You cut it off and it grows that much faster. But it never gets any bigger than your arm. Let it go, let it get that big, it'll die. But when it dies off, it'll come right back up again.

Then there's another plant, called lobeely [Lobelia siphilitica]. Cut that root off and throw it away, and take the rest of it. A fellow could leave that root in the ground, but it's like a lot of other stuff, it dies off in a year's time. It's just gone. It makes a medicine, I forgit any more what they did say in that book I got.

And there's another one, grows up about that high and got a long bloom on it. Skullcap [Scutellaria incana]! Bet you know what skullcap is too. Lot of that grows around this country, grows along the ditch and along the edge of the woods, about six inches high. Has oval-shaped leaves on it, and a bloom looks like a cap—that's the reason it's called skullcap. Whole lot of differnt ones. I always took the top off and left the roots in the ground, but I've got ahold of some books here since that says the roots—the roots are medical—y' dry the root.

Not too many of 'em I used for myself. Mostly I used snake root, and—let's see, there's somep'n else I used. Dittany. And I'll tell you somep'n else that's good, and I bet you know what this is, too. Field balsam [Gnaphalium obtusifolium]. Balsam grows in fields. Not very often you find it in the woods. That's quite a thing to make tea out of. It's nice t' drink. You boil that out, it's just got a smooth taste. It's got little long slim leaves on it, they're a kinda gray color—not brown—they're white, betwixt white and gray. Grows about twelve inches high, and after so long a time the bloom is white, a bunch right at the top. Any more you can't hardly find any of it, but used t' be a lot of it around. A lot of this stuff I used t' gather y' can't find any more, it's died out.

And another one is sweet-anise [Washingtonia longistylis]. Fer tea. Most of the teas like that, things like that I gather up, keep 'em, have 'em t' make tea for colds.[5]

I'll tell you somep'n that's nice. I don't know as I ever saw it, but I was told it grows wild, and that's marijuana. They call it "happy grass." Lots 'em said, "You ought to get that." I don't want that around [chuckling], *might be an officer, sheriff come around here an' get me, happy grass and all! Did you see the picture where Jimmy Jones* [the Hocking County sheriff] *was standin' beside that big stalk of it? We had it here in the paper, a big stalk of that marijuana, and it was ten feet tall! Took his picture standin' beside of it. He found it someplace and destroyed it. It was a big one. A lot of 'em plant that; the leaves of 'em is awful purty, and a lot of 'em plant it just t' have the leaves. They didn't look at the leaves on that one very long, he destroyed that 'n in a little bit. I don't want any of that around! It's illegal. You never know when somebody is gonna come around lookin' fer somep'n like that and that's what they want t' find.*

You take berries: *now a lot of people think a pokeberry [Phytolacca americana]—pokeweed—is poison, but it's not. I used t' gather that, big pokeberries, and dry 'em and sell 'em. That fella Leemaster down there'll buy all the pokeberries you'll get, he'll buy all you can get. You know pokeberries: people want to get rid of them. There's nothing that'll eat 'em. And they're a regular nuisance growing around, spider webs stuck together in 'em. I'd dig the root of that. There's some kind of medicine they used to put that in. I don't know any more what it is.*

Some plants you find just t' sell for decoration. *They was a man lived up here where my son-in-law was raised—it was my son-in-law's uncle—by the name of George McGrady. Him and Guy Green, they was gettin' herbs, roots, ferns, and stuff like that. And I got started with 'em, found out where all I could sell it. We gathered pitch pine [Pinus rigida] and hemlock [Tsuga canadensis] t' make decorations with, and wreaths. A lot of these pretty wreaths you see around town 're made of pitch pine. Any amount of it grows back up here. And ground pine [Lycopodium complanata], it grows just a few inches high off the ground, kind of a fluffy ball, a lead or a gray color kinda. Makes about the prettiest wreaths you ever seen. Spruce pine* [the local terminology for hemlock], *gather it the same way.*

I'll tell you another fella used to get a lot of stuff, Oscar Bainter. He digs blackberries mostly. He still gathers that stuff; but not very many gathers any more. Bet you knowed Andy Carr. Paul Carr. He lived out the ridge out the other side of Jess Vorhees. He's dead, got hurt in an automobile wreck. Him and his dad used t' gather a lot of ferns. They got me started gathering ferns back years ago, when ferns were a pretty good price. They use them to decorate with, in stores. Cut 'em off and put 'em in a bundle—so many ferns in a bundle. You can sell them live too. Put 'em in a pot, put two in there and hang 'em up, and they'll grow out and grow down over. You cut the stem and all—right on top of the ground—on them ferns. Sort 'em out, the nice ones, and lay one right on top, put twenty, twenty-five to a bundle. Put them in where they keep cool. And they get so many thousands gathered, take 'em and sell 'em. I picked so many, till I got so tired I just quit and [laughing] wouldn't pick any more. That time money was hard to get ahold of, and a fella would do most anything—in wintertime y' had nothing else t' do—t' get a little bit of money to keep a-goin', back in the thirties, early thirties.

Bet you know what Indian turnip [Arisaema] is. Got that big leaf on. Lots of 'em wants that in the yard, got such a nice-shape leaf on 'em. It'll grow up about that high, with pretty good size leaves on. The fall of the year they have a big ball of berries about that big around on a big stem, just all right up in solid, like your fist. You've seen many a one of them. Jack-in-the-pulpit is what it is. If you want to get a hold of somep'n: Did y' ever taste the root? I bet you'll get some water or somep'n and you'll have a time gettin' that out of your mouth. You'll think you're afire! Ohhhh, they're hot!⁶ I never tried none of the berry. One time I was out in the woods and I seen one, and I said, "I'll just dig that up and take a little nip of it." Everyone told me, "You don't want to take very much until you try it out and see what it is. You'll find out!" So I took my knife, took a little nip of it on m' tongue, and gee whiz! I thought that thing would burn my tongue off. Just that little bitty piece. Boy, it's just like fire!

I got herb trays out here yet, back of the garage. See, I'd make trays out of plaster lath; they'd be about two inches square, 'n three-quarters of an inch across the bottom, with the top open. I'd set 'em out in the sun with mosquito cloth t' keep 'em covered in the daytime, keep 'em clean. Cheesecloth and "mosquito bar"—it's a little bit finer than cheesecloth.

They's people comes here yet, wantin' herbs like sassyfras bark, if I still had some to sell. I ain't got any more though. Baskets 'n rugs and stuff like that keeps me a-goin'.

I used to be out lookin' through the woods, 'n I'd get a cane now and then along. After I moved here was when I got to gatherin' them in, that is t' have any amount of them t' have around. I'd get any that had a wrap on (I mean, a vine that goes 'round and around). I pull that out, all back in and around again. That makes a pattern in the wood then. And I've found 'em with big knots in 'em, or funny shapes and differnt sizes.

I use all kinds of wood. Some hickory and poplar, white maple, oak, wild cherry, sassyfras, and quakin' ash (or quakin' aspen, some call it). Cut a hickory and bend that, bend the handle on it, tie it down. And when it's tied, it'll just stay there. Now you take the quakin' ash or a shoemake [sumac], the roots of them makes the handle. Take a shoemake: that root starts in and goes right straight out on them (some of them has three, and sometimes four roots, goes out like that). You can go around there and find out which one'd make the nicest handle, the most uniform, and leave it on, cut the rest of 'em off.

Oncet in a while you kin get a sugar tree. That's the maple family, but it's altogether a differnt tree. Them's the ones you tap. You know, you've heard 'em talkin' 'bout tappin' sugar trees. I've seen sugar camps where they have—the whole woods was prett' near all maple trees. That was their "maple sugar camp," they called it. They tap them maple trees in the spring of the year, boil sap down 'n make maple syrup. The sugar tree has got a rough bark, it's checkered 'n it's rough down. But the regular white maple tree's got a real smooth bark on. That's the differnce.

Oh, and I've made canes out of dogwood. It does that too. And I can think of somep'n else: bittersweet. I've found 'em big enough to make a dandy cane. Yeah, they make a nice one. And grapevine, sometimes that bends just right t' make a handle on it. I also make canes out of this white oak. They're called "cattle canes." Heavy. "Stockmen's canes" is what they are. They have a bent handle on 'em, just like the other canes, only they're a whole lot heavier.

I like to work on 'em, clean 'em up and polish 'em out. I like t' set and whittle 'em down, smooth 'em out. Make 'em smooth. I take the bark off all but the shoemake, but I leave it on that, 'cause it turns black if you don't. Leave the bark on and smooth it down with a little fine rasp. It'll get just as pretty and smooth! But now Ed Fassig told me a new trick: you take them shoemake out when the sap is up in 'em, take the bark off and leave 'em lay out until they do turn black, 'n

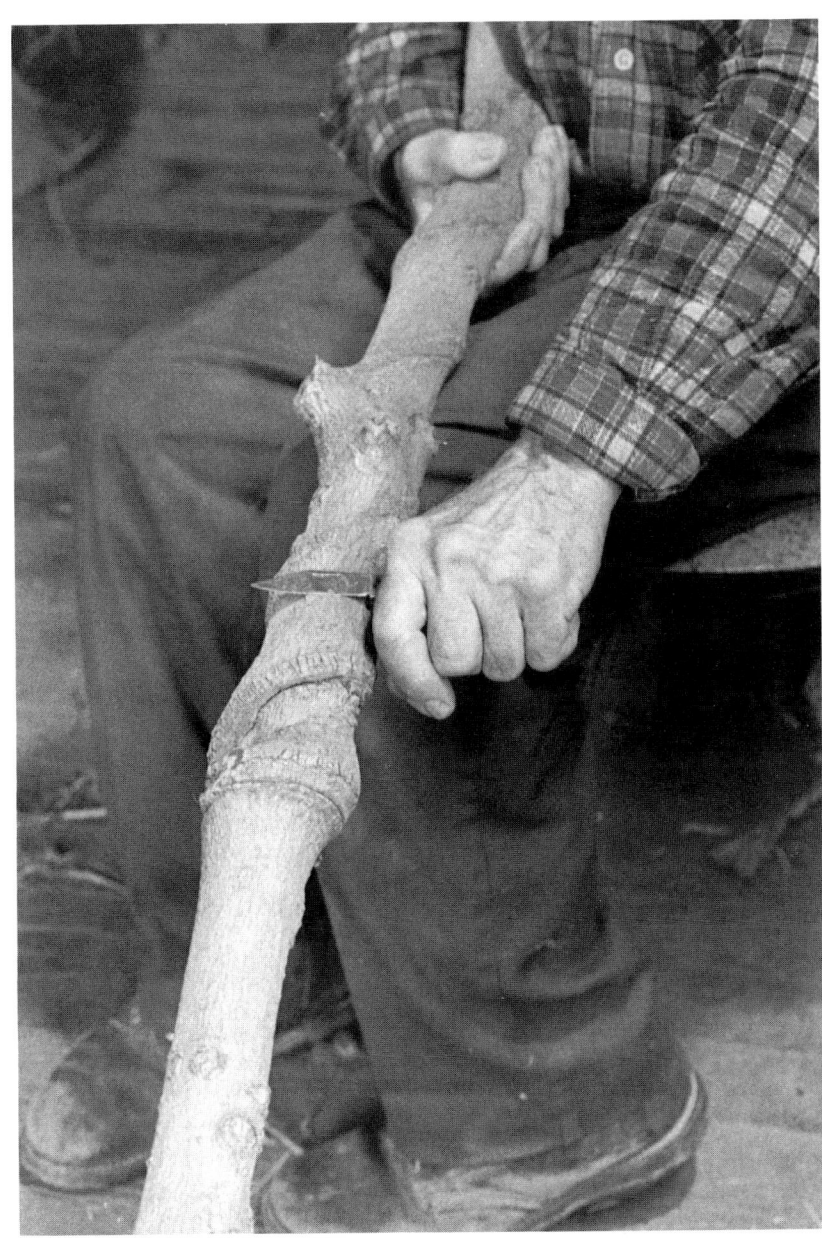

Whittling bark off to make a cane

after they get a little dry, take a cloth and rub back and forth on 'em like that. And he said, "It'll look like it's been painted with black polish. They really shine!" And I got at it, and that's what I done. Ed got me started on those.

Mostly I like the ones that are twisted—twisted growth, or else vines twisted up around 'em. Some of 'em the vines grow into *the bark, into the wood even. I usually pull that out. A few I leave in, if it's in there with a nice shape and everything. I take the bark off, an' if it don't look right, I take that on out so it shows in deep around on 'em. Some, the vine grows on the* outside *of the bark, and that usually grows up right nice. I leave that on, put a little tack through it, so it'll stay into the holes. If it'd be loose, I'd take it off.*

When that vine grows in there, y' take it all out, work it all out, 'cause that vine rots and gets dry. What I do is get this brown vine all out of here and round this, round and up here—see that brown in there? I take my blade, little knife blade, get down in there (there's a tool you can get to take that out, but I ain't got it). I take that brown all out of there, and sandpaper that all down. See, places like that, I sandpaper all that off, white like that there, and when I get done it'll all be white. You won't see no brown whatever on it. It's a lotta work, but it makes the cane show up better.

And then there's no place for anything to crawl back in—insects or bugs. Sometimes there's a egg or somep'n in that vine inside that will hatch out, eat right out through it. It's insects. Person wants to shellac them—cut that out of 'em and you can shellac them clear around, shellac them out. Now I watch and don't get no termites in nothing. Never had no cane yet that had a termite. They will get into stuff like that, but they mostly get in soft wood—they can't work anything that's very hard.

See, you take that bark off, all off there, and after it dries just enough where it won't crack, then I take a file and file it all—cut them all off—file them all down smooth. Rasp the whole thing clear down from the top to the bottom, handle an' all. I got a wood rasp t' do that. Yeah, I got all kind of wood outfits t' work with here.

But looka here: this one's split. If I'd waited till the sap went down and then took that bark off, that wouldn't have done that. But I took the bark off and there's sap still in there. After you cut it, it's wet in there. And when you take the bark off, that leaves the air in a little too quick. Mostly I let it sit with the bark on for a while. I get them in the summertime, I won't take the bark off them atall until they're prett' near dry.

But it won't take them too long; you get a bunch of them and lay out in the sun, they dry pretty quick. Fix them so they won't warp side— that's a funny thing about a cane, they'll warp sideways if you don't watch. If you get one that's a nice one, but twisted a little bit, you can take and put that on a board, put a clamp on that, and hold it on there and put it someplace where it'll dry; when that cane dries, that's as straight as the rest of them. I have took kinks out of many of them like that. Hickory's the worst.

Mostly the ones that grows around 'em is bittersweet vines, most all I ever found. That vine grows in there and it'll stay alive till the tree grows over that vine. Soon as it cuts the air off—that tree bark cuts the air off—that's the last of the vine. It's died right now. It's gone. That's the reason a grapevine grows on the outside—it stays alive. Sometimes I have found little grapevines inside, but mostly it's bittersweet. Now I don't monkey with the poison ivy vines. I know not t' get one o' them! *I can get pizen off them, and* nobody *wants that!*

I've got some of the prettiest ones with honeysuckle on that you ever saw, growed right around onto that honeysuckle vine. Honeysuckle will grow on there, but it's the same as bittersweet; after the tree bark grows over one, it's gone. Y' find one where honeysuckle grows around, they're prett' near perfect around as anything I ever saw. They grow right around like that and go so fer and then they come out. Mostly when the bittersweet vine grows in, he'll grow in a couple of circles around, and then he'll come out and come up here, and a couple more circles again. They won't hold like a honeysuckle vine.

It's funny about that—most of the vines grow in them trees clockwise. About all the ones I found, right around clockwise in the doggone tree. They don't grow the other way. Every one *seems to be clockwise.*

Now here's a differnt *one. This 'un my grandson found. You see, this one row of vine runs clear up here. Now watch where that goes— I'll put my hand down on that. Now you see there's* another one—*that you didn't see foller up. See, it went clear down there into that one. So there's two vines. There's the other 'un. I told the boy, I said, "You'll never find another one like that again." Look there, see that goes up* that far, *it's double. Now that ain't—if I'd been finished with it when them women were here a little bit ago, they'd a give me five dollars for that thing if I'd a had it done. But it ain't done yet.*

I've also found bittersweet canes. *And you take a dogwood when it's twisted like that, they make an awful pretty cane. Dogwood makes an awful nice cane.*

I found one one time up here, I don't know why I sold it, it was sugar [maple]. *You hardly ever find sugar; but this one, the sugar was exactly cane size and had one of the* prettiest *twists, 'n handle right over like that. I sold that one fer five dollars, and I wished time and again I'd never sold it. That's the only one I ever did find had that pretty twist on like that—growed right over it—like a regular cane. Lot of them seen that, said, "How'd you bend that like that?" Said, "I didn't bend that—nature bent it like that." They never saw anything like that.*

Dwight's grandson Jeff had come to visit that afternoon and chimed in, "Some people come down and ask how you grow them. I say, 'No, you *find* them. You find wood, you don't grow them. You don't grow those type of curlicues, you *find* them.'" And Dwight agreed, "Yeah, you have to find them. You got to find them."

Oh, I'd get them and make with them fer other people. I got handles here now, boughten handles to put on some. Somebody had a cane and wanted a boughten handle put on. I got some pretty ones. Like some are cloth bound.

As far as size, well, whatever height I thought'd make the cane, I cut it off there. They're all heights. I just kinda guess on where to cut them off. Let's see. This one here is about the average size—might be a little bit long. Let's see once what they are. Right there is the mark— thirty-seven inches. Thirty-six is what it's supposed to be, length of a standard cane, but this'n's a little bit high. Sometimes I measure them. That one there I cut out in the woods—got it pretty close though, within an inch of what I wanted.

Now this here, that's sugar [maple]. *That's for a lampstand. Cut that off wherever you want. I couldn't cut this'n any shorter than that, so I left it like that. They can put that on a pedestal down at the bottom and build up on it. And then they got a outfit they can drill a hole right down through that center, and run a wire right up through there—and put a lamp right on top there. There's a man down on this side of Cincinnata comes up here, he got one once off of me. He was supposed to come up here and get this big one, but he never come back yet. He's got a shop down there, works 'em down. That one will make the nicest lamp out of the whole bunch there when I get it cleaned up. It'd make a cane, but it'll make a nicer lampstand. My friend, Ed Fassig, has that furniture 'n wood-makin' shop down on 93, I give him that big sassafras one. He's gonna make a lamp outa that.*

They was four women here yesterday about this time, and they got about all I had back in there in the back of the shop [laughing]. *Yeah,*

**Sugar maple, ready to be
made into a lampstand**

A selection of Dwight's canes

prett' near got all of 'em, any I had finished. They kept a comin' and buyin,' and gettin' 'em and buyin' 'em.

There's differnt ones—individuals—comes here and buy them. I don't often sell any amount at one time unless it'd be—there's a gallery down in Athens, she's got her gallery in the university building. She buys rugs, baskets, 'n canes. Comes here about once a year, in her pickup truck. If I've got 'em, she buys 'em up, takes them down there and sells them on a commission. Oh, for the last five or six years she's been doing that, comin' up here and gettin' 'em. Pat Green. Nancy Crow knows her. I have been to her place down there. You'd be surprised what all she's got in there. Baskets of all kinds and make.

But that drum back there's almost empty. I haven't been makin' 'em anymore. Can't see to get 'em, and my grandsons won't. They've got to the age they won't go out. I've about had t' quit on that.

Water Witching

When I was just a boy, I seen the old people do that. I just thought it was fun. I got up pretty good size, and my stepmother's dad, old Ben Clark, by gollys he showed me. Got a witch and showed me how it worked.

The wood has *t' be green, with a fork, fork-ed so each side'll fit your hand onto it. You can use willow, peach limb, or witch hazel. That's the only kind I ever use, one of them three. I'd find a peach limb; if I couldn't find a peach limb, I'd get a pussy willow.*

Now see, you hold that out in front of you, goin' over the ground slow. You'd think by grippin' it like that, holdin' it down here tight, you wouldn't think that'd pull down like it does. See, that's pullin' down right now! *That vein comes through under the building here.*

I don't know how many differnt places I used t' dig fer water. One whole summer, when the depression was over, I dug water wells for twenty cents a foot. I used that tool on every well I dug, and I found water with it too! The fellas'd laugh at me and make fun. I'd say, "Where do you want your well?" And they'd tell me. And I'd say, "Now you wouldn't want a fella t' dig a well there and find no water there, would you?" "No. But how're you gonna tell?" I'd say, "Just wait till I get me a green limb, or any kind of green limb, witch hazel, or any of 'em." And I got that and showed 'em where they would dig down and get water every time. I never missed a one. Never missed a well with one of them. I don't know how many wells I dug that summer.

Dwight as water-smeller, waiting for the branch to dip toward water

Over there at Snuffy McGrady's, he's got a well there, right there beside the house, and that's how I found that one. I dug that 'un by hand, fer his dad, it was. Ain't so awful deep. And you can't pump that well dry! They got plenty o' water. They just pump all they want.

I dug a well out here, but got down on rock and didn't do no good. I had t' get that one drilled. I can't pump it dry with that electric pump. I could dig down level with the land down there and it would be an artesian, run all the time. But I didn't want that. When they drilled it, they had water runnin' out of it, ran right down the lane, down the side of the ditch. I told him, "I don't want that." "Well, I'll just put a six-foot pipe on, shut it off." So he did and that shut it off.

I've showed differnt ones how t' do it. But not just ever'body can do that water smellin'. I've seen people try it and couldn't get nowhere with it. Must be a gift of some kind. Must be the sign they was born in or somep'n like that. Now Bobby here, he can. I and him one Sunday we was playin' around here, right cattywampus by the house, 'n found one stronger yet than that. It come out down by the road and they had t' doze up the road. Had t' put a whole truckload of brick in there t' shut it off. Shut it off and it went someplace else. But we found it.

Boooy, if you get a picture of me doin' that, John'll say, "I know *that fella's crazy now!"* [laughing hard]. *You kin take this branch along and show it to him, and he won't believe you, will he?* [Enjoying his joke tremendously.] *You tell him what you seen me do!*

Well Drilling with a Spring Pole

Once you found that water with the "smeller," you usually wanted t' drill a well. Nowadays they drill 'em with a machine, of course. But used t' be they did it sometimes with a spring pole. That's a hickory pole that bends way over, and on the end is a rope fastened to a bit goin' down into the ground. Put another rope on the spring pole—it's called a foot treadle—and pull your foot, up and down. As that goes up and down, it cuts, goes down in the ground each time. After so long a time, the bit won't hit the dirt any more, 'n you have to loosen it, slack it, then it'll go right on back down in again, keep on a-goin'. You have to keep water in there so the bit'll cut. Get too much water, y' have t' bail it out. Keep that water in there, 'n that mud gets so thick in there you have to get it out, pour water in and bail it.

I've drilled 'em, oh yeah, I've drilled 'em with a spring pole, but that's a long, hard job! A terrible hard job! I've worked on one a week to ten days, on one well. Go down maybe thirty, forty feet. But you wouldn't get over about five, six feet in one day. And when you got down into the rock, well, you was just about done there. You could drill pretty good till you got down there. Then quit.

Over on Drums Ridge where I was tellin' you about, I had two un- cles lived over there, with only one farm between them. And they each one had what they call a "treadle drill well." There was an old man at that time come through that part of the country a-drillin' them wells. He had his bits s' thick he could drill into rock! He'd drill down, drilled three wells out there for my uncles, and he got good water. That was back when I was just a little fella, 'n them wells are still there.

So you just keep drillin' till you hit water. Just keep on drillin'. But most of the time they already found where the water was with a water witch. After they hit water, they bail that mud and water right on out of there, just keep bailin' it the same as these people that drills with a machine. They use a bit too, but it's a bigger outfit. Some of the bits we used 'd be two and half to three inches, once in a while they'd be one four—anywhere from two and a half to four inches. You use a regular drill bit, a well *drill bit. A blacksmith can make 'em. They make 'em and tamper 'em, so that the ends has a tamper to it, won't wear off s' quick.*[7]

But the hickory pole would hold it. You get a big long hickory pole (a smooth-bark hickory, a pignut), it'll bend good. They get 'em good and stout, and they'll just swing 'em out, swing up and down like that. And that bit's right on the end there; it goes up and down with the swing. You can use your hand on that treadle, or your foot, or put a rope on the pole and pull it up and down.

The hickory doesn't have to be too big, about four inches in diameter. You see, they're stout, and they're fastened in the back, anchored back down. Y' have t' have somep'n solid t' hold the end down. Sometimes they can anchor fast to a tree, or set a post in the ground, or drive a stake in the ground. Mostly I drove an iron pipe slaunchways in there, then wrap, wrap that big end of the pole right around that and out. Then the pole went out over, come around, bends right back.

When you get down to the water, you don't have to dig a well, you can put a pipe down in there. That man drilled over on the ridge road for my uncles, he took what they call a "well bailer." It's a long piece of pipe made out of the spouting of a house. It goes down—it's a smooth spouting—and they put a plug in the end here, and they put a bolt up through that's got a head on it. The other end goes up in through a plug, and that plug's bound in there real tight, down in that bit, in that casing. That's got a bailer on, a rope on, and they move that down in the water, then they can bail it right out with that.

Not many people ever did that. I drilled one for Harley Glenn, right under his house. We put a hole in the floor, spring pole in, went down. Then I drilled one up here for Millie Morse, up here on 180, with a spring pole. I and Sam Wolf drilled that. He had the bit, and I and him drilled that 'un. There's a long, hard job, Rosemary!

8. Recycling Nature's Bounty

Because raw materials are so precious, Dwight has supplemented his ingenious uses of nature's bounty by recycling scraps and discards; often those are natural materials already used by others. His braided rugs are made from reclaimed baler twine—someone else's use of sisal. He has unearthed artifacts from nearby fields and caves—Indians' uses, primarily, of rock. And he has sold his service of locating buried clay tile with a tool made from scrap aluminum—still others' uses of metal.

For the most part, such recycling is a boon to our endangered natural resources, and far less consumptive than the use of natural products. This is especially true of the twine used in the braided rugs and even of the small amount of aluminum used in tile locating. The Indian artifacts, however, are quite a different story. Dwight is but one of a small army of enthusiastic amateur archaeologists who have worked across the country since the early part of this century. Unfortunately, most of them have lacked the knowledge with which to do that collecting without at the same time destroying valuable historical information. To combat the problem, many historical societies now offer courses on collecting by using the least harmful or most helpful methods. Those courses were not available for Dwight. Still, by carefully questioning his eager buyers (many of them experts in the field), he has gained a better understanding of his ancient predecessors in the land of the Hockhocking.[1]

Generous neighbors provide Dwight with his most valuable recycled product: lengths of used baler twine, which ultimately become hairy-looking braided rugs. A heavy piece of twine about seven feet long is automatically wrapped and tied by a complex machine, the baler, around a bale of hay (in this area usually a cube approximately two by five by two feet). Farmers feed their animals the hay by simply cutting the twine away wherever the stock have access to the bale.

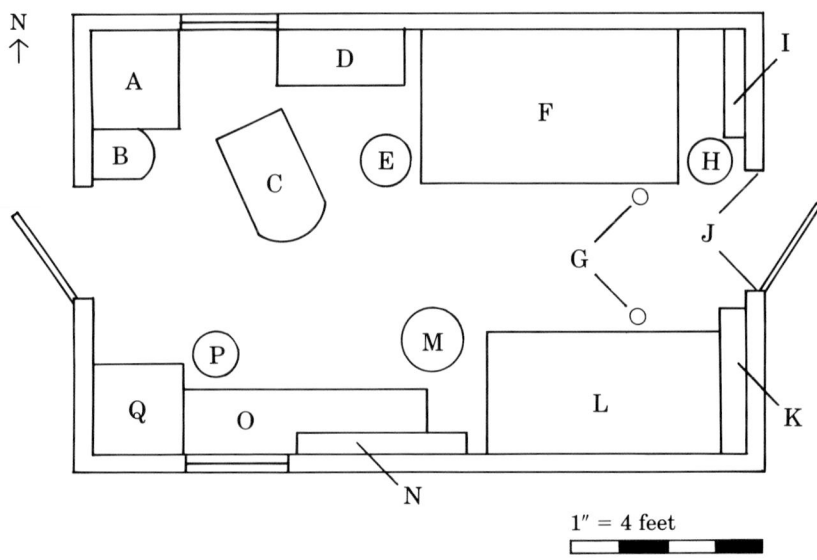

1″ = 4 feet

A. Table
B. Washbowl
C. Chieftain stove
D. Pipe-leg table
E. Chair
F. Plywood table
G. Inside die brackets
H. Drum for canes
I. Hanging shelves

J. Outside die brackets
K. Hanging cupboard
L. Table for braid spools
M. Dwight's chair
N. Open tool shelves
O. Workbench
P. Chair
Q. Pump cabinet

**Figure 3.
Diagram of Dwight
Stump's Workshop**

These braided sisal rugs are, after his baskets, Dwight's most important craft product. The rugs have several positive features. They have no overhead cost, as they are made entirely from the donated, used baler twine. They provide a perfect complement to the baskets: when the sap freezes in the white oak and basketmaking is finished till the spring thaw, Dwight simply turns to braiding and sewing. Further, the rugs mollify those disappointed customers who have traipsed back to the head of Toad Hollow only to discover that not one of the touted baskets is available. So they buy rugs—odd, different, but obviously serviceable.

Dwight's penchant for using available resources, natural and discarded, is evidenced in his shop (fig. 3) and his tools and labor-saving devices, as well as in his products. The shop itself is a study in both the ingenuity and the storage needs of the confirmed recycler. In addition to the reused lumber and ancient tables used as workbenches or for storage space, the shop contains a bewildering stock-pile of potential somethings: for example, varied lengths of wire, a rusted latch, a bleach bottle cut into a scoop, a cardboard box full of empty aluminum beer cans, ends of cut bottles, a rusted long-handled dipper, a V-shaped wooden container, a glass jug, an extension cord with no plug, three rusted sickles on a nail, a bundle of used half-inch molding, empty oil cans, a rusty tin wastebasket, every kind of cardboard box and paper sack.

The rugmaking process is yet another illustration of Dwight's aptitude for recycling—as well as his innovativeness. Note his names for each tool, some of them derived from his carpentering trade: spool, lapping, wrapping boards, turning journal, reel fork, and roller stand.

First he braids onto a spool, a cross with vertical lathe (lapping) supports (which he refers to as wrapping boards), all of them second-hand building materials. Using an iron rod, or turning journal, as an axle, Dwight fits this spool down onto the notched stand he dubs a reel fork, or roller stand. They are homemade devices as well: "I just studied that out, how to make them."

Using this receiving spool to wind braid, Dwight reaches for the successive lengths of twine—or sisal—from one of the bundles on an adjacent hook. Beginning with a basic three-strand braid, he

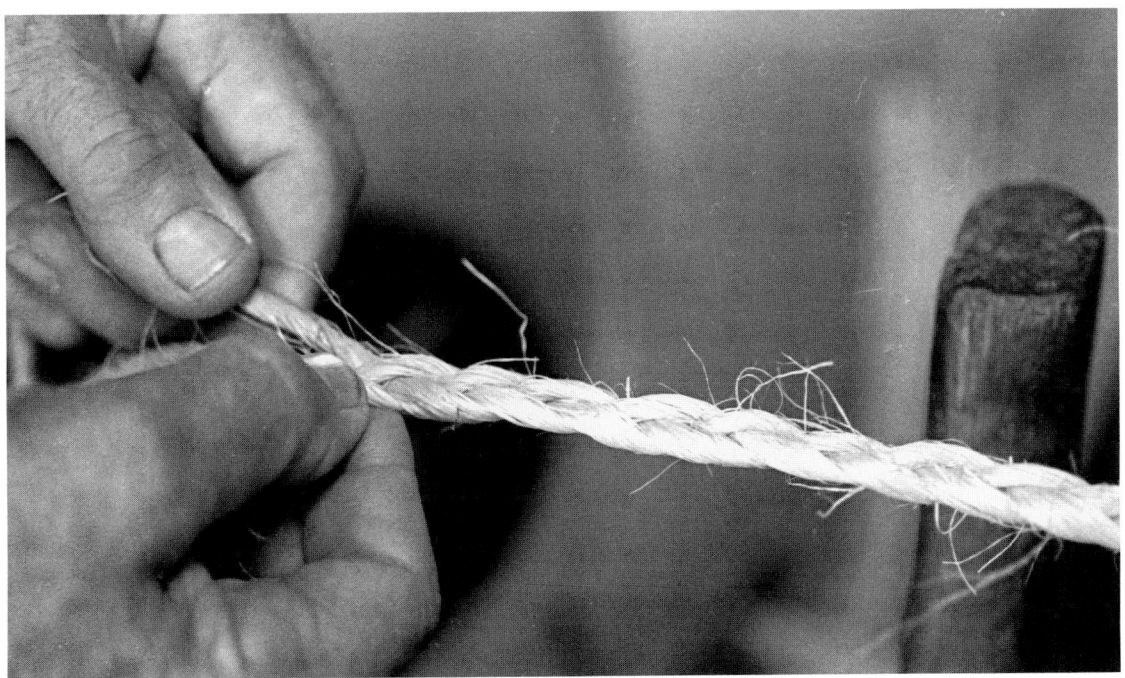

methodically wraps and twists yard upon yard of even, tight pig-
tail ribbons the same thickness, the same uniform width. A nail
pounded onto the front side of his worn workbench holds the very
top of the braid, while Dwight backs and braids, braids and backs,
stopping at intervals to wind this newborn product onto its waiting
spool.

Filling spool after spool (on one of my visits, on a chill late-
November day, there were twelve stockpiled), Dwight finally decides
to assemble three or four rugs. The receiving spool, originally
wound up on a rod seated on a roller stand, now reverses to feed the
fat lengths of braid into Dwight's hands as he maneuvers them
around a pattern board.

One of the pattern boards is twenty-four by forty-five inches. The
other, twenty by thirty-six inches, features a painted circle. From
these two patterns Dwight turns out a range of oblong squared and
oblong rounded, round and half-round rug sizes, in addition to thirty-
six-inch-wide runners (see table 3).

Beginning on the *outside* edge of the rug—a surprise to me, since I

Table 3. Sizes and Prices of Dwight Stump's Braided Rugs

| Rug Names | Sizes[a] | Cost | |
		1978–1982	1988
Round	20″–34″ diameter	$1.50	
Square	17″		5.00
Half-Round	19″ × 32″	1.50	
Oblong	20″ × 36″–24/26″ × 45″	1.50–6.00	15.00–20.00
	29″ × 33″[b]	4.00	15.00
	30″ × 48″[b]	8.00	
Squared Oblong	24″ × 5″	6.00	
Carpet Runner	36″ wide	—	
Room-size Rugs	9′ × 13′	50.00	
	6′ × 6′	30.00	

a. Dwight remembered—and comprehended—the sizes perfectly; they were the
same ones he'd given me years before, ca. 1978.

b. Dwight added these sizes in 1979.

have seen rugs braided from cloth begun in the center always—
Dwight *hammers* that original (outside) row of braid down with carpet tacks. He then begins sewing it to the next row in; with either a
steel or a homemade wooden needle, he loops and pulls the binder
"thread" in and out, from one braid to its next (parallel) counter-
part row.

Again, Dwight is careful and methodical, bringing just the right
pressure into the stitching to make the joints tight enough so that
no gaps will appear, but not so tight that the rug heaves and lumps
and—the bane of every owner—won't lie flat.

Braided Rugs

*I don't know how I got started on those rugs. When I lived on Dunlap
on Harley Glenn's place* [circa 1968], *I got started on that. I seen an
advertisement in the paper to send fer instructions on how to use baler
twine to make rugs. M' boys said, "Why don't you send for those?"
"Don't need to." I just did it. Come to find mine are completely differnt
from the ones in the advertisement.*

*Fella by the name of Azbell, Pete Azbell, lives below Laurelville, he
brings the sisal up here. He uses a lot of hay—feeds a big bunch of
cattle—'n saves the twine for me. People roll it up in sacks and give it
to me. It's called "recycled sisal."* [Dwight pronounces it "sisal," as in
"sister."] *If I was t' go buy that, I think a ball of that twine would cost
me about eighteen dollars for an eight-pound ball of that, at the hardware. I haven't bought any yet.*

*They buy it new in a bale, and that stuff's expensive! They said they
don't know what t' do with it, and I say "Don't throw it away. Put it in
a pack and I'll make you a rug for some of it." And I do. I make them
one, they pick them out a rug, whatever they want. Last time Pete was
here, he wouldn't take no rug, said "You've only got a few of 'em." I
said, "Take 'em, I'll make some more." "Oh," he says, "wait till next
time I come up." First time he comes, I'll give him three or four.*

*I cut the knots off the baler twine with m' knife, then I sort it into
two differnt colors, brown and white; I put the white to itself 'n the
brown to itself. It's not hard to untangle. I just sit down and sort it
out, loop it over an old broomstick. When I get a bundle I hang it up,
then pull out one strand at a time as I braid. I wouldn't have the least
idee how many strands're in one bundle. Or how many strings are in
one rug. I never measured it out.*

**Sorting neighbors' used
baler twine**

Get ready t' braid, I put nine *of them together and tie a knot in the end. Take a little nail that ain't got no head on it, drive it in the bench, then stand back and just keep goin' right on out with it. Sometimes I sit down, but I most generally always stand. I keep moving around, see, keep moving back. It don't seem t' bother my back any. The* worst *thing on my back is pullin' the basket splits through that die!*

Now I use nine pieces of twine in each strand, three in each piece, and lock the strands as I go. I used t' use three, then next I used six, but I think nine makes a nicer, wider braid. When I run out of one strand, I just put another on top of it 'n lock that one right down over. The short one is underneath the long one; the new one is on top. Then I take my nippers and cut them raw ends off.

It's called "endless braid," the store boy up here told me. Keep braiding, keep braiding, don't stop, it don't have no end. This flat side will be underneath when it's finished. The flat side is on top when I braid—I call that the "bad side"—my thumb holds it down flat. Then when the rug is made, that part is on the underneath side. (I learned this braiding when I was in school down at Hemphill; m' cousin Max Steele was the teacher.)

I braid onto a spool as I go, ones I made out of lapping. Some of 'em are twelve inches high, but mostly they're fourteen inches high, sixteen acrost. Pretty heavy? I'll say they're heavy! Try to pick one o' them up. Two of 'em come from Lancaster Glass, had electric cable on 'em. One of m' boys works there, they give it t' him, 'n he brought them two down here.

I fill two or three spools o' braid at a time usually, then use that up. But it takes practically all day *to fill one of them spools full. That braidin' goes slow. There's between 500 and 1000 feet of braid on one spool, accordin' to the size of the braid. You can get 100 feet of it on there pretty quick.* [Actually there were 340 feet of nine-strand braid in the roll we measured, which meant over 3,000 feet of sisal.] *I mostly aim t' keep two or three ahead. But last month I had* twelve *ahead! Then I'll sew up about four door mats. I aim to sew three or four of each size when I'm sewin'.*

I turn the turning journal around by hand, wrap the braid close together on the spool, just like thread. Same way. Takes less room that way. I wind it around clockwise. Then I turn the roller stand clear around [180 degrees] *to sew, and unroll it the same way, clockwise. I even sew the rug clockwise too—lefthanded.*

I make round ones twenty inches across on this pattern board, or oblong ones twenty by thirty. Then the big oblong is twenty-four by

Braiding onto a spool

**Partially filled spool
seated on roller stand**

Stockpiled rolls of braid

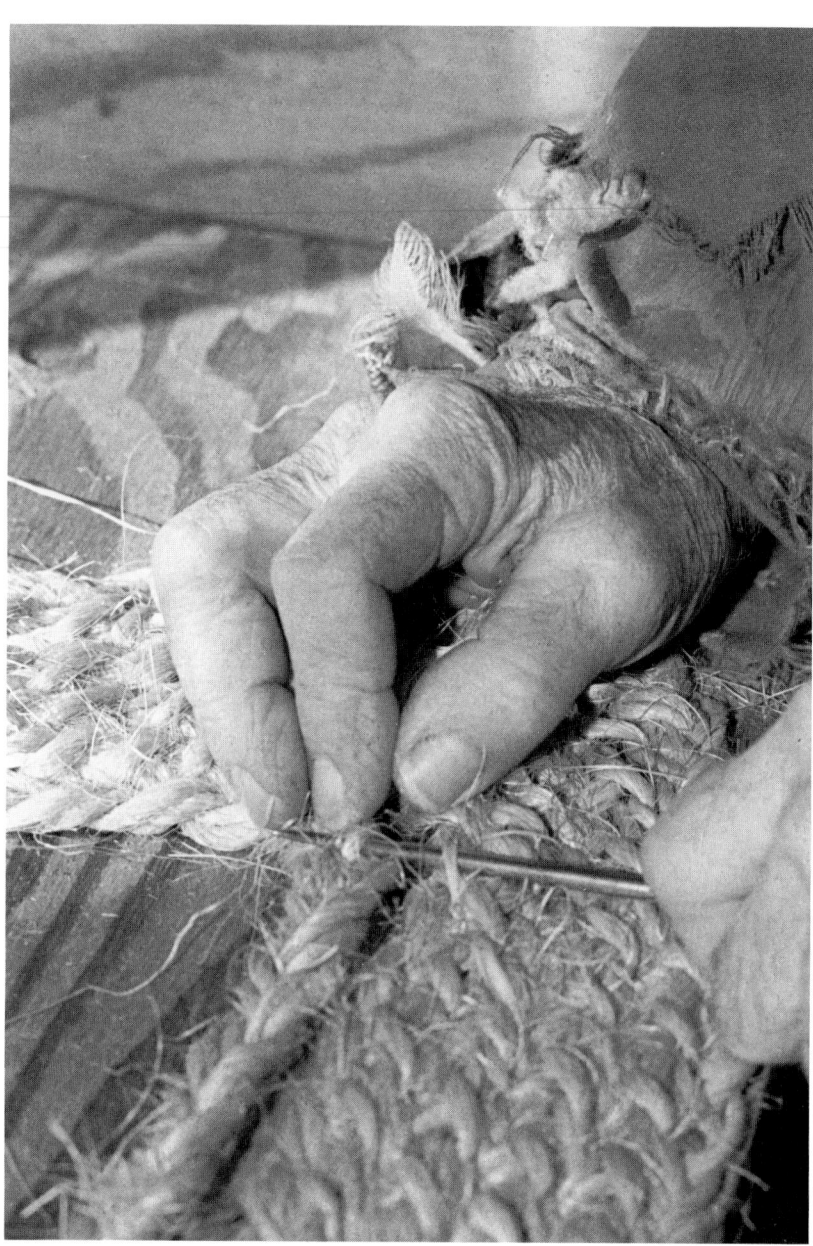

Sewing braid together onto plywood pattern board

forty-five. You'd be surprised how that size rug sells. You'd think that's just too big a rug, but them's the kind that go first. You wouldn't think it. [Dwight has made a nine-by-thirteen room-size rug but would never tackle such an onerous chore again, especially since he received only fifty dollars for it!]

I tack the first round with carpet tacks. Then I start to sewin' right on around. I don't pull the tacks out till I'm all done. I take good care t' get them all out too, fer no one wants those!

I always used t' use wooden needles, make 'em outa white oak— start a hole in there with a penknife. But they get thin 'n break off. I even made one out of a sardine can "key"; I straightened that out and sharpened it, made a needle out of it. But it got monotonous t' work with, too hard t' thread. Then I got one your neighbor woman, Mary Zeisler, brought. Her man, Harry, made me a steel needle t' use; it's the end off an iron curtain rod I give him. (I've still got the other end, fer when I need one.) That steel needle, the eye's gettin' pretty well wore out in it [laughing]; *it's pretty hard steel, but yet it'll wear out, wear through.*

If I bust the eye out of that one, I can always use these white oak ones—same material I make the baskets out of—make as big a needle as I want. It's a little tedious. But the eye is thin and'll just break off. Oh, I've had them to last maybe a month, three weeks, then I've had them maybe wouldn't last till I got one rug made. They'd break— certain way it'll catch comin' through—'n snap right off, like that. But that steel needle, I've made two, three hundred rugs with that!

I use a single strand of the sisal, the same material, for the binder as the rug. Only I go through and sort out the little—it's slim—sisal.

**Rug-sewing needles, two
wooden and one steel**

Makes a pure sisal rug, no other kind connected with it. Some of it's only about half as thick as the rest! I go through a bundle after I get the knots cut off, 'n sort out that thinner stuff to sew with. I do that right after I hang it all on the hook.

I have t' watch the sisal; they's a color they get differnt sometimes. They's a roll or two back there that's real brown, then some is real light. Sisal grows in the water, and I have an idee it's the water what colors it more than anything else. Maybe that real brown might've been where they's darker water or lighter. But I never did learn, or give it a study to find out. They claim it grows in Brazil. But I never did trace it up. I was talkin' to the fella down here that runs the hardware at Laurelville, 'n I said, "Now you sell that sisal, where did it come from?" "Well," he said, "from Brazil." I said, "You right sure?" "Yeah, I'm right sure." I said, "Don't be too sure, maybe it don't come from Brazil any more!" He looked at me so funny.

My boy down by Laurelville brought that green twine up here t' me. That's the first I ever got ahold of any that was green. Lots of 'em likes that light green color, though. There's one kind of twine I used t' use, but it's hard t' find. It's a black plastic and I mix that with the sisal. And boy! that makes one of the prettiest rugs you ever saw. The light shines on the rugs like them there hanging up on the wall, and that there black after night just glistens! I had two down at the Logan Fair here, I fergit how long, what year it was, I got a prize on both of them. They had them hanging on the wall, the light shined down on them— they judged them after night—and the judge come along, they said that judge stood there and looked at them 'n said, "I can't pass them up" [laughing], 'n I got a prize on both of them. I've prett' well quit using it, though, it don't prove out satisfactory; too much give to it.

See this stuff here? A weather balloon came down on Carl Anderson's place a few years ago. Do you remember that? I got the cord off of it, and I've used that to sew with! Makes a good sewin' thread. It's white, but I can sew it so it won't show up in those rugs atall. Only thing is, it ravels out so bad. It's either nylon or somep'n next to nylon. But it won't rot. That was one thing, it didn't get wet.

My grandsons got me somep'n differnt one time: binder twine. But they can't get it any more. Azbell's is all the same color. Binder twine is lighter, on account it hasn't got that treatment on it—it's purt near white. I'd like t' get that, it's nice t' sew with.

I'm gonna make up some colored ones. They're after me t' do that. After they're made, y' take liquid Rit—or most anything you'd color cloth with'd do it—and color both sides. Lots of 'em wants 'em col-

A finished rug, sturdy enough to withstand constant use

ored. I can't get the package Rit t' work right, but the liquid'd work, go all the way through. I never tried it m'self, but anyone wants to can.

These sisal rugs'll last years and years, Rosemary, take all kind o' wear. And all ya gotta do is just hose 'em off to clean 'em. Guess that's why so many people buys 'em. I can't keep no rugs around here. I had two piles layin' there last week. They just grab them up! They're like m' baskets; I can't keep them ahead either.

Yeah, I had a pile of about thirty-six of 'em back here, and they're 'bout all gone. I don't charge so awful much fer 'em, since I hain't got no money in 'em, just m' labor. I raised m' prices a good bit this last year though, ever'body had such a fit about it (see table 3). Pat Green, down at that gallery in Athens, comes up and buys 'em, picks so many of each size. And a woman named Edwards comes every summer when she's stayin' down here on Snortin' Ridge, gets a bunch. I think she's from the Edwards Carpet Company in Columbus, takes 'em up there and sells 'em again. Mostly it's people that comes here t' buy baskets that buys 'em.

I like to make the rugs, but it gets tiresome. I work on them a while, then I have to change off. Yeah, it's more tedious than the baskets is, to make them and get them right. When I start to making on them rugs and get started good on one, then I have to quit, 'cause it gets so

Piles of spools and
braided rugs after a
busy season

tiresome. You stand there so long on your feet—you don't do much movin', and it gets monotonous in a little bit. Nobody ever showed me anything about these. Been those here that wanted to learn it, said they could make braid, but didn't know how to start.

Indian Artifacts

I got to findin' Indian artifacts when I was only a boy. First one I saw, my grandmother was with me. I said, "Funny-lookin' stone." She said, "No, that's an Indian arrahead. Keep all that y' find." I'd get out and walk in the fields, find arraheads right out in the open field, mostly in plowed ground. I used t' get in the cornfield, when they were plowin' corn, 'n follow the plow. I found a lotta arraheads that way. I found some of the prettiest arraheads you ever saw. They'd come right up on top, I'd pick 'em up and put 'em in m' pocket. Another way, after I got big enough to plow corn, I'd see 'em on the ground and I'd get 'em. Over on Clear Creek there were some caves, one right there above the road. They'd eventually work down the hill and I'd find 'em layin' right aside the road, layin' right there.

My stepmother's daddy, Ben Clark, he was a great fella to find that stuff. He'd take me with him. And on Sundays he'd say, "Come on, we'll go find some arraheads." And away we'd go. We'd go to a cornfield someplace, walk around and look. He'd explain to me, tell me about how they made 'em. I don't know how he knew. He said they'd take one pretty good size piece of flint, then take another one that was sharp, then strike down acrost it, 'n take a piece out of it. It'd chip out, a chip out of it. He used t' take two pieces of flint at night and say, "I'll show you how the Indians started a fire." 'N he'd take two pieces of flint like that 'n hit 'em together, get a spark, catch it in dry stuff 'n start a fire! Showed me how they done that.

Then I got to findin' caves around places and under the rocks, shelf rock, where the Indians stayed. We'd always tell by the ashes in there. And there was always arraheads and flint in them ashes. You could take an old sieve, and shift them ashes and the arraheads'd show right up, come up in them ashes. I got on to that siftin' by myself. Oh no, wait: Harley Glenn, he had a cave over there on his place, 'n he was quite a artifacts man. So he said to me one day—it was rainin' and we couldn't work outside—"I've got an old sieve out here, let's go out under the cave 'n see what we kin find." We found some purty arraheads in there.

Yes, I found any amount o' nice arraheads, some of the nicest, biggest ones you ever saw. Biggest I ever found was about five inches long and wide as m' three fingers! You find a lotta little artifacts in that sifting. Sometimes you'd find a wee little arrahead, not much bigger'n your finger. They made them little fellas prett' near as perfect as the big ones.

I found five artifact collections over here below Snuffy's on Harley's place. He didn't think I'd dig around in them caves and find anything. Wound up I had five collections and he bought all five off of me. He says he didn't think I had nerve enough to get in that cave and get 'em.

There was a man named Tracy Heft (he died not too awful long ago; he lived close to the edge of Rockbridge), 'n he had found Indian flint knives in Harley's cave. Same cave I found the five artifact collections. He was there 'fore I was, but he didn't dig deep enough. He worked on top and secured these knives, either six or seven Indian flint knives.

In the meantime I hunted other caves, and I have quite a number of Indian hammerstones. I have 'em here, I'll show you what those hammerstones was, if I kin find 'em [rooting through myriad boxes under the worktable]. *They use that t' pound the corn up with; had a round place in a big rock, and they put that down in there, then take this an' hammer down in there on that corn, grain. It's pointed so it'll go down in, and that round part hits that down in. I found spearheads—any number of those—and arraheads. I also found the second atlatl handle been found in Ohio.*[2] *(I'll tell you the man's name got that. His name is Ray Baby. He got the collection and took 'em up. I found out about that through Harley, he was in that, one time he was president of that—or some—outfit.)*[3]

You wanna see what they look like? I've got some little pieces back here if I can find 'em. I'll set 'em out where you kin see 'em. I had an Indian mill, a fella by the name of Dick Green, he bought the complete mill. He lives at New Straitsville. I'll bet you have saw the Indian pots. Here's a piece of one, see how it's smooth on one side and rough on the other? Here's a piece that's been part of a scraping knife. Surprising how sharp they got those edges! Here's a piece of a needle. That's bone; they cut that and work it down. That's out of a wild turkey wing.

Yeah, differnt ones told me all about this. Ray Baby was the first one to tell me. He's read up on it. Then Bob Goslin told me a whole lot about lots of it. There's a sarpint mound back in there in the woods too. From the Indian grinding mill[4] *you can't see what it is. Not everyone knows that; it's a sarpint mound. I know through the arkology books I used t' get. It said there's more of them, but they've growed up with underbrush so people couldn't find 'em so good. A fella used to—he's from Columbus, Dr. Soday—I worked with him a while. He worked out of Columbus, and he worked out in the West a good bit. He worked on the Aztec treasures, tried t' find all the Aztec stuff he could. (They worked in metal, 'n he was looking for pieces of metal.) He only found two pieces of Aztec artifact here in Ohio, the rest in the West and the South. I have a book someplace where he and someone took down a mound, told what all they found.*[5]

A man up there at the Ohio State University gets these art collections. I had a bunch one time 'n I sent him word that I had two collections. He came over there, when I lived on the other side of the hill there. And he said, "I want to see your collection you sent me word you got," and I said, "All right." And I got them. He picked out any amount and said, "The American Indian never saw this. This is Ordenas."[6] *He says, "Ordenas was a tribe that was here before the Indians." (That's why I call my baskets "Ordenas color" when they get old and darken.)*

The differnce between the Ordenas and the Indians: the Ordenas was cave dwellers, that is, in the beginning they was cave dwellers, and they was here before Indians were. And they left, got extinction, and then the Indians come, they took over. The Indians, the American Indian, work their flint out more smooth, their arrahead, and the Ordenas, they notch their arraheads. They was made pretty much on the same type, in shape, only the Ordenas made theirs a little more blunt. The American Indian made their arraheads more long and slim. The Ordenas arraheads was what they call "bearded," a bearded arrahead.

I found a collection of spearheads in the cave on Pansy Wylie's place, also on Dunlap Hollow. I was lookin' for artifacts when I found a whole skeleton *one time! Tryin' to think where. I think I found that in that cave on Harley Glenn's. No, I dug that up on the McKinley Hanson farm on 180. Yeah, that skeleton laid all right in there together, in a cave. Couldn't tell how he died. I took it out a piece at a time. When I dug down on it, it was layin' like that, the bones of the legs laid up side by side. I dug down first where the feet was; I dug back, and there they all were, right on there! One of the boys was along, 'n they got so excited too! I watched careful how I dug it up. I think I lived over on Dunlap, brought it down there, and I had a burlap sack, folded it out, 'n I laid it on that sack and rolled it up. I'd unroll it 'n you could see it. It was a complete skeleton, the whole thing! If I could find the papers, I've got the date wrote down on that.*

Here's a thicker piece of pottery. Oh say! I found something else. I had somep'n else called transparent flint. One looked like glass and one was a gray color. And somep'n else: See the color of this flint? This black flint come from Zaleski, and the tricolor (I ain't got any of that here, m' buyers was slick enough to get all that out) but them kind come from Flint Ridge, kind of pinkish and gray and also white. I have two or three—not in here—they're all white. And another, all white on one side, all black on the other. Someone said, "I'll give you twenty-five dollars fer that." "Oh no, my wife's keepin' that, you won't get that for any amount of dollars." Nobody gets that, she's got it all put away.

People come from Cincinnata and all around come here. I used t' have five-gallon buckets of this stuff, but they've sorted 'em and picked 'em all out. Oh yes, I got paid for 'em [but not much, I'm sure]. Then there's flakes, flakes o' flint, is what them is. I'll tell you somep'n else, Rosemary, they make a certain design on a board and make designs out of those flakes, the collectors.

'N I've found skulls, and then that one complete skeleton. Sold 'em. Used t' be people come far 'n near, found out I was findin' that stuff, 'n bought it from me. I can't remember who did buy that skeleton. I used to sell an Azbell a lotta stuff. The historical society bought a whole lots too. They coulda bought it. Oh! Doc Copeland got that, he bought the skeleton off of me.

Azbell comes down here yet, from Lancaster, 'n there's been differnt ones wants to know what I had. Well, I didn't happen t' have any— and won't, fer I can't see t' find 'em. My grandsons, Harold's boy Kelly and Homer's boy, they're findin' 'em. They was down here way early this spring and they had some stuff.

Locating Tile

Now I kin do the same thing fer findin' tile, clay tile, as I do t' find water, only I use a "tile locater" fer that. You know, these farmers in the bottoms and places, they got tile down in their fields t' drain 'em. That tile gets plugged up and they don't know how t' find 'em any more. Or say, fer instance, somebody had a bunch of money buried in a jar, buncha gold. They know where it's at but can't find it. Come t' me, I'll take my tile locater and find it, find the jar.

Recycling Nature's
Bounty

An aluminum "tile locater"

The tile locater is the same thing almost as the water smeller, only it's made out of aluminum or copper—either one—fence wire. You fit the wire down in these pieces of aluminum pipe (two pieces off of a television antenna is what it is). The wire is just ordinary fence wire, aluminum; must be no rust on 'em, has to be clear of rust. That's why you use aluminum. I can take them things and—I don't care how deep down in the ground the tile is or where it's at—I'll find that tile exactly. I just walk slowly along, hold these still right in front of me. When you come across to a jar [clay tile], the crock, they'll come right over like that. The wires'll cross over one another. See, they're straight now. As soon as they come over that jar, they'll come right across over, turn over that tile. Aluminum or copper, either one, I can take them things and put it on my hands and it'll work the same way. Somep'n about the jar, I don't know what it is.

I found out about that in Lancaster, when I worked for the Gorsuch Construction Company up there. We was diggin' foundations fer houses, 'n the city had some sewers in there they was afraid we'd dig down on. So they sent a man out there one day. He come out, walkin' around lookin', and he said, "I come out here, the city sent me out here to locate them sewers so you won't dig down on 'em." I asked him, "What you gonna find them sewers with?" He commenced to laugh, and he says, "You'd be surprised! I'll get the thing and show you."

What he got was copper, but it worked just the same as this one, made just exactly like it. And he said, "I'll find them, 'n I'll put a stake down where I do." He put the stick down and he said, "If you don't find it right by the stick it will be right beside of that." There was four sewers went through there; he marked all four off and sure enough, every one of 'em! I took a rod where he marked, and run that rod right down on top of 'em and hit 'em. That's how I got on t' how that was done. I don't even know what his name was any more. Just a young fella the city sent out to locate those sewers. Back in the fifties, I think it was.

Conclusion: A Weaving Together

Climbing once again to my meadow-crowned hilltop, I realize it has been more than a year since I first sat here mulling over questions about Dwight and his life. The season has progressed too, and now a vast greening embraces the land, as succulent berries and swelling vegetables add a different, maturing dimension to the landscape. The waterfalls only trickle now, but the caves remain sweet and cool. Surrendering the woods to poison ivy, wildflowers decorate the fields instead. I am jolted out of contemplation when carbon-paper crows scold and berate me for impinging on *their* land. Back to business.

After reviewing all the materials Dwight and I have put together, I repeat my questions of a year ago: Why *is* Dwight drawn to life in these southeastern Ohio hills? Does his work satisfy more than basic food and shelter needs for him? Or is his sustenance here purely economic? Do Dwight's and my attitudes and aesthetics and values mesh at all? Would a positive answer simply betray that I had fallen into the "romantic sentimentalist trap," a Rousseauian pastoralization? In this trip across cultural boundaries, have I misinterpreted his personal and regional subtleties of speech? Have I wanted to hear positive answers simply to comfort myself with some common denominator in the human experience? Whatever the answers are, they have not come easily.

Dwight is eighty-eight this year. For many years, as evidenced by a few comments from different time periods, aging affected him little. Despite his octogenarian status, Dwight's plans for the future attested to his optimism: where he would get another supply of white oak when there was none left in the woods nearby; how he planned to experiment with different ways to store wood; how he wanted to build a bigger basket shop; what he planned to make for whom; how he hoped they could find funds for him to teach classes at the vocational school in Nelsonville; how Harold made a basket this past summer and might begin to make baskets in earnest one day.

My father came from a big family, twelve or fourteen of 'em, and most of 'em lived t' be pretty old, hardly ever find that many that old. My father, he lived t' be eighty-nine. I don't know whether I'll pull through that fer or not. I might!

I'm in that Medicare and I could get glasses, get m' teeth fixed too. But I'm like ever'body else, haven't got the time to go. I will some of these days. I used t' go around lookin' pretty sporty, spiffy, but I don't any more. Yeah, I looked spiffy! I'd keep m' hair cut short—it's longer now 'n I've had it fer a long time.

Last winter I planned t' make a fancy, complete shop in the garage, 'n use this one for a display room. Shop and basket store, so people kin come 'n look. Have it heated and warm. Then I got that bad flu and didn't get to it. I'll mebbe still go ahead with it, even if I am old.

I have headaches once in awhile. One good thing, I rest good at night. I go to sleep, nothin' bothers me till I get awake, anywhere from five to six of a morning. I go to sleep and I rest good. I'm awful tired, 'n then I get so doggone sleepy—I stay up and get the eleven o'clock news—I prett' near go to sleep sittin' in the chair with the news on.

I ain't like a lotta old fellas, get grouchy 'n snappy. I was always in t' have a lot of fun, enjoy it. I like t' see other people enjoy life, 'n entertain 'em. I ain't much of an entertainer, but I try. But if I start t' do something I don't enjoy, I soon quit.

Yeah, I suppose I'll make baskets as long as I can work my hands. If I can keep my hands from swellin' I'll be all right.

Dwight's low-key humor surfaces, in this case to make light of a serious problem: "I'm so slow now that when I take the inside bark off, it grows back on 'fore I get the basket made!" However, his hands were not to be the problem. Not long after he turned eighty-two, Dwight began mentioning vision loss.

I worked last night after supper, 'n listened to the ball game. The Reds; I've listened t' them fer years. I split reeds into squares. I don't weave too much at night any more, 'cause I can't see too good. But I can see t' split.

I'm almost blind in one eye, 'n sometimes I make a miscue. But I catch it pretty quick. I only go a coupla rounds weaving till I see it. See that miscue there, right there? I just go back and fix it.

Oh, any more I don't care nothin' 'bout teachin'. I've got where I can't see t' do anything. Make too many mistakes. I used t' like teachin', used t' go round far and near. But I'd be a lookin' fella now when I can't get these whiskers off, and I can't see t' shave 'em off now. I'd look like an old fella if I'd let 'em grow.

At first I thought Dwight's difficulty in seeing was simply a natural part of the aging process. But gradually his eyesight worsened and his health deteriorated, and he became more and more frail. Alarmed, I arranged an appointment, and my husband took him to a specialist in Columbus. The doctor diagnosed a disastrous condition: glaucoma, with no chance of regaining the lost vision. Only the dedicated use of drops would prevent complete loss of sight.

Rather than describe Dwight's health problems earlier, I wanted readers to identify with him as I first had: as a vigorous person, full of self-sufficiency and vitality. The blindness has, of course, changed him somewhat from the wonderfully positive, forward-looking, future-oriented man he had always been. Yet he has never asked for any kind of pity, even though he must surely have felt sorry for himself many times.

His comments do point to the loss of sight as being an enormously destructive development. Since work *is* his life, near-blindness is incapacitating. *I'm just trippin' around m' shop somethin' awful, knockin' inta things. Bobby helps me with the parts I can't see, like trimmin' off the inside pieces. Sure, we kin sit outside, long as it ain't too bright. When it's real bright, then's when I can't see outside atall.*

Rosemary, here's a spool of green *baler twine, first I ever got ahold of. I can't see it, but leastways they say it's green.*

Still, he remains stoic and philosophic, seldom complaining about *anything,* even this severe a blow. The demonstrations, the teaching, the opportunity to socialize and be recognized, have all come to a halt. Though Dwight never had traveled much, now he has become almost a hermit.

But still a hard-working one.

True, sons and grandsons must bring him the oak logs he once hefted to his left shoulder to carry home. But once they provide the wood, he has continued to strip withes through die holes he can only vaguely see, weaving and handling baskets he can only feel, blessedly unaware that they are now marred by hairy splints and broken weavers.

Even so, Dwight tries to maintain his humorous twinkle: "As the old sayin' goes, I'm like a blind horse, y' might have t' lead me."

We now have biographical and biological facts. But there is far more to knowing about a person's life than chronologies or health status or even crafts methods. My plan for collecting Dwight's life story was to learn about his life and his basketmaking, but also through gathering the facts to discover more about his values and beliefs. For the study of folklore makes its greatest contribution to scholarship and the advancement of knowledge by providing keys to a people's—and its culture's—basic attitudes, beliefs, and values. And biography can further our understanding of humankind, by illuminating the values and philosophies of a single individual.

Consciously or unconsciously, we then sift and compare that other person's values with our own, introspectively forging and cementing, perhaps even altering, our personal beliefs. In that process, we can come to know ourselves better, to sense better our particular niche in this time and this space.

But few of us are practiced in clarifying our personal values. How, then, as folklorists and oral historians, can we find answers to questions of value that may have seldom, if ever, been examined by our consultants either? Often we must simply speculate or piece together clues to clarify their attitudes and beliefs.

Asking direct questions about values is not always successful. In addition it can create subtle barriers between biographer and subject. My own value-seeking questions seemed to disconcert Dwight, especially since he enjoyed providing ready answers and they were not forthcoming. "Rosemary, you caught me on a bad day; can't think of anythin'. Let's see, am I supposed t' take stuff along t' weave at that demonstration in Worthington?"

While the book offers many aspects of Dwight's life through photographs and tables and figures, the primary clues to understanding many of his values and beliefs must come through his narrative. His words must fill out the drama of his particular life's stage, carrying us in temporal space from the beginning of a new century to the second appearance of Halley's Comet, from helping a grandmother work in her garden to eking out a precarious living for eight children.

Many characters have been cast in his story: a much-loved young mother, a disciplinarian grandmother, an encouraging great-uncle, an insensitive stepmother, a crafty farmer-employer, dedicated grade-school teachers, a shadowy wife, eight children, numerous—but unnumbered—grandchildren, demanding employers, striking fellow workers, friendly neighbors, hopeful customers, unwilling students.

The plot is an unraveling of the sinewy fibers tangled in the thick fabric of Dwight's memory, a reweaving of the textured goods of his life. The central theme is, of course, *work,* and hard work. We know that Dwight's life has been a homely one. He has traveled little: to work in Alabama, to demonstrate in various Ohio cities and in Washington, D.C. "I guess I've been everywhere and everyplace, 'n haint' been no place either."

But what has sustained him during those years of "being no place"? What has he liked and disliked? What attitudes and values can we perceive from his many reminiscences? What does he think about such institutions as the law, the government, the church, the city? Is he aware of tradition in his crafts? How does he relate to the basketmaking? Does he like innovation, order? Does he articulate his obvious belief in hard work? Does he experience pride in his accomplishments?

Dwight has ambiguous feelings about the law: some respect, some scorn, some fear. He was proud to have been a deputy sheriff. He scorned the "dry officers," the sheriffs, and the judges who were too hard on moonshiners. But, even though he must be aware of marijuana growth—ardent herb gatherer that he is—there was an element of fear in his remark, "I don't want that 'happy grass' around. Might be an officer, sheriff, come around here an' get me, happy grass and all!"

Before we went to Washington, he unabashedly thought we might get to see the president, then rethought that: "Mebbe if he hears about me bein' there, he'll send me congratulations or something like that. I know I won't get t' see *him,* 'cause they wouldn't let me in there. I've seen him time and time again in the movies, when he was a cowboy in Hollywood. That's quite a high step from cowboy to president!"

He respects the Lord, though his is not a vindictive, Calvinist God. *Longest day in the whole week fer me—I don't make baskets on Sunday but mebbe get some papers through the week I don't get t' look at, and I'll go in the house biggest part of the time 'n look at that. I don't make any on Sunday. Lotta people say, "Why don't you make on Sunday too?" Oh, I wanta take Sunday off. They call that the Lord's Day. The Lord didn't make this world all in six days. Said he worked six days and rested the seventh. But he finished up somethin' on the seventh. Now I might finish one up on Sunday, if I have t' put a handle on, or weave it down. Get that done, I quit right there. So many people say, "Oh, you oughta take the Sabbath Day off." That's 'cause they got nothin' else to do.*

Dwight values a rural setting, choosing to live in the country, primarily in Hocking County, except for the time he worked in the glass factory and lived in nearby Lancaster. And, again with the exception of the factory job, he has worked outdoors, either on the land itself or with organic materials. He lives in and from his environment, works in it and draws pleasure from it, as we see from his various comments.

I've lived in town a little bit, but you see I'm back out in the country again. There's a lot of 'em raised out in the country, they ain't much interested in goin' t' town.

You've got more advantage. A person workin' has got more advantage out in the country than he has in town. You gotta go accordin' t' this in town and accordin' t' that in town, t' do this and to do that. Have t' have a permit t' do this, a permit t' do that. And out here, why that's the important part of that, you don't have t' have all that stuff.

And it's more quieter, and you get around and get about. You can see things out in the country you don't see in town. You can get around through the woods, fields, walk around. If a person wants to, he can walk around the rocks and see differnt sights. City people just don't know till they get out and see once, then they find out. I'd like t' tell people, if they wanted t' live a good, natural life and want t' enjoy nature, they should get out in the country where nature formed differnt things they could see.

Dwight's rural culture has always rewarded the ingenious producer in this area marked by poverty. Thus Dwight has developed a reliance on the products of nature's bounty, either in an organic or a recycled state. But this use *seems*—although he has never directly said so—to answer personal aesthetics as well as a monetary need.

His mother's proficiency inspired an early interest in working with his hands. This, coupled with his own affinity for the natural environment and his interest in using recycled objects, led Dwight into the broad spectrum of crafts he pursues. He developed them all within a framework of tradition—a traditional rural setting, traditional occupations and crafts, using traditional tools and methods, turning out traditional products. The words *old-fashioned* and *tradition* have high value for him.[1] "Yeah, basketmakers all kind of link in together, carryin' the tradition on, keepin' the tradition up. Lots of people come here, they say I'm workin' at a forgotten art.

And I say, 'No, it's not forgotten, people just quit and didn't work at it, it ain't forgotten yet.'"

But all of his traditions have been marked too with the stamp of his own personal innovation.[2] He manufactures many of his work aids and tools, often by modifying "store-bought" ones (such as the mallet or the bark scraper), or by using found objects (the victrola-turntable dies, the reed guide, the turning journal, the rug patterns, the roller stand). He remodeled and reworked his father-in-law's old 1880 Chieftain stove, and the water pump. When Dwight worried over the dwindling supply of white oak, he announced one day, "I'm startin' t' use maple t' weave. It dries out while you're workin' on it, but it makes a real purty white basket." He enjoys the experimenting and inventing, bragging, "I've got a patent on that!"

Dwight likes order. He has always kept the shop swept up, understanding and maintaining order in what I perceive as chaos, jumbled corners, and saved materials, all of the might-come-in-handy-someday collection of found objects so dear to the heart of a confirmed recycler. He also attempts to schedule work in an orderly manner: "Mostly I like to start on Monday morning to weave. And I like to weave on Mondays and Tuesdays. Sometimes I can't, but I try to aim that way. Wednesdays and Thursdays sometimes I have to get out and hunt up wood 'n stuff, so I don't take on and weave up. And mostly—I did there 'fore my back got to bothering me—on Friday and Saturday I'd pull a bunch through the dies, 'n sort 'em up fer rods t' weave with, t' start on Monday morning then t' weave." John and I visited him one Sunday, and as he pulled splints through a die board, he explained carefully: "I never weave on Sunday, but I'm pullin' through today, gettin' *ready* t' weave tomorrow." Even though the pulling-through process is actually more work than the weaving, it nonetheless satisfied his no-work-on-Sunday restriction.

As Dwight has related the details of his many and varied work activities, he has enlarged most upon his basketmaking. While this is no doubt due to my continued focus on that craft, he does receive the most recognition, both monetary and personal, from the basketry. It gives him his strongest sense of identity: "I carry credentials in my pocket. On my Social Security I'm supposed t' be a retired carpenter. I think of myself now as a basketmaker, 'n havin' a basket 'factory.'"

As he described his craft, his attitudes toward its materials and its process became quite evident. Dwight always enjoys going to the woods. In a rare use of the verb *love,* he admitted: "The young oak tree is mostly what I love!" He gains great satisfaction in realizing that round-rod basketmaking is complex, often remarking: "See, Rosemary, there's a whole lot more to it than most people think! There's all differnt ways t' work things out." He visibly enjoys that competence: "There's lots of tricks—tricks t' all trades. Y' gotta trick t' know how t' do 'em." And tricks mean the difference between a Dwight Stump basket and, say, a Wade Huffhines basket. "Never a one brought a basket back frazzled out. I never had t' change a handle a second time. And I hardly ever get a bulge in my baskets. Way I weave 'em, I've never had a basket t' come back with a thing wrong with it."

Still, he is rather casual about the end result of his weaving. He hasn't "kept tab" on the numbers of baskets he's made over the years. Nor does he sign any, expecting us to recognize his left-handed weave just as he does. He has not kept even one of them: "I don't like stuff settin' around. I did have one real old one o' mine 'round here fer awhile; I don't know what possessed me t' sell it, but I did. I wanted t' keep it 'cause it was old. I just kept a-sellin' 'em as I made 'em, never did keep one, fer some 'cause or other. Guess I always figured I could make another'n if I needed it."

Dwight knows what he likes. While he wants very much to satisfy his customers, too, even experimenting to make new sizes and shapes at their request, he pleases himself first. To Dwight, a basket is a *container,* an object made for use, and usually for a specific function, not merely for aesthetic pleasure. When the web of stays is tied up together, he declares: "I kin make 'em with the top pulled in like that, lotsa people think that looks purty, but *that's* no *basket!*"

Dwight's sense of aesthetics evolves from one central idea: function. Not "Will it sell?" but "Will it last?" Not "Is it beautiful?" but "Is it useful?" Yet that very observation warns of a potential ethnocentric or art-criticism approach here, a culturally biased use of judgmental terms. For Dwight, and for many traditional artists yet to be studied as individuals, useful *is* beautiful.[3]

Despite the claim of most basketmakers that round baskets are the most difficult to make, Dwight has always returned to that one shape. He gains tangible satisfaction in seeing that particular one "take form," a sense of accomplishment in doing something difficult well. Though he has woven flat-splint baskets, he comments tersely: "I've made 'em, but I don't like 'em." He does not paint or dye the splits, nor create openwork designs. And while people "talked him into it," he makes only a few odd sizes and shapes. Mostly those remain fly-specked orders still hanging on a nail, ignored. Dwight likes the plain, unadorned, uncolored, sturdy, round, round-rod baskets that the old-timers before him made: "They had them baskets just as purty around, round as you'd want t' see 'em, and they was all about the same."

One day he laughed: "At times I have a notion t' quit. Like everythin', it gets monotonous. Sometimes I have t' stop 'n do somethin' else, mebbe fer two, three months. Then I get t' thinkin' 'bout I wonder how I'd go to make baskets. And I go back to makin' baskets again. Yeah, it's like the old basketmakers used t' tell me, 'When y' get in the Basketmakers Row once, it's hard t' get out!' I don't know why, it just grows on a person. You get 'tached to it."[4]

For Dwight, *work* is the motivating factor, the organizing principle, his reason for being. As we have seen, he lives that primary value daily. In responding to my query concerning "the most important things to you in life," Dwight answered: "Oh, I don't know. I've worked with so many differnt things, that—well, carpenter work is pretty important t' me."

And I replied, "But I don't mean what your most important *work* is—just what is most important to you in life."

"Oh, I don't know, I can hardly tell it. Fella said, 'You're kinda gettin' me up a limb now.' I was gonna say, it's pretty important t' me t' see everybody get along with ever'body, and see ever'body get along betwixt themselves."

Pursuing the enigmatic question, I later tried switching to what he thought was "the most important thing to your neighbors." Dwight answered, "A lot of 'em raise cattle, sheep, hogs, that was one time an important livelihood." At another time, the same question brought the same kind of answer: "Oh, farmin' mostly, farmin' and timberin' lumber."

"Well, not what do they do, but what they consider most important in their lives?"

"Oh, most of 'em work at differnt things. A lot of 'em work in town now. Funny 'bout that, fella says, 'I can't think.' My land!"

Because Dwight does so much repetitive work, and because he creates his own "assembly line" as he works, I often wondered if he would have made a good factory worker. Only later did I discover that he had been one for four years.

It's all right workin' in a factory. But I'll tell you about that. If a person has a job of his own he's a little better off, I think. You've got a lot of imposition in a factory.

You don't know what you're goin' up against, what's gonna happen. That paper mill I worked in, at that time was a pretty dangerous place. They had what you call a "slewer," and wet paper and stuff went through that. The one that throwed the paper in there, stood there, and if he ever fell on in there, he'd be gone! Said one time they was one did *fall in there, and that was the last of him!*

Dwight is an independent: he gathers, manufactures, and sells his own products, much as did his nineteenth-century forebears. Occasionally he refers to his shop as a "basket factory," but it is the kind in which he achieves that status so prized in Appalachia, in America: he is his own boss. However, as is true for most of those fortunate yet beleaguered persons, the "boss" is a hard taskmaster. His hours are long ones, with no coffee breaks, no "benefits" or financial perks, no paid vacations—no vacations at all, in fact.

I always liked a job fer myself pretty good. I could work t' suit myself, didn't have no boss t' tell me what t' do. Ohhhh, watch out! There's a yellow jacket's nest in here. No, I take my good old time, no one t' hurry me up. I always liked something that was construction, that is, to promote, to build up. See something come up and take form. *That's what I like!*

Even with need such an obvious factor, Dwight does not work simply for the money generated. He is not a materialistic person, and I realized with some shock one day, he *owns nothing,* not the land he lives on or the house he dwells in, no car, not even one of his own baskets. Again, he lives his values. *I'll tell you, Rosemary, money's just the same as watchin' a picture in the paper. It's funny that way, but money is something that never concerned me much. I made it, but I always told people I was more concerned with my work than I was with the money that was in it.*

They's some people comes here thinks I'm too high priced on my baskets, and I said, "High priced! I give 'em away fer fifteen years, now I just begun t' sell 'em. How am I too high priced on 'em?" "Well, there ain't much work t' that." And I say, "There's fifty dollars' worth of work in a twenty-five-dollar basket."

I started doin' m' rugs double thickness just lately, but I charge the same price fer 'em. No, I don't make 'em fer money—just t' keep busy and have somethin' t' do. Oh, I could set around, but myyyy [chuckling] *that'd get monot'nous t' me just in a little bit!*

When I'm makin' a basket I enjoy settin' an' weavin' 'em, and when I'm makin' rugs I enjoy sewin' 'em. That's what I get my enjoyment out of, settin' there, usin' my hands and keepin' my hands a-goin'. I like t' exercise my hands. I always like to make something. Create something. I like to create something if I can.

In 1981 his work gained another dimension: solace. His wife, Maisie, died in February, just before they celebrated their fifty-ninth wedding anniversary. In an unusual reference to feelings, Dwight tearfully admitted, "I just can't get over it. The only way I can keep goin' is t' come out here to the shop and work."[5]

Dwight is not a braggart. In fact he was highly amused at his son's reaction before Dwight and I went to Washington for his demonstration at the Library of Congress: "Bobby said, 'When you come back your head'll be so swelled up you won't be able t' get in the door!' I told him I didn't think so."

Occasionally, though, revealing bits of pride slipped into our various conversations.

My sisal rugs'll last years and years, take all kinds o' wear, 'cause they're sewn together with the same thickness o' twine as the braid's made of. Guess that's why s' many people buys 'em.

M' daughter Mary was here this mornin'. They're all fixin' up the house. The roof got t' leakin', they're gonna fix it. The house has been here fourteen years, all built out of used lumber, stood that long without havin' t' have any repair work done on it, so you know I built it.

If I ever make a basket that don't come out right, t' suit me, nobody gets that. If it starts going bad, I just quit there. Either tear it up, tear it apart, use what I can out of it. If I don't feel right of a morning when I'm making baskets, I won't bother with it. I just wait a day or so until I get t' feelin' differnt. Go on t' something else, and kinda forgit about it fer a little bit.

I've never had t' hunt fer a job! *I've been around a whole lot, done a lotta work, on lotta differnt jobs. But* [talking slowly here to emphasize his seriousness] *whatever I started, I made a success. I aimed t' make good money, but I aimed t' learn the trade, keep the trade up at the same time. Whatever I done fer a man, a year or so later, if he wanted anything done, he'd be right back after me. Somebody'd come wantin' me t' do a job of some kind, wanted t' know if I could do that. "Yep." Well, I'd go do it, the job's done. "You got any more work fer me t' do?" And then I'd do it again. And I always got t' go back. I never, never had t' hunt fer a job.*

I don't think I work hard. Musta got kinda used to it. I guess all my life I've worked hard. Worked hard and never saved anything either. A lotta people say, "Much high-priced work as you've done, you oughta be a millionaire." I said, "I don't care about bein' no mil-

lionaire, just so I can live and enjoy life. That's all I'm out fer. I enjoy life when I'm a-workin', that's all I get out of life anyhow." And I let it go at that.

Dwight claims he doesn't work hard, but the work is obviously of primary importance.

Nooo, I don't work hard. I've done a lot, been pert' near oncet around. I've just liked t' see how many different jobs—what all I could do and what I could get into. I enjoy makin' the baskets now. It's kind of a hobby for me now. You can't make no money at it. And publicity, that don't mean nothing either. M' baskets and rugs keeps me goin'.

Other craftspeople have echoed similar sentiments: Dwight's friend Omen Beavers for example, liked to "make something useful, something creative." The Georgia potter Lanier Meaders offered this assessment: "It's a gift that a person come by. I could no more stop this than I could fly an airplane. . . . All of my movements, all of my work that I've done all my life has led straight to this place right here." Roger Morigi, a stone carver, said, "The more you work, the better it comes out, you feel good inside. . . . it fills you with some kind of emotion—such a sense of satisfaction." And Elwood West, a Kentucky basketmaker, concluded, "Well, there's definitely an art to it. When you spend a lot of time making something like that, a lot of pride gets built right into it."[6]

Work may well share the stage with family in Dwight's hierarchy of values. But that remains supposition, since Dwight seldom talked about his family. He once said, "The old sayin' is, I seen m' best times after I got married and settled down. I knowed once I was married that was time t' settle down and look forward to the future. Now all they think about is 'do ever'body 'fore they do you!'"

We do know, however, that from the time he was small, the family affirmed the community value of work. Dwight was "taught to work and work hard." His grandmother and uncle, the compelling influences in his early life, exhorted him to do so.

Uncle Eli always said, "If you want to have anything, you'll hafta work t' git it." Grandmother told me, I'll never forget, she said, "Boy, as long as you're able t' work you won't starve. Try t' save something, though. But if you work, even if it was from hand t' mouth, you'd still be livin'."

Yeah, all the people around here, they all said, "Get out and work and earn your money!" (Nowadays, politicians are the ones makin' the money.) I had an uncle said, "Boy, don't never start t' do any work unless you know you kin make a success at it." He wouldn't do any-

thing unless he could make a success at it, accomplish! *That was Harvey, father's oldest brother.*

However unarticulated his thoughts may be, Dwight has a philosophical view of life, a view that I glimpsed between the cracks of reticence as he talked.

I've been in so many differnt things, worked s' many differnt ones, that I just couldn't tell y' exactly what's most important t' me. There's an old saying, "Always take life as it comes."

When I was a boy, just a little fella, I was sick a whole lot. I don't know how I lived t' be so old. Well, I get all the rest I kin and sleep, and not let anything worry me. I am one fella that never worried about what tomorrow would bring, for I knowed tomorrow would come, regardless of what I planned or not. And I never worried about what tomorrow's gonna bring. Lots of people said to me, "Why don't you plan ahead? Plan a year ahead." "Oh, no." I talked to one man, said, "Why I got my plans all made a year ahead." And that man made his plans a year ahead, wasn't long after I seen him, he died. His plans didn't work out. Differnt ones say, "Oh, you ought to plan six months, a year ahead." I always told 'em, "Take care of today and tomorrow'll take care of itself." Yeah, I've always tried t' be well-contented as much as I can. Don't try t' leave anything worry me or nothing.

Well, it ain't twelve o'clock yet. They call it daylight savings time. I call it race-horse time. It don't make any difference; it's daylight till it's dark anyhow.

I never worried much about anything. Ain't nothin' to worry about, so I never let nothing worry me. What's the most important in life? All I know t' tell you is: make life enjoyable and enjoy what you're doin' as you go through life.

Besides combing his verbal testimony for glimpses of Dwight's thoughts and beliefs, I found one other window to his world. Spoken language often expresses meaning in a covert or subtle way, in metaphor. But physical action—performance and work of all kinds—also expresses meaning, the meaning expressed by movement rather than words. Dwight overtly expresses multiple layers of meaning—beliefs, attitudes, and values—through performance as well as speech.[7] Verbal metaphor enables us to comprehend abstract ideas or complex values by comparing them to a less complex object or activity. By using action as metaphor, we can further comprehend Dwight's abstract, largely unspoken beliefs and complex values by letting his basketmaking speak more simply for him.

For Dwight's basketmaking is truly a metaphor for his life. As he attends to the many steps of the process, he twists the strands of daily existence into and around the oak withes, in an unconscious weaving of the textures of his life. His making of these baskets ultimately speaks for him and for his culture. Metaphors, either verbal or physical, are culturally determined, always relative to the way of life from which they spring, inseparable from their social context. Consequently, metaphor reinforces and affirms societal beliefs.[8] By placing Dwight's basketmaking in its own social context, we can see that it also reaffirms many of his culture's values as well as his own.

The product, the basket itself, is useful, functional, and necessary, qualities prized far more than mere aesthetic "beauty," reflecting life in his rural culture. In their community, useful is both revered *and* beautiful.

The basketmaking process first of all embodies, and then reinforces, the valuing of hard work that characterizes Dwight and his community. The basket is white oak, the sturdiest of natural materials, but also one of the most difficult to gather. The basketmaking process—preparing the wood, splitting it, then pulling it through metal dies—is also one of the most time-consuming methods known. And the basket's round shape is one of the most difficult to weave. All of these stand for Dwight's convictions about doing well *any* job worth doing, regardless of the hard work or the difficulties involved. The process requires many "tricks of the trade" and many competences.

The basketmaking represents Dwight's knowledge of and respect for nature's materials (he has even expressed love of the young oak tree), as well as his reliance on using those natural elements. The making also denotes his choice of place, since basket oak, dense and heavy, matures in deep woods found only in that rural environment. It is the location Dwight prefers for raising a family, for working, for finding all his pleasure, for living.

On another level, making an oak basket stands also for his desire to exert control over that environment, one that many have construed as hostile in a continuing nature-against-culture battle. Dwight and his basket claim European sources, and that heritage—like many other heritages—includes a view of nature as a force to be subdued, not conserved. (The increasing scarcity of white oak is mute testimony to the problems that must ultimately be faced as a result of this viewpoint.)

Basketmaking symbolizes the need for creativity in Dwight's life. He most enjoys working with his hands, sitting and weaving, seeing something take form. He derives his greatest satisfaction from creating some product. The basketmaking exemplifies Dwight's nonmaterialistic approach to life. Its product is ephemeral, a temporary possession to a person who owns nothing. Dwight asks only for the opportunity to work. *That* is what he enjoys, what he "gets out of life."

The basketmaking personifies Dwight's ability to maintain his independence, his pride, his sense of dignity and purpose, even long past the period when other people are retiring. Through that work, he is still a complete person, one recognized for his ability to contribute to the society in which he lives. Basketmaking keeps him going.

Basketmaking also stands for the force of tradition in Dwight's life, in the lives of all of us. Dwight continues to make the same round, unadorned baskets, by the same process, out of the same materials, that he learned as a boy to make from the community of traditional makers. As primarily urban dwellers, we tend to lose sight of the strong pull that our traditions still exert on us, too, whether they originate from family, age, sex, church, school, recreational, neighborhood, regional, ethnic, or racial groups. But that pull is there, daily influencing our own habits and attitudes and beliefs and, yes, values.[9]

As in one stage Dwight visually and expressively creates a "spider web" (readying the formation of the basket's side frame), he presents us also with a web of oppositions, opposition between maker and perceiver, nature and culture, rural and urban, function and decoration, continuity and discontinuity, stability and change, thus conveying a whole body of metaphorical meaning within the simple structure of the basket.

A Weaving Together

In presenting Dwight as a happy, satisfied person, I do not paint a facile watercolor, blurring the edges of reality with a poor-but-happy-craftsman palette.[10] I am all too aware of the darker side of that picture: the deprivation of a stark childhood, the concerns of feeding eight children, the sorrow in losing a newborn child. But I admire and attempt to emulate Dwight's own emphasis on the positive in his life, his patient, nearly saintlike perseverance, as he loses himself in his beloved work. And goes on, making tools, making baskets, making himself.

Putting this book together has been a long process. In some ways it reminds me of Dwight's basketmaking, since for me it became "more complicated than y' think." Perhaps my writing was not so well organized as his basketmaking process; but, in slowly piecing and working and weaving its parts one by one, back and forth, in and out, the book finally took on a shape with which its maker can be satisfied. With Dwight, I applaud the enormous satisfaction to be gained from such shaping, "seeing something come up and *take form*. That's what I like!"

I have answered my original hilltop-inspired questions. Dwight not only "shares" my great love for these hills, he goes beyond my own considerable appreciation. His sustenance here is far more than economic. His work satisfies much more for him than basic needs of food and shelter.

I have also attended to my stated purposes: presenting a book dedicated to extending and deepening our understanding of the circumstances of another person, especially a person from another culture. For with that broadened perspective, we can better interact with and more sensitively contribute to others in our world. Most important, we ultimately bring that new understanding into focus on ourselves.

As a common-person life story, the book moves us from a great man/significant event focus to an appreciation of the excellence possible in humble living. We see not only the depth of a traditional culture, but also the importance of an ethnography/biography in placing that tradition into its own time and space context. One more set of description, it does not "answer our deepest questions" but makes more answers available for inclusion in the "consultable record."[11]

Featuring an individual rather than simply an object, the book focuses on the creator of the form, amplifying some of the attitudes and aesthetics involved in that creation and reminding us that the creative act is an important, even vital, part of daily life. There is a necessity for art in the richness of life, "for art and life have an inextricably entwined rootage . . . . it is the modern world of 'high culture' and 'high technology' that makes sharper and sharper the difference between art and non-art, between artist and the ordinary citizen, rich or poor."[12] It also alerts folk-art enthusiasts to the potential dark side of selling production.

Dwight is a model for maintaining pride and a sense of accomplishment and self-worth into old age. His story may help others, the aging or those who work with them, to pursue his methods and philosophies. Certainly older persons, either as practitioners or teachers, can offer important contributions to their respective ethnic groups by maintaining their culture's continuity.[13]

Folklorists may consider the life-history format more often. The genre not only enables them to cast a wide net for consultants, but also offers the subjects themselves benefit: the life-review process has empowered Dwight by underscoring his sense of personal accomplishment and well-being, his job well done in the strictest, truest sense of the word. By traditionalizing everyday experience, workers can, in some degree, empower their own lives. Further, a recounting of one's life story can "help to demystify experience and redress loss."[14] As Dwight repapers the rooms of his past with recollections of everyday experience, his humor and straightforward accounting fight the dehumanization of poverty, helping to demystify that experience both for himself and also for his less visible contemporaries.

The book presents Dwight's basket as a symbolic form of his culture, as metaphor designating cultural and individual meaning. Adding a small clue to the search for regional patterning, it documents a nearly vanished tradition, oak round-rod basketry, a link to the past and possibly the future as well. In so doing, it fulfills a responsibility of "cultural custodianship" by preservation and interpretation (a reminder of the poignant saying, "Each time an elder dies in Africa, it is the library of Alexandria that burns").[15]

Dwight's whole life has been and still is lived in poverty. He owns nothing material. He does, however, own the knowledge that he must take life as it comes, that he needn't let anything worry him because, regardless of what he plans, tomorrow will come. And when it does come, it will, essentially, take care of itself. He has made his life enjoyable, he has contributed to others' enjoyment, and he enjoys what he is doing. Dwight is a successful person.

He has shared with us both the beauty of his baskets and the wisdom of his approach to life before the Basketmakers' Row here finally becomes empty. Then Dwight will contentedly weave again, clear of eye and facile of finger, in a grove of heavenly white-oak trees.

Appendix A

National Survey of Traditional Basketmakers

In 1985 my assistant, Cerena Miele, and I surveyed sixty-four persons by mail, including the state folklorists (as the one definable group presently contacting traditional craftspersons) and a number of individuals known for their work in the field of material culture or of folk art. Our goal was to enlist their help in compiling a gross estimate of current traditional American basketmaking.

We arbitrarily divided the thirty-five replies by region (West and Southwest, Plains, Midwest, Appalachian South, Deep South, Northeast, Alaska, and Hawaii)—a chancey proposition at best, since many people have strong feelings about which state goes where in such divisions.

The survey consisted of two parts. In the first, a comprehensive paragraph requested the general status of traditional basketry in the respondent's state or region, with reference to areas of the state included, ethnic backgrounds involved, natural materials used, methods used (coiling, plaiting, or weaving), and the density of the activity (that is, whether there were a few individual standouts or a more pervasive group participation).

The second part of the survey dealt with outstanding or well-known individual makers, with spaces provided for the name, area of the state, racial or ethnic background, age, sex, whether he or she works alone or in a group, method used (coiling, plaiting, or weaving), materials used, shapes and sizes produced.

To our surprise, the second section proved to be the large stumbling block in our search for full information. The survey faltered substantially at that point, since numerous respondents left many or all lines of section two blank. Most were frank in stating the reasons for their omission, reasons which were, frankly, shocking. They all shared a strong belief in the need to protect the anonymity of the artists they knew or with whom they worked (I referred to this obliquely in the Preface).

Even though I have myself received requests for anonymity from various craftspersons whom I interviewed, I attributed their fear of The Government (writ large) to a sort of paranoia, stemming from either naïveté or simply a lack of personal experience. For it was beyond my comprehension—recognizing as I did the poverty of these craftspersons and the low prices they received for their labor—that "revenuers" could conceivably target this population. Nonetheless, judging from the replies I received and from the numerous instances of abuses cited, I was wrong.

Further, some of the entrepreneurs are, allegedly, not only purchasing the baskets of traditional artists at extremely low prices, they are also claiming the baskets—and the recognition for making them—as their own! Some of these buyers, when denied sales at rock-bottom prices, have angrily reported the "recalcitrant" craftspersons to the "authorities," who prosecute them and attempt to take away their old-age pensions. For obvious reasons, I cannot disclose my sources at this time. But I recount these allegations to reiterate the complexity of the seemingly uncomplicated act of marketing a few baskets.

This, then, explains the paucity of information about individual makers. On the basis of the facts we did receive about them, Miele devised an interesting computerized profile, on which the table at the end of this appendix is based.

General Status of Traditional Basketry: Regional Summary

Alaska

Aleut. Probably forty to fifty women are currently weaving twined-grass baskets of very, very fine scale.

Athabascans. Numerous craftswomen (no estimate of the number) make folded birch-bark baskets and also coiled split-willow trays and baskets, maintaining a very active tradition.

Tlingit, Haida, and Tsimshian. A few women are making spruce-root and cedar-bark baskets. More are learning now through workshops and apprenticeships, as part of a larger cultural revival effort (sponsored institutionally by, for example, the Institute of Alaska Native Arts and the Consortium for Pacific Arts and Cultures).

Yupik Eskimo. Several small villages of only three hundred to five hundred people may have as many as thirty women who make coiled-grass baskets. Many women also make twined-grass bags for everyday use in carrying things, sometimes also to be sold in gift shops.

Inupiaq Eskimo. A small number of men make baleen baskets, although some women are now making them as well. Birch-bark baskets, different from the Athabascan ones, are made in one or two northwestern villages.

—Suzi Jones, contributor

Hawaii

Hawaiians used three basic materials for their craft: 'ie'ie (*Freycinetia arborea*) vines from a high-elevation creeping plant, Lau niu (coconut leaves) and Lau hala (pandanus leaves). And very fine weaves were lavished on sleeping and floor mats plaited from makaloa (a sedge grass reported extinct now).

They lavished their finest skills and attention on baskets made from the 'ie'ie vines, utilizing various twining techniques, often making them over gourds to protect them from cracking. Other articles were helmets, fish-traps, handles for dance rattles, and frameworks for images of the war god Kukailimoku. Today there are only two or three people pursuing this art form, which virtually died out in the late 1800s. Those people practicing today have researched the techniques on their own, using photographs and objects in the collection of the Bishop Museum in Honolulu.

The least complex baskets were made from coconut leaves. These baskets, as well as hats, fans, and mats of the same material, were made for daily use and were not long-lasting, because of the relative impermanence of coconut fiber. There are a number of people now who weave excellent coconut hats and baskets.

The baskets made from pandanus leaves, plaited at ninety-degree angles, were much simpler in design and coarser in weave (approximately three-quarters of an inch). Today one can find in certain districts a great variety of plaited lau hala hats, fans, and some square-bottomed baskets, usually referred to as "coffee-picking baskets."

Filipinos came to Hawaii in the late 1800s as contract labor for the sugar and pineapple plantations. Some had brought their bamboo and rush-plaiting skills with them, and continue to weave today. Two rather elusive gentlemen who weave bamboo coffee baskets are probably the last of that line.

While some islanders have attended the community classes offered at various locations around the state, only the dedicated ones are involved, for baskets are not economically viable because of the fierce competition from Taiwan and the Philippines. —Lynn Martin, contributor

West, Southwest

Idaho. While there seem to be no Anglo-American basketmakers (one older man has stopped producing) in Idaho, traditional basketry does exist on the five Indian reservations: Kutenai (far north), Coeur d'Alene (north), Nez Percé (north central), Duck Valley Shoshone-Painte (southwest), and Fort Hall Shoshone-Bannoch (southeast). They use willow and grasses in all areas, plus cedar and cornhusks in the north. Root- and berry-gathering baskets, cradleboards, cornhusk bags and hats, back rests, and winnowing trays are some of their products. However, only a few older people at each reservation make baskets regularly. —Steve Siporin, contributor

Utah. The only known group currently producing traditional basketry is a Native American one, the Allen Canyon Utes, who reside near Blanding. Although historically they seem to be Paiutes with geographic connections in the White Mesa area near Blanding, they consider themselves Utes (a tribe with more social prestige). They are best known for, interestingly, the coiled Navajo wedding baskets they have made for many years to sell to neighboring Navajos. They also use the same locally gathered willow (or squaw bush or sumac) for weaving shades on cradleboards. Only a handful of active makers, all female, seem to have knowledge of the tradition.

—Carol Edison, contributor

Arizona. Traditional basketry *means* Native American basketry. The Papagos are the biggest producers (and are considered some of the finest weavers in the country), with the Hopis next. Pimas, Apaches, and Navajos make as well. Almost all the basket production today is for display rather than domestic use, except for looped baling-wire baskets made by Papago men for their own kitchen storage. All the groups do coiling, but the Hopis also make plaited sifter trays and wicker plaques.

—Jim Griffith, contributor

Colorado. Only one basketmaker, a Native American born on the Creek reservation in Oak Grove, Oklahoma, is still active, but she learned from formal teaching-workshops at a church in northwest Denver. The Ute tribe has no basket tradition now (presumably they made water baskets before their cultural activities were so changed after being driven into reservations). Now they tend to make pottery, beaded clothing, and jewelry. There is no Anglo tradition, presumably because there are so few potential materials in the state.

—David Brose, contributor

Wyoming. Since there are few native hardwoods in Wyoming, and none suitable for basketmaking, the tradition seems not to have developed here. There is material culture evidence to indicate that there was a tradition among the Eastern Shoshoni on the Wind River Reservation of weaving green willow, especially for cradleboards. But extensive fieldwork indicates that that tradition is moribund.

—Dennis Coelho, contributor

The Plains

Kansas. Because materials on the prairie are so difficult to find, the tradition is not strong. There are many revivalists, but only one known traditional basketmaker, a Cherokee Indian who uses willow, honeysuckle, buckbrush, oak, ash, cattail, reed, and cane to make excellent plaited and woven baskets.

—Jennie Chinn, contributor

Nebraska. As near as we can tell, the tradition is nonexistent, with the last basketmaker (a Czech) deceased. Most American and European immigrants apparently left their basketmaking traditions behind. In addition, there seems to be no revival basketry in Nebraska.

—Lynne Ireland, contributor

Midwest

Iowa. There is a great deal of revivalist and nontraditional basketry interest, centered in the Iowa Basketweavers Guild, but no indication of traditional work.

—Steven Ohrn, contributor

Illinois. Little information is available on Illinois basketmakers, none of it standardized. There is one "seven-generation family" of basketmakers, and there are numerous examples of nontraditional makers.

—Egle Zygas, contributor

Indiana. The traditional craft has been moribund for some years now, but there are many revivalists. There seems to be only one traditional basketmaker left in the state, and she is a transplanted Kentuckian. Nonetheless, not all areas of the state have been surveyed, so that it is possible—though not likely—that some of the Anglo white-oak weaving persists.

—Geoff Gephart, contributor

There used to be round-rod basketmakers in Indiana, but the Hovis family (according to Gary Stanton) moved to southwest Missouri, probably in the early twentieth century. And there are some historic photographs of the Bohall family, who used to make round-rod baskets in Brown County. Today there is a Greek émigré, about forty years old, who decided to try making an olive basket like the ones he had watched his grandfather make twenty years before in Greece. He uses whatever materials he can find in nearby ditches, presumably some type of willow, and splits it in thirds with a sharp wooden tool he made in the steel mill where he works.

—Betty Belanus, contributor

Michigan. Generally speaking, black-ash basketry has never completely died in the state; some individuals have always made baskets. However, there is a revival of basketmaking on community levels, for example among the Potawatami, among whom the women weave, while the men prepare the wood and carve the handles. One or two individuals who have maintained the tradition have taught other women, who are now making and selling at powwows, and demonstrating at artist-in-the-school programs. The Ojibway in the Upper Peninsula have craft outlets for their products, and a few gift-shop trading centers also act as outlets. Black ash and sweetgrass are the more common materials used, the sweetgrass sometimes being embellished with quillwork. —Yvonne Lockwood, contributor

Ohio. Historically, the state has never been known for its basketry tradition, and very few traditional basketmakers work in the state of Ohio today. Those who do are elderly, live in some part of that eastern and southeastern area (more than one-third of the state) designated as "Appalachian Ohio," and make flat-splint baskets—except for Dwight Stump, who makes the round-rod. None seem to be passing their skills on. One possible exception is a descendant of one of the "old makers" Dwight talks about: Bruce Steele's daughter, Ocea Steele's granddaughter, became interested in flat-splint making after a demonstration by Omen Beavers, one of the old makers who is no longer weaving.

The Longaberger family in Dresden, eastern Ohio, has moved its traditional flat-splint expertise completely into the realm of commerce. Using their traditional patterns on traditional wooden molds, they have a factory setup from which they market numerous sizes and shapes (many of them contemporary) in a handsome catalog.

—Tim Lloyd, Susan Colpetzer, John Lieser, and Rosemary Joyce, contributors

Appalachian South

Kentucky. A white-oak-splint basketmaking tradition continues to exist in Grayson, Hart, and Edmondson counties in central Kentucky. Wax, Cub Run, Big Windy, Winesap, Dog Creek, and Center Point are communities which have historically supported the tradition. Several of today's basketmakers no longer live in the communities where they learned the craft. Although many families made baskets, it was an activity performed within the family, not in a community setting. The primary material of white oak is woven into a number of styles, including variations of rib baskets as well as spoke-construction baskets. The Red Bird Mission in Beverly purchases baskets from traditional makers in their area of eastern Kentucky.

—Beth Hester, contributor

The traditional split-oak maker is still active in Kentucky and represents a continuing folk craft in this region. All are white, rural southerners whose families have practiced Kentucky basketmaking for a number of generations.

—Annie Archbold, contributor

Edmondson, Grayson, Hart, and surrounding counties still support an active tradition, which has thrived since the development of Mammoth Cave as a tourist site in the 1920s. The communities of Wax and Cub Run are especially notable. Many makers around Wax have turned from the increasingly scarce white oak to water maple instead. Many of the senior "celebrity" makers have died in the past decade. The Higdon family is one of the best known, but the difficulty of finding timber is making them dependent on an exploitive marketing situation.

—Roby Cogswell, contributor

Tennessee. Traditional basketmaking is still practiced throughout the state, with the most notable concentration in the eastern Highland Rim and the upper Cumberland Plateau, especially in Cannon and Warren counties. Split white-oak baskets of all types are made, and the tradition shares much in common with that of east Tennessee. Family traditions persist, but there is also wide overlap with revivalist production. The western tradition is more culturally diverse but less active, with a few isolated Anglo split-oak makers, a small number of black split-oak makers, and a Choctaw woven split-cane maker.

—Roby Cogswell, contributor

Virginia. There is a great deal of activity in the Blue Ridge area of central Virginia, but most of it is a revivalist, or popular-contemporary type. For example, several artists have become aware of the tradition, and have adapted the methods and forms to create new ones, advertising and exhibiting locally and in Washington, D.C. This is a large part of the contemporary scene and should be documented and studied by someone, since it does affect the traditional maker. There may well be traditional makers who, after some hiatus, have returned to the craft because of contemporary interest and resultant new markets.   —Nancy Martin-Perdue, contributor

North Carolina. North Carolina's files are neither comprehensive nor updated. However, from fieldwork activities, folklorists do not think there is any longer a vibrant basketmaking art here, even though there are still a few outstanding makers.   —Mary Anne McDonald, contributor

Deep South

South Carolina. Several hundred Afro-Americans continue their African-derived coiled sea-grass basketry, in the low country centered around Mount Pleasant. The craft is passed on in families and is practiced generally by women, with help from the men in gathering materials and marketing the product. The foundation grasses used are sweet grass, bullrush, and longleaf pine needles. These are sewn with strips of palmetto leaf, using an awl most commonly made from the handle of a teaspoon, broken off and filed smooth. The tool is called a "nail-bone," whether it is made from a spoon, an animal bone, a nail, or another sharp implement. The baskets come in all shapes and sizes, and the craft has evolved from its agricultural origins into a highly inventive folk art produced for sale.
                    —Dale Rosengarten, contributor

Alabama. Many Anglo- and African-American basketmakers (almost always male) are weaving with white-oak splints statewide; most work in isolation. Afro-American women in the extreme southern end of the state work both in isolation and in small informal neighborhood groups making their traditional coiled pine-needle baskets. They are less decorative than those made by the Anglo-American women there, who learned their highly decorative coiling and stitching technique from home-demonstration workers in the 1930s. Black females in west-central Alabama work in isolation and in small informal groups, twisting and coiling corn-shuck baskets. A few mother-daughter pairs of white women in isolated areas plait honeysuckle vine in small family groups.   —Henry Willett, contributor

Mississippi. Basketmakers are still very abundant here. One can buy handmade baskets at roadside vegetable stands, suggesting the common nature of the art form. Most are white-oak flat splints, a pervasive form made by both whites and blacks. The skills are still being learned and practiced traditionally, and are considered by many to be some of the least changed and most authentic traditions in the country. Choctaw Indians continue to make beautiful dyed-cane baskets, along with ones from pine needles, some from white-oak splits. There is also trading of forms and technique among Indians, blacks, and whites.   —Tom Rankin and Dan Overly, contributors

Louisiana. Basketmaking is still strong here. A number of basketmakers, both black and white, work almost full time selling at fairs, while others work part time to supply their own and their neighbors' needs.
                    —Maida Bergeron, contributor

Northeast

Except for occasional outstanding individuals, most traditional basketry has apparently died out in the Northeast (including Vermont, Massachusetts, New Jersey, New York, and New York City). However, Abwesasne Mohawk and a few Seneca in New York State are continuing and revitalizing their uninterrupted tradition.

—Jane Beck, Nancy Sweezy, Ethel Raim, David Cohen, Rita Moonsammy, Janis Benincasa, and Varick Chittenden, contributors

Our thirty-five correspondents agree that traditional basketmakers still work today, though not in great numbers. Many of them have returned at retirement age to a craft they either enjoyed or made money from—or both—when they were young. Thanks to the renewal of interest in "the old crafts," prices have climbed for handmade objects, certainly not enough to be regarded as adequate compensation for the hours of work involved, but better compared to the rock-bottom prices of earlier days. This, along with encouragement from cultural revitalization programs, has stimulated much of the renewed activity, in traditional music as well as in crafts.

Further, much of the traditional basketmaking activity today occurs among Native American Indians in both the lower forty-eight states and Alaska. White-oak flat-splint basketry in Appalachia and the Deep South accounts for the two other strong areas.

Individual Traditional Basketmakers

Classified by Method, Materials, Region, and Racial or Ethnic Background

Region and Racial or Ethnic Background	Weavers				Plaiters		Coilers		
	Oak	Maple	Willow	Cane, Black Ash	Coconut, Bamboo, Panadus, Ie'ie	Honeysuckle	Pine Needles	Willow	Corn Shucks, Ie'ie
Appalachian South									
Caucasian	25	3							
Native American				1					
Unspecified	12								
Deep South									
Black	5						1		1
Caucasian	4					1	1		
Native American				1		1			
Unspecified	6						1		
Hawaii									
Caucasian					2				1
Pacific Islands					12				
Midwest									
Caucasian	2	2	3				1		
Native American				1					
Unspecified	3								
Northeast									
Caucasian	1		1						
Plains									
Native American						1			
West, Southwest									
Native American								4	
TOTAL	58	5	4	3	14	3	4	4	2

Appendix B

The Old Basketmakers of Fairfield and Hocking Counties

In the annotated list below, the "old makers" are classified by the type of basket that they wove: round rod, flat splint, or both. Each entry gives the year of birth, place of residence, and additional information about family relationships, where known. Dwight Stump's comments about several of the makers appear in italics after the appropriate entries.

Round Rod

Arter, Denzel (ca. 1930). Residence unknown. Adopted son of Isaac Arter. *He helped his father make. He's got a big machine shop now, though, and he won't look at baskets hardly. He bought a two-thirds bushel basket of me here a couple of years ago, said he wanted one of my baskets to keep.*

Arter, Isaac (ca. 1880). Tar Ridge. *Ike used t' be my neighbor. There was only one man from around there that wove clockwise* [left-handed] *like I do, and that was Isaac Arter. The rest was all right-hand weavers.*

Arter, Jimmy (ca. 1882). Tar Ridge. Brother of Isaac Arter.

Arter, Leroy (ca. 1885). Tar Ridge. *He was a half brother t' Isaac. His wife was Noah Cisco's daughter, Ruby. I knew him well. He was the only one who colored 'em.*

Arter, Pearl (ca. 1886). Tar Ridge. Brother of Leroy.

Buzzard, William (ca. 1860). Revenge, Tar Ridge. *Bill stopped in there and helped Hines and Cisco once in a while.*

Cisco, Albert (ca. 1893). Tar Ridge. Second son of Noah and Nettie Cisco.

Cisco, Arthur (ca. 1890). Tar Ridge. Eldest son of Noah and Nettie Cisco.

Cisco, Harry (ca. 1899). Tar Ridge. Youngest son of Noah and Nettie Cisco.

Cisco, Nettie Hedges (ca. 1870). Tar Ridge. Wife of Noah Cisco.

Cisco, Noah (ca. 1866). Tar Ridge. Brother of ——— Hines, mother of the largest basketmaking family.

Cisco, Ruby (ca. 1895). Tar Ridge. Third son of Noah and Nettie Cisco.

Cisco, Sam (ca. 1870). Tar Ridge. Brother of Noah Cisco and Mrs. Hines.

Cox, Phil (ca. 1870). Tar Ridge. Brother of John and Wade Cox. *He made a clothes hamper fer me one time. But none of his children made.*

Cox, Wade (ca. 1882). Tar Ridge, Cola Valley. *His wife was Hines's daughter. Their children didn't make though. He started out on Tar Ridge but lived a good bit of his life over on Coley Valley. That's where he made a good bit of his baskets. He had a boy and a girl, but they didn't want no part of basket makin'.*

DeLong, ———— (ca. 1890). Clear Creek.

Fetheroff, Harvey (ca. 1870). Above Toad Hollow. *Dropped a gun on his hand, partly shot it off, two fingers clean off, the whole outside of his hand! That stopped his basket career.*

Flowers, William (ca. 1860). Pisgah Ridge. *That was Ross Anderson's father-in-law.*

Glenn, Johnny (ca. 1930). Route 180. *That was Joshuay's father, 'n Harley's grandfather. Sold his cabin to John Cox, so three basketmakers lived there.*

Glenn, Joshua (ca. 1865). Route 180. Son of Johnny Glenn and father of Harley Glenn.

Graham, Daniel (ca. 1880). Poe Ridge. *That was my son's father-in-law. So m' boy, Junior, his children had both granddads basketmakers.*

Hedges, ———— (ca. 1876). Clear Creek. Wife of Bert Hedges.

Hedges, Bert (ca. 1872). Clear Creek. Brother of Nettie Hedges Cisco.

Hedges, Reuben (ca. 1876). Clear Creek. Brother of Bert and Nettie Hedges.

Hendrickson, George (ca. 1870). Buena Vista.

Hines, ———— (ca. 1855). Tar Ridge. Father of the largest basketmaking family.

Hines, ———— (ca. 1858). Tar Ridge. Mother of the largest basketmaking family; sister of Noah and Sam Cisco.

Hines, ———— (ca. 1881). Tar Ridge. Youngest daughter of the Hineses; married ———— Smires.

Hines, Charley (ca. 1883). Tar Ridge. Third son of the Hineses.

Hines, Dewey (ca. 1893). Tar Ridge. Seventh son of the Hineses.

Hines, Jay (ca. 1880). Tar Ridge. Second son of the Hineses.

Hines, Jury (ca. 1888). Tar Ridge. Fifth son of the Hineses.

Hines, Kate (ca. 1878). Tar Ridge. Oldest daughter of the Hineses; married Wade Cox.

Hines, Martin (ca. 1885). Tar Ridge. Fourth son of the Hineses; Dwight's teacher.

Hines, Sam (ca. 1875). Tar Ridge. Oldest son of the Hineses.

Hines, Truby (ca. 1896). Tar Ridge. Youngest son of the Hineses.

Hines, William (ca. 1890). Tar Ridge. Sixth son of the Hineses. *Used t' run a junk yard over t' Clearport.*

Huffhines, Wade (1880). Tar Ridge. Remembered for his poor baskets.

Leisure, John (ca. 1855). Leisure's Hill.

Minic, Pearl (ca. 1860). Tar Ridge. *He made with Ciscos a lot of the time.*

Poling, Link (ca. 1880). Tar Ridge. Brother of Wesley Poling.

Poling, Wesley (ca. 1865). Pleasant Ridge. Brother of Link Poling. *He had a store out on Tar Ridge, about 1915. Said about* ever'body *out there made 'em. He was a township trustee at one time over there, 'n his boy, Charlie, was deputy sheriff at Logan during Prohibition days.*

Rackley, Al (year of birth unknown). South Bloomingville.

Smyres, —— (ca. 1870). Big Pine. *Married a Hines. He was Judd's father.*

Springer, Henry (ca. 1900). Dry Tavern Ridge. *Henry was a preacher. His mother lived on Blackburn Hill over there on Jack Run.*

Steele, Bruce (1900). Stump Run. Son of Ocea Steele. *He was here visitin' not too long ago, with a friend of his. He don't make any more, though.*

Steele, Ocea "Osie" (1872). Stump Run. *He's a relation of mine, a second cousin, if I ain't mistaken.*

Tucker, Hollis (ca. 1870). Residence unknown.

Tucker, William (ca. 1895). Toad Hollow. *That was Holl's son. He made a* mighty *good basket!*

Waters, Amos (year of birth unknown). Tar Ridge.

Waters, Bert (year of birth unknown). Tar Ridge. Brother of Amos Waters.

Flat Splint

Beavers, Omen (1903). Stump Run. *He's a retired carpenter. Makes kids' egg baskets once in a while, but it's hard t' get him t' make any more.*

Downs, Emery (ca. 1875). Long Run.

Leisure, —— (ca. 1850). Brimstone.

Leisure, —— (ca. 1855). Brimstone. *They* [the Leisures who made flat-splint baskets] *were brothers, 'n I don't think they was related to John* [Leisure, who made round-rod baskets].

White, Johnny (ca. 1850). South Perry. *He's the one made m' grandmother's market basket.*

Round Rod and Flat Splint

Barkley, —— (ca. 1855). Brimstone.

Barkley, —— (ca. 1860). Brimstone. *They was two brothers, 'n they made with Leisures* [the flat-splint makers] *sometimes.*

Cox, Clarence (ca. 1900). Pleasant Valley Road. *Made with his dad, John. Owned a sawmill on Pleasant Valley. He had a brother, but he didn't make, worked up there at Anchor Hocking when I did, way I knowed him.*

Cox, John (ca. 1865). Tar Ridge and Route 180. *He bought Johnny Glenn's house; his son, Clarence, made too, so that's three basketmakers lived in that little cabin on 180.*

Kinser, —— (ca. 1855). Revenge. Father of Salem; experimentally planted willow for baskets. *I think they were Dutch.*

Kinser, Salem (ca. 1880). Revenge. *Said he made 'em when he was just a boy.*

Notes

Introduction

1. This remains a problem for me—as it does for most folklorists and anthropologists—even though I have had fifteen years of field-research experience in Appalachia and Appalachian Ohio; see my *A Woman's Place: The Life History of a Rural Ohio Grandmother* (Columbus: Ohio State University Press, 1983), 27–30.

2. For technique, see, for example, Virginia Harvey, *Techniques of Basketry* (New York: Van Nostrand Reinhold, 1974). For cultures and geographical areas, see George Wharton James, *Indian Basketry* (1909; reprint, New York: Dover, 1972); Gloria Roth Teleki, *Baskets of Rural America* (New York: Dutton, 1975); Sue Stephenson, *Basketry in the Southern Appalachian Mountains* (New York: Van Nostrand Reinhold, 1977); John Rice Irwin, *Baskets and Basket Makers in Southern Appalachia* (Exton, Pa.: Schiffer, 1982). For a genealogical study, see Nancy J. Martin-Perdue, "Case Study: On Eaton's Trail: A Genealogical Study of Virginia Basket Makers," in *Traditional Craftsmanship in America: A Diagnostic Report,* ed. Charles Camp (Washington, D.C.: National Council for the Traditional Arts, 1983), 79–100. For contemporary work, see Ed Rossbach, *Baskets as Textile Arts* (New York: Van Nostrand Reinhold, 1973). For a wide range of sources, see Susan S. Whisnant, "Traditional Craftsmanship in America: A Bibliography of Published Sources," in *Traditional Craftsmanship in America,* ed. Camp, 105–27.

Two exceptions to the general dearth of studies concentrating on an individual basketmaker are the articles by Henry Glassie, "William Houck, Maker of Pounded Ash Pack-Baskets," *Keystone Folklore Quarterly* 12 (Spring 1967): 23–54; and by Howard Wight Marshall, "Mr. Westfall's Baskets: Traditional Craftsmanship in Northcentral Missouri," *Mid-South Folklore* 2 (Summer 1974): 43–60, reprinted in *Readings in American Folklore,* ed. Jan Harold Brunvand (New York: Norton, 1979), 168–91.

Michael Owen Jones introduced the emphasis on the individual rather than the product in his seminal work *The Hand Made Object and Its Maker* (Berkeley and Los Angeles: University of California Press, 1975). For similar focus in material culture, see, e.g., Ralph Rinzler and Robert Sayers, *The Meaders Family, North Georgia Potters* (Washington, D.C.: Smithsonian Institution Press, 1980); John Michael Vlach, *Charleston Blacksmith: The Work of Philip Simmons* (Athens: University of Georgia Press, 1981); William Ferris, *Local Color: A Sense of Place in Folk Art* (New York:

McGraw-Hill, 1982); R. Gerald Alvey, *Dulcimer Maker: The Craft of Homer Ledford* (Lexington: University Press of Kentucky, 1984); Simon J. Bronner, *Chain Carvers: Old Men Crafting Meaning* (Lexington: University Press of Kentucky, 1985).

This approach has become evident also in nonacademic writings on folk subject matter; see, for example, John Rice Irwin, *Alex Stewart: Portrait of a Pioneer* (West Chester, Pa.: Schiffer, 1985).

3. I am indebted to Edward D. Ives for underscoring my belief in this genre with his excellent article (in spite of the unfortunately gender-specific title) "Common-Man Biography: Some Notes by the Way," in *Folklore Today,* ed. Linda Dégh, Henry Glassie, and Felix Oinas (Bloomington: Indiana University Press, 1976), 251–64.

4. For an exposition of the need for finding new ways to assess women's narrative, see my "Toward an Analysis of Personal Narrative," in *Papers in Comparative Studies* 2 (1983): 119–35.

5. See Richard M. Dorson, Introduction to *Folklore and Folklife,* ed. Richard M. Dorson (Chicago: University of Chicago Press, 1972), 45, for an early definition of the contextual method of analyzing and presenting folklore texts.

6. Defined by Michael C. Howard, *Contemporary Cultural Anthropology* (Boston: Little, Brown, 1986), 14. Howard cautions: "Cultural relativism does not mean that anything a particular people does or thinks must be approved or accepted without criticism. Rather, it means we should evaluate cultural patterns within the context of their occurrence." One of its most articulate spokespersons was Melville J. Herskovits; see his *Cultural Relativism: Perspectives in Cultural Pluralism* (New York: Random House, 1972).

It is obviously impossible in this abbreviated space to make much sense of the complex subject of cultural politics and political power with these simplistic kinds of statements. See Milton Gordon, *Assimilation in American Life: The Role of Race, Religion, and National Origins* (New York: Oxford University Press, 1964), for summaries of the "melting pot" and "cultural pluralist" theories.

7. Using a historical background, Simon Bronner traced the symbolic power of the whole range of folk material culture in America, showing how politics are framed by history and culture; in *Grasping Things: Folk Material Culture and Mass Society in America* (Lexington: University Press of Kentucky, 1986). See also Nathan Glazer, "The Universalisation of Ethnicity," *Encounter* 44 (February 1975): 8–17, on the accentuation of ethnicity in political, social, and economic conflicts.

See especially David Whisnant's pioneering work, *All That Is Native and Fine: The Politics of Culture in an American Region* (Chapel Hill: University of North Carolina Press, 1983), in which he graphically illustrated the concept and the importance of the politics of dominant culture as it has influenced Appalachians. Most important, Whisnant demonstrated the far-reaching implications of imposing dominant culture attitudes on any other culture.

See also Loyal Jones's brief but important discussion of the politics of culture in *Minstrel of the Appalachians: The Story of Bascom Lamar Lunsford* (Boone, N.C., Appalachian Consortium Press, 1984), vii–ix.

8. For a brilliant exegesis of the political power inherent in art and definitions of art, see Eugene W. Metcalf, "Black Art, Folk Art, and Social Control," *Winterthur Portfolio* 18 (1983): 271–89. Metcalf used the history of black American art to demonstrate the aesthetic control and social consequences inherent in manipulating definitions of art. The article is mandatory reading for anyone interested in sorting out the historical ambiguities of definitions of folk art as well as their very tangible implications. I am indebted to Metcalf for helping me clarify my own perspectives on this complicated issue.

See also his "The Politics of the Past and the Myth of American Folk Art History," in *Folk Art and Art Worlds,* ed. John Michael Vlach and Simon J. Bronner (Ann Arbor, Mich.: UMI Research Press, 1986), 27–50. He begins with an apt quote: "A people . . . which is cut off from its own past is far less free to choose and to act . . . than one that has been able to situate itself in history. This is why . . . the entire art of the past has now become a political issue" (from John Berger, *Ways of Seeing* [London: Penguin, 1972]).

9. These problems generate great intensity of feeling among some folklorists. Consequently, several who did not know me personally would not include any knowledge of their region's basketmakers in my "National Survey of Traditional Basketmakers" (see Appendix A for further details) because of their fear of further exploitation of the artists and their products; survey answers, and an interview with Roby Cogswell, Cincinnati, 20 October 1985.

For one example of such intense feeling, see Cogswell's charge—backed by multiple examples—concerning outside buyers in Kentucky: "Some . . . by capitalizing on the discrepancy between local and outside economics, have in the worst way abused the region's folk artists and their traditional birthright ("Folk Arts, Outside Markets, and Exploitation of the Folk in Kentucky's Lincoln Trail District" [Paper presented at the annual meeting of the Great Lakes American Studies Association, Oxford Ohio, 9 April 1983], 2; quoted also in Robert Teske, "'Crafts Assistance Programs' and Traditional Crafts," *New York Folklore* 12 (Winter–Spring 1986): 75–83).

Evidence that folk-art objects are indeed attracting widespread interest may be seen in such articles as Bradley Hitchings's "Finding Folk Art with a Future," *Business Week,* 10 June 1985, 126–30.

10. See my "'Fame Don't Make the Sun Any Cooler': Traditional Artists and the Marketplace," in *Folk Art and Art Worlds,* ed. Vlach and Bronner, 225–41; and my "To Market, to Market, to *Sell* Some Folk Art: Introduction," as Guest Editor, Special Section, Marketing Folk Art, *New York Folklore* 12 (Winter–Spring 1986), 43–47; see also the other articles in that section of the issue, especially Teske's "'Crafts Assistance Programs' and Traditional Crafts."

11. John Michael Vlach, "Commentary," *New York Folklore* 12 (Winter–Spring 1986): 88–89.

12. In 1974 Robert B. Edgerton and L. L. Langness favorably surveyed the anthropological literature that included personal comments and experiences as an integral part of reporting the fieldwork experience, in *Methods and Styles in the Study of Culture* (San Francisco: Chandler and Sharp, 1974), 78–82. Langness and Gelya Frank offered detailed and convincing reasons for *not* being detached and objective, in *Lives: An Anthropological Approach to Biography* (Novato, Calif.: Chandler and Sharp, 1981), chap. 5.

13. Joyce, *A Woman's Place*, chap. 1, "Doing a Life History."

14. Following Michael Owen Jones, *Hand Made Object*, vii, I do not distinguish between "art" and "craft," considering that to be a pointless distinction.

15. According to the oral historian Willa K. Baum, an hour-and-a-half interview can take up to sixty-three hours to process, including transcribing, editing and chaptering, final typing, proofreading and indexing, preparing introduction and supplementary material, final preparation and arrangements with the narrator; see *Transcribing and Editing Oral History* (Nashville: American Association for State and Local History, 1977), 18. See also Barbara Allen and Lynwood Montell, *From Memory to History: Using Oral Sources in Local Historical Research* (Nashville: American Association for State and Local History, 1981); and Edward D. Ives, *The Tape-Recorded Interview: A Manual for Field Workers in Folklore and Oral History*, rev. ed. (Knoxville: University of Tennessee Press, 1980).

16. Few fieldworkers have written openly about their field experiences. Refreshing exceptions are documented by Inta Gale Carpenter, "Introspective Accounts of the Field Experience: A Bibliographic Essay," *Folklore Forum* 11 (Winter 1978): 191–219. Carpenter lists numerous references to such sharing and quotes Jean Guillemin's acknowledgment that when she found glimpses of Boas and Firth and Malinowski as fallible people, it was "genuinely pleasurable," because it was "an assurance that the stuff of fieldwork, whatever the objective stance assumed later, was unavoidably a human experience" (p. 207).

See also Robert A. Georges and Michael Owen Jones, *People Studying People: The Human Element in Fieldwork* (Berkeley and Los Angeles: University of California Press, 1980).

17. For detail, see Joyce, *A Woman's Place*, 13–30.

18. Dennis Preston, "'Ritin' Fowklower Daun 'Rong': Folklorists' Failure in Phonology," *Journal of American Folklore* 95 (July–September 1982): 304–26.

19. Elizabeth C. Fine, *The Folklore Text: From Performance to Print* (Bloomington: Indiana University Press, 1984), 140. Fine (pp. 137–41) presents a thorough and insightful analysis of the whole area of text presentation, including a critique of Dennis Preston's stance (see n. 18 above). See also Gail Jefferson, "Transcript Notation," in *Structures of Social Action: Studies in Conversation Analysis*, ed. J. Maxwell Atkinson and John Heritage (Cambridge, England: Cambridge University Press, 1984), ix–xvi.

20. Clyde Kluckhohn, "The Personal Document in Anthropological Science," in *The Use of Personal Documents in History, Anthropology, and So-*

ciology, ed. Louis Gottschalk, Clyde Kluckhohn, and Robert Angell (New York: Social Science Research Council, 1945), 155.

21. The "pompous and presumptuous" quote is from Vlach, *Charleston Blacksmith,* xii. Several other examples of the many using nonstandard English are: Richard M. Dorson, *Buying the Wind* (Chicago: University of Chicago Press, 1964); William Lynwood Montell, *The Saga of Coe Ridge* (Knoxville: University of Tennessee Press, 1970); Archie Green, *Only a Miner* (Urbana: University of Illinois Press, 1972); Jones, *Hand Made Object;* James Seay Brown, Jr., *Up Before Daylight: Life Histories from the Alabama Writers Project* (University: University of Alabama Press, 1982); Henry Glassie, *Passing the Time in Ballymenone: Culture and History of an Ulster Community* (Philadelphia: University of Pennsylvania Press, 1982); Amy Shuman, *Story Telling Rights: The Uses of Oral and Written Texts by Urban Adolescents* (Cambridge, England: Cambridge University Press, 1986); Richard Bauman, *Story, Performance, and Event: Contextual Studies of Oral Narrative* (Cambridge, England: Cambridge University Press, 1986); Theodore Rosengarten, *Tombee: Portrait of a Cotton Planter* (New York: Morrow, 1986); Kathryn Galloway Young, *Tale Worlds and Story Realms* (Dordrecht, the Netherlands: Martinus Nijhoff, 1987).

The second quotes are from Rinzler and Sayers, *The Meaders Family,* 13, 14.

1. Gathering Materials

1. Henry Glassie, "William Houck."

2. "The technology for making the [oak rod] baskets has now been lost in the Appalachians" (Stephenson, *Basketry in the Southern Appalachian Mountains,* 90); none were mentioned or photographed in Teleki's *Baskets of Rural America.*

3. Compare with the discoveries of Rachel Nash Law and Cynthia W. Taylor, who, in an exhaustive historic-geographic search for their manuscript "Handing Down the Basket: Appalachian White Oak Basketry," have seen over five hundred white-oak baskets, flat- and round-splint, many with varying shapes and interesting, innovative details.

4. In Santa Fe a series of baskets is available with a set of slides, as well as an accompanying manuscript for researchers, "Dwight Stump, Traditional Basketweaver of Southeastern Ohio," a copy of my paper presentation at the annual meeting of the American Folklore Society, Salt Lake City, Utah, 12 October 1978.

5. For further reference, see J. Ernest Carman, *The Geologic Interpretation of Scenic Features in Ohio,* Ohio Geological Survey Reprint Series 3 (Columbus: Ohio Geological Survey, 1972).

6. Those wishing a fuller summary of Ohio and southeastern Ohio history may see the beginning sections of chaps. 3–7 in my *A Woman's Place;* and Eugene H. Roseboom and Francis P. Weisenburger, *A History of Ohio* (Columbus: Ohio Historical Society, 1976), 3–4.

7. *History of Hocking Valley, Ohio* (Chicago: Interstate, 1883), 179–86,

421, 816, 829–33, 859, 1148–49; Francis Gordon, "Early History of Hocking County" (M.A. thesis, Ohio State University, 1940), 33–47.

8. Roseboom and Weisenburger, *History of Ohio,* 130–32; Gordon, "Early History," 99.

9. Roseboom and Weisenburger, *History of Ohio,* 122; Thomas H. Smith, *The Mapping of Ohio* (Kent, Ohio: Kent State University Press, 1977), 127; George W. Knepper, *An Ohio Portrait* (Columbus: Ohio Historical Society, 1976), 74–76; Emilius O. Randall and Daniel J. Ryan, *History of Ohio: The Rise and Progress of an American State,* vol. 5 (New York: Century History, 1912), 439–70; Eugene Roseboom, *The Civil War Era: 1850–1873,* vol. 4 of *The History of the State of Ohio,* ed. Carl Wittke (Columbus: Ohio State Archaeological and Historical Society, 1944), 73; Henry Howe, *Historical Collections of Ohio,* vol. 1 (Cincinnati: Krehbiel, 1888, 1908), 106.

10. Roseboom and Weisenburger, *History of Ohio,* 219, 241, 247; Knepper, *Ohio Portrait,* 154; Roseboom, *Civil War Era,* 15; Simeon D. Fess, *Ohio: A Four-Volume Reference Library* (Chicago: Lewis, 1937), 13–18, 52–56; Walter Havighurst, *Ohio: A Bicentennial History* (New York: Norton, 1976), 142–44; Ohio Community Development Division, *Ohio Appalachian Development Plan* (Columbus: Department of Economic and Community Development, 1974), hereafter referred to as OCDD; Philip D. Jordan, *Ohio Comes of Age: 1873–1900,* vol. 5 of *History of Ohio,* ed. Wittke, 124, 243–46, 309, 343–45, 335.

11. John Falconer, *"Agricultural Changes,"* in *Ohio in the Twentieth Century,* comp. Harlow Lindley, vol. 6 of *History of Ohio,* ed. Wittke, 134; OCDD; John M. Weed, "Business—as Usual," in *Ohio in the Twentieth Century,* 185–90; Ohio Writers Program, Works Progress Administration, *The Ohio Guide* (New York: Oxford University Press, 1940), 35.

12. Ohio Department of Development, Community Development Division, *Profiles of Change, Ohio Appalachia: 1965–1984* (Columbus: Ohio Department of Development, 1985).

13. OCDD.

2. Growing Up

1. It was an unusual but effective twist on transmission of folklore: by example, *but* from an unsuspecting teacher/craftsman to an adept and diligent apprentice! A similar kind of informal learning process was related by Peter Alston, a black basketweaver in South Carolina; see Gerald L. Davis, "Afro-American Coil Basketry in Charleston County, South Carolina: Affective Characteristics of an Artistic Craft in a Social Context" in *American Folklife,* ed. Don Yoder (Austin: University of Texas Press, 1976), 178.

Leon Peck Clark, a black flat-splint basketmaker in Mississippi, recounted his learning process: "I'd go and sit down and just watch. I didn't know nothing about baskets, and so I'd go down and look at him, maybe six months before I started. And so finally one time he said, 'It's easy to learn.' So I said that I was going to try it. I've been making baskets ever since" (Ferris, *Local Color,* 44).

3. A Hard-Working Man

1. Worry would not be misplaced in such a situation. Many men are injured or killed digging wells; see, e.g., a report on the death of two young men who were working in such a shaft, in the *Columbus Dispatch,* 20 August 1985, 2D.

2. In some areas "moonshining" was considered a legitimate and reasonable way for a man to help feed his family. One woman recalled, "Just everybody was trying to make a living. I mean they wouldn't report them. If you walked upon them . . . and you told your mother or dad, they'd say, 'Well, just don't go back there no more . . . stay away from that section of the woods.' They was making a living. If you'd turn them in, there'd probably be a house of little kids starved over it" (quoted in Michael Korn, "Report on Basketry in the Mammoth Cave Area in South-Central Kentucky" [Student paper, Western Kentucky University, 1977], 6).

3. Compare with the similar attitudes of chain carvers toward factory work, in Bronner, *Chain Carvers,* esp. 30–33, 64, 151.

4. Making a Round-Rod Basket

1. Some argue this particular division. I am following Rossbach, *Baskets as Textile Arts,* 138.

2. *Webster's Third New International Dictionary,* 16th ed., s.v.

3. Jeannette Lasansky, personal correspondence, March 1979. Stephenson, *Basketry in the Southern Appalachian Mountains,* 90, 11. Dorothy Wright, *The Complete Book of Baskets and Basketry* (Newton Abbott, England: David and Charles, 1983), 196.

4. Dwight was typical of most basketmakers in not considering it his full-time employment. See, for example, Marshall, "Mr. Westfall's Baskets, 173; Glassie, "William Houck," 24–25; and Jeannette Lasansky, *Willow, Oak, and Rye: Basket Traditions in Pennsylvania* (University Park: Pennsylvania State University Press, 1979), 3.

5. According to botanist and basketmaker Cynthia W. Taylor, American basketmakers used the term *white oak* to refer to a number of white-oak species available, usually stave oak (*Quercus michauxii*) in the South or *Quercus alba* (letter to author, March 1983). Obviously, makers use the species native to their region, and Dwight uses *Quercus alba.*

6. Dwight refers here to his own local predecessors in Ohio. Makers in the Mammoth Cave area of Kentucky reported using hickory for the hoops and ribs of their flat splint and ribbed baskets, because, even though it is harder to work with than white oak, it is stronger. Maple and sassafras are sometimes used for their baskets, but are exceptions to the rule. They consider a six-inch diameter tree the average size, or eight-inch for a bushel basket. Some get their wood in the spring "when the sap is up," others in the fall or any time except when the trees are frozen; Debbie Hall, "Preparing Timber for Basketmaking" (Student paper, Western Kentucky University, 1977), 1.

7. Elmer Knott, interview with author, 10 September 1980. Kentucky peddlers quoted in Hall, "Preparing Timber for Basketmaking," 12.

8. Some of the makers in the Mammoth Cave, Kentucky, area dug a trench to put the timber in, then covered it with water to store till ready for use; Hall, "Preparing Timber for Basketmaking," 2.

9. Dwight has a favored chair in his shop but has used other ones too for the weaving. Compare with a weaver of willow baskets in Britain, where it is traditional "to sit on a plank on the floor, back to the wall, with perhaps his tool box or a cushion to lean upon, so he is almost at ground level" (Alistair Heseltine, *Baskets and Basketmaking* [Aylesbury, England: Shire, 1982], 13).

10. Glassie noted the same circumstance, in "William Houck," 23.

5. The Finished Basket

1. In contrast, there is much resentment among makers in the Mammoth Cave area toward similar gift-shop owners who mark their baskets up considerably. George Childress complained, "You just make reasonable wages at it, you see. Still the man who makes something [profit] is the man buying them. They just double on them. You sell them for five and they sell for ten": (Lyndell Payton, "The Process of Basketmaking: A Personal Interview with Mr. George Childress" [Student paper, Western Kentucky University, 1977], 7.

On the other side of the fence, Marie Nolte, a gift-shop owner at Fort Falls Trading Post, Kentucky, explained her position in an interview with the author, 13 September 1982: "I used to buy chairs, footstools, furniture, weaving, I had a great big barn for storage, and a workshop too. But I had to quit buying much, 'cause m' customers won't pay as much as they're chargin' fer stuff now. I go to the gift shows in Dallas and Atlanta (used t' go to Chicago, but that was Housewares and Gifts combined, and I don't need that). Now I can buy from China, Haiti, the Philippines, wherever I can buy nice ones."

2. Elmer Knott, a Glouster, Ohio, basketmaker, uses the checkerboard effect extensively, though by using sapwood and heartwood in contrast, rather than actual dyeing. This same method was used for the same effect by makers in Kentucky, along with numerous dyeing methods (see n. 3 below); in Martin Ostrofsky, "Aesthetics of Basket Making in the Mammoth Cave Area of Kentucky" (Student paper, Western Kentucky University, 1977), 11.

3. Nora Rutter, another Glouster basketmaker and the sister of Elmer Knott, uses either egg coloring or crepe paper (interviews with author, Glouster, Ohio, 10 September 1980 and 7 December 1985). She also explained how her mother, Jane, colored her baskets:

> My mother colored 'em, too. She colored this one here with, let's see, it's what
> they call "indigo," I don't know whether you ever heard tell of indigo or not, it
> makes a blue if you use it full strength. But that's just laundry blueing on this
> one. She used pokeberries for red, you know what pokeberries is, and we used
> to color with elderberries. They make like a wine color. You'd just crush up the

berries and mash 'em, you didn't have to cook it. Pokeberry is just like a berry, mashy and juicy. We never did try to color 'em with real berries like you eat, you know, but we'd use pokeberries. And there was some kind of a bark she boiled, too, to make 'em brown, if you wanted brown splits. I don't know what kind of bark it was now, it's been so long, but she used to boil it, I know, and drop the splits in it for a little while.

She used to use andalene [aniline] too. Well, that made more than one color. It looked like diamonds, some of it, 'n it would sparkle, look like little beads with all kinds of sparkles in them. You boiled that, put it in water and boiled it, and it would get it real thick, real darker. If you'd get it thinner it'd make it a lighter color, red and wine color, mostly. You'd get it at the drug store. She'd use blueing and andalene and another stuff, a dye, like you dyed clothes with, two or three brands of that in differnt colors.

A number of makers in the Mammoth Cave area of Kentucky dyed strips of their baskets, since it added sales appeal. "'The people that bought them, they liked all sorts of colors—bright colors, black and red and gaudy colors.' Stripes, checks, and chain-link designs were popular. Susette Barret's grandmother alternated colors, 'a row of white, then maybe three splits of brown, then maybe three of orange, and the rest of the basket white. . . . And it was really pretty, it was something to see. . . . She even used to make a few in solid colors. . . . It was a whole lot more trouble, but it was something to see.' After the Depression, makers used Putnam's Fadeless Dye extensively, along with Rit. But more traditional colorings remained in use, too, such as walnut hulls for a dark brown, coffee for varying shades of brown, and polkberries [sic]. Walter Logsdon believed 'those stripes helps the looks of the small basket'" (Ostrofsky, "Aesthetics of Basket Making," 8–11). Kentucky peddlers (see n. 7) paid a little more for baskets with colored splits, since they "made the wagons look pretty" (Elizabeth Harzoff, "The Long-Distance Basket Trade" [Student paper, Western Kentucky University, 1977], 9).

And in Mississippi, Leon "Peck" Clark, colored his flat-splint baskets with well water. "No rain water or pond water will color it. Only thing . . . is the water in the well. . . . A lot of people thought it was some sort of stain or paint. It's not any sort of stain; this is done by water" (quoted in Ferris, *Local Color,* 46).

4. It is important to note that, as Dwight intuitively realized, the continued thrust toward collecting pieces which "reflect our American heritage" makes *plain* baskets prized now. See the Special Issue on Folk Art in *New York Folklore* 12 (Winter–Spring) 1986, especially my "Introduction: To Market, to Market, to *Sell* Some Folk Art," 43–47.

Ostrofsky observed this in Kentucky: "Rather than increasing the popularity of decorative dyeing, plain baskets are now prized, since they serve as links to the past, even the pioneer past. Age rather than strength is the new preference" ("Aesthetics of Basket Making," 13).

5. The book he found was a very old one: Charles Crampton, *The Junior Basketmaker: Home Basketry,* published in England. Unfortunately, he could not find it again for me to complete the reference. Coincidentally, his

son Harold had ordered the same book, a newer version, which may still be available for those interested: Charles Crampton, *The Junior Basketmaker,* 16th ed. (Leicester, England: Dryad Press, 1972).

6. Dwight refers to O. K. "Red" Pierce, who lives near Ewington, Ohio, and Nora Rutter of Glouster, Ohio.

7. *If* they received cash, the Ohio makers probably had a better deal from their local hardware stores than Kentucky makers had with general-store merchants in south-central Kentucky. Craftspeople there were allowed a certain amount of groceries or supplies along with due bills—a form of scrip, for example, "Due Sam Jones, $1.50"—for the remainder. That way any excess funds still remained with the store owner and, according to a maker there, "the merchant usually got a fair deal—and then some"; in Keith Ludden, "Ten-Cent Coffee and Twenty-Cent Baskets: Local Basket Trade in the Mammoth Cave Area" (Student paper, Western Kentucky University, 1977), 2.

A far more complex marketing system developed in the South, where in many areas enterprising peddlers loaded up covered wagons and sold to general stores, to warehouses, or from door to door. In Kentucky, cross-ties, grinding stones, kerosene, pottery, and other regionally specific crafts and products were traded and sold through a network of peddlers and traveling merchants, who covered a large area into southern Illinois, Indiana, Ohio, and middle and eastern Tennessee. The basketry trade was the most tenacious, lasting into the 1960s, whereas the others declined well before World War II; see Korn, "Basketry in the Mammoth Cave Area," 5–6.

Often peddlers bought from local merchants, who had themselves filled their attics and lofts with baskets bought from nearby makers for credit exchanges. One peddler remembered buying fifteen hundred baskets at one time from a local merchant; Harzoff, "Long-Distance Trade," 2.

Jean Crawford described these entrepreneurs: "Moving slowly through North Carolina, South Carolina, and Virginia, the wagoners were gone two or three weeks, sometimes months, at a time. The pottery was either sold for a few cents or traded for needed merchandise, such as nails and horseshoes. Peanuts, onions, dried apples, tanned leather, and other foodstuffs were also taken along to sell" (*Jugtown Pottery: History and Design* [Winston-Salem, N.C.: Blair, 1964], 8; reference in Jim Brown, "Zen and the Art of Basketry: A Manifesto" [Student paper, Western Kentucky University, 1977], 12).

8. The same marketing strategy used by black coiled-seagrass basket weavers in South Carolina; in Davis, "Coil Basketry," 154, 172–73. It is reminiscent, too, of the mobile advertising utilized by the Kentucky basket peddlers in the early part of this century, who used the frames of their wagons as display racks for white-oak flat-splint baskets; Harzoff, "Long-Distance Trade," 8–9.

9. These prices are not included in table 2, because the book does not list sizes.

10. These prices are nearly identical to the ones received for baskets in south-central Kentucky as late as the 1920s and '30s: "Prices . . . ranged

from ten cents for half a peck to 25 cents for a peck and 50 cents for a bushel basket" (Ludden, "Ten-Cent Coffee," 1).

Peddlers marked up the baskets they bought for 25 or 50 cents to $1.00 or $1.25. Stanley Cottrell, one of a family of peddlers, sold peck baskets—his cost $1.80—to wholesalers for as little as $3.00 a dozen, though usually he received much more; Harzoff, "Long-Distance Trade," 14.

Folklorist and basketry researcher Nancy Martin-Perdue related visiting at a doctor's office with a Virginia neighbor whose mother had been a basketmaker: "She said her mother had made baskets to help support herself and her ten children, and had sold them to the Syria store for 10 to 25 cents apiece. Recently she has been seeing some of her mother's baskets being sold at auctions around here for upwards of $100. She said, 'Mother would turn over in her grave to know what they were bringing now, when she had such a struggle trying to support her family and selling them for so little'" (personal communication with the author, 14 January 1986).

11. Much like the cobbler's children we always hear about, Dwight has no baskets. But this may well be common. See, for example, Michael Owen Jones's quote of the chairmaker Charley: "I've heard that all my life, a chairmaker never has a thing to set on. That's about the way it is here, ever' time I get one made pretty an' I wanna keep it I al'ays sell it—somebody talk me out of it" (quoted in *Hand Made Object*, 87–88).

12. This becomes a pervasive problem. For example, even in 1967, the master potter Cheever Meaders also lamented his trouble in finding a successor: "I'm the only fellow that's at work, nobody ain't a-learning it. Can't get 'em to learn it. I'd teach boys and girls up here, but no, it's get in a car and down the road. They just won't learn it"; and, "They's none of these young boys'll learn it at all. Oh, there's some of 'em did learn but they won't work at it"; in Rinzler and Sayers, *The Meaders Family*, 41, 138.

6. The Old Makers

1. After this book evolved into a common-person biography rather than one strictly on basketry, the chapters detailing my historical research no longer fit, and a detailed report became inappropriate here. These statements concerning the status of basketmaking in Ohio and in the United States are based on the literature, my own research, and a survey I conducted.

In working with Dwight on this book, questions arose in my mind about the number of traditional basketmakers working today, and whether Dwight is really one of the last round-rod weavers in this country. But there were few answers. No one book, archive, or museum offered any kind of summary of information on basketmakers or making. Reliable information about the quantity—or quality—of traditional basketry today was sorely lacking, for a variety of reasons. My research became more extensive.

Because of this lack of available information, in late 1985 my assistant, Cerena Miele, and I conducted a mail survey on the status of traditional basketmaking in the United States at that time. Of the sixty-four persons to whom we sent the survey, thirty-five replied, supplying us with much excellent information and often including bibliographic suggestions and invaluable books and articles as well.

Nevertheless, we cannot make statistically viable pronouncements about the state of the art on the basis of such a low percentage of replies. We can, however, offer Appendix A as a sampling of the activities of traditional basketmakers in America up to 1986. While these results are certainly a bare bones beginning, we hope they will encourage someone with the necessary financial resources to mount a full-scale survey.

2. None of the historical research adequately answered questions concerning the ethnic origin of the round-rod tradition itself. Even after exhaustively studying white-oak forms, Rachel Nash Law and Cynthia Taylor still found questions of origins to be enigmatic (see "Handing Down the Basket: Appalachian White Oak Basketry"). They conjecture that German settlers brought the round-rod tradition to this country and adapted it to oak. In fact, many of the old makers Dwight refers to had Germanic surnames, and a predominance of Germans settled the Hocking and Fairfield County area. Dwight's baskets resemble photographs of German antecedents, not British, as Appalachian crafts are ordinarily designated.

To summarize the little we do know: the round-rod tradition appeared in the United States in the nineteenth century, probably (much like folk music and so many of our American folk traditions) as a hybrid of both the knowledge and skills of settlers from varying backgrounds and the availability of new materials. The round-rod type, never as widespread as the flat-splint type, has nearly disappeared because of the difficulty of preparing the materials, along with the other reasons so much traditional basketry is disappearing (little compensation for long hours, the availability of better-paying jobs, and the competition of a variety of cheaper or sturdier containers).

3. For a validity check on Dwight's ability to remember such an astounding number of old basketmakers, I interviewed the surviving relatives of old makers, interested local historians, and two former makers, Omen Beavers and Bruce Steele. Subsequently I realized that Dwight's recall, however faulty now on detail, is far more accurate than that of most others.

4. Dwight refers here to Stephenson, *Basketry in the Southern Appalachian Mountains,* 6–8, nos. 5 and 6.

7. Using Nature's Bounty

1. See Verni Greenfield, *Making Do or Making Art: A Study of American Recycling* (Ann Arbor, Mich.: UMI Research Press, 1985), who demonstrates that recycling is not always a practical act spurred only by necessity.

2. For further reference, see Evon Zartman Vogt and Ray Hyman, *Water Witching, U.S.A.* (Chicago: University of Chicago Press, 1959); Kelleigh Nelson, "What? Where? Which? . . . Just Ask the Water Witch," *Country Living,* September 1987, 18–20.

3. Dwight's son Harold, who uses the book now, obligingly returned it for my perusal: Joseph E. Meyer, *The Herbalist* (n.p.: n.p., 1918; rev. ed. 1960).

4. This was in 1980. In autumn 1987 the price for ginseng was approximately $160–$180, or perhaps even more, according to Tom Lemaster at Lemaster Herbs and Metals in Londonderry (Ross County, Ohio): "I'd have t' see it; if it's nice, I'd pay more." In autumn 1988 the price was $220, because of shortages caused by the severe summer drought. LeMaster has a printed price sheet listing the various roots and herbs they buy ("Items must be CLEAN and DRY to bring full prices"), such as clean wild ginseng (no price listed, just "subject to change"); yellow root or goldenseal at $10.00 a pound: serpentaria or snake root at $8.00; wahoo root bark at $4.00; blood root at $3.00; blackberry root, blackberry root bark, slippery elm bark, rossed ("what is left after outer bark is scraped off. Herbs are the leaves and stems of plants"), rossed sassafras root bark, and lobelia at $2.00; may apple root at $1.50; rough sassafras root and pignet root at $.75; wahoo bush bark at $.50.

5. After turning off the tape recorder that day, I asked Dwight what medicines he'd used for the flu bug from which he was just recovering. (He'd been in bed for over two weeks.) He replied that he used Four-Way Cold Tablets and Dr. Sloan's Kidney Pills: "A lot of people think you don't need that with the flu, but your kidneys *are* involved. Drink a lot of water and take those pills, and that will help flush that out."

6. Actually, Dwight understated the effect of tasting a Jack-in-the-pulpit root or fruit. The plant forms "needlelike crystals of calcium oxalate, particularly in the rhizome, which if taken into the mouth become embedded in the mucous membranes and provoke intense irritation and a burning sensation." It is generally believed—and disputed—that it is not fatal, primarily because ingestion of more than the first mouthful rarely occurs, since the pain is compared to "eating a mouthful of needles" (John M. Kingsbury, *Poisonous Plants of the United States and Canada* [Englewood Cliffs, N.J.: Prentice-Hall, 1964], 472). My source for the reference, Emmanuel Rudolph, professor of botany at Ohio State University, related that in botany departments it has long been traditional—albeit cruel—to offer the "tasty" fruit to freshman students.

7. Dwight refers here to "tempering," a process of controlled softening which strengthens and adds resiliency to the metal. After the steel has been hardened with heat, it is cooled by rapid quenching in a brine bath, both steps requiring some degree of experimentation. See Alex W. Bealer, *The Art of Blacksmithing* (New York: Funk and Wagnalls, 1969), 149–55.

8. Recycling Nature's Bounty

1. I am indebted to Martha Potter Otto, curator of archaeology of the Ohio Historical Society, for her extensive help with the section on Indian artifacts.

2. *Atlatl*, or "throwing stick," is an Aztec word referring to an instrument which hooks onto the throwing end of a spear, allowing hunters to hurl their spears with much greater force and power. It has been used all over the world by Eskimos, Australian aborigines, and Indians. Used by the Archaic

Indians in Ohio, ca. 8000–500 B.C., it suffered a decline in popularity in Adena times, ca. 800 B.C.–A.D. 1000. The main part of an atlatl was made from wood and so would probably deteriorate. However, the use of antler handles and hooks, along with stone weights, was a later improvement, so these could have been preserved and subsequently found. Martha Potter Otto, personal communication, 28 August 1985.

3. Raymond Baby was the curator of archaeology for the Ohio Historical Society from 1948 to 1974. Harley Glenn was at one time president of the Archaeological Society of Ohio, an association of amateur archaeologists.

4. Dwight refers here to a worked hole in the sandstone floor of a nearby cave. There are at least two in the area, referred to in local tradition as "Indian grinding mills," or "corn-grinding holes" (sometimes "hominy holes" in other areas). Chipped out of the floor of caves, they are approximately five or six inches wide and six inches deep, cylindrical-shaped holes, in which Indians hunting and traveling in the area are said to have ground their corn. (Otto agreed that this could well be the case. It is known that the Indians used long, narrow grooves in the sandstone rock outcroppings there for polishing the bit ends of their axes. However, she continued, some of the holes are deep and narrow, and it is difficult to see how they could have had any such utilitarian purpose as grinding.)

5. Presumably Dr. Frank Soday, an employee of the Skelly Oil Company in Tulsa, Oklahoma, who was mentioned in Olaf Prufer, *The McGraw Site: A Study in Hopewellian Dynamics* (Cleveland: Cleveland Museum of Natural History, 1964), 8. See also Frank Soday and Mark Seeman, "The Russell Brown Mounds: Three Hopewell Mounds in Ross County," *Mid-Continental Journal of Archaeology* 5 (1980): 73–116, based on Soday's excavations in the 1960s. References from Otto.

6. Dwight's pronunciation of *Adena*. The Adena Indians lived mainly in central and southern Ohio, ca. 800 B.C. to A.D. 100. They are particularly known for their mounds built over burial sites, as well as for the earliest pottery in the Ohio area, and distinctive art styles. For further reference, see Don Dragoo, "Mounds for the Dead: An Analysis of the Adena Culture," *Annuals of the Carnegie Museum* 37 (1963). Reference from Otto.

Conclusion: A Weaving Together

1. Also true for Philip Simmons, in Vlach, *Charleston Blacksmith,* 9, as well as for the artists in Ferris, *Local Color,* xvii–xviii.

2. See Jones, 68–74, for amplification of the tension between conservative and innovative behavior.

3. For elaboration of ethnocentrism in our depictions of "beauty" (and "art"), see Robert Plant Armstrong, *The Affecting Presence* (Urbana: University of Illinois Press, 1971), 10–11.

4. See also the Lake Erie fishermen's similar sentiments about their work, in Patrick Mullen and Timothy Lloyd, *Work and Identity: Tradition Among Lake Erie Commercial Fishermen* (Urbana: University of Illinois Press, 1989).

5. For a treatise on the role of creativity in processing grief, see Jones,

Hand Made Object. See also Bronner, "Carvers mark pain and sorrow also . . . . the carvers can block out troubles and also think and feel more deeply" (*Chain Carvers,* 69).

6. Omen Beavers, interview with author, South Perry, Ohio, 3 February 1986. Lanier Meaders, in Rinzler and Sayers, *The Meaders Family,* 43. Roger Morigi, in Marjorie Hunt, "'Born into the Stone': Carvers at the Washington Cathedral," in *Folklife Annual,* ed. Alan Jabbour and James Hardin (Washington, D.C.: Library of Congress, 1985), 134. Elwood West, in Ostrofsky, "Aesthetics of Basket Making," 14.

7. I am indebted to Claire Farrer for introducing me to the concept of metaphor in other than linguistic applications: she used children's play as visual metaphor giving access to culture specific patterns of communication, in "Play and Inter-Ethnic Communication: A Practical Ethnography of the Mescalero Apache" (Ph.D. diss., University of Texas, 1977). See also Judith Shulimson, "The Quilt as a Visual Metaphor" (Paper presented at the annual meeting of the American Folklore Society, Minneapolis, 17 October 1982).

Terence Hawkes used the overt/covert description of metaphor in *Metaphor* (London: Methuen, 1972), 60. Robert Plant Armstrong spoke of metaphor as a "miraculous process," in *The Affecting Presence,* 57. Dwight's basket is not an "affecting presence" in Armstrong's definition, because it was not made with the intent of creating a potent, affectively powerful object. But Armstrong's discussions expanded and informed my own thinking on this complex subject, especially on using metaphor to designate a process not characteristic solely of literature.

J. David Sapir believed metaphor basic to creative thought, quoting Ortega y Gasset's elegant cosmological definition: "an instrument necessary for the act of creation, which God forgetfully left . . . in the inside of one of his creatures, as an absent-minded surgeon sews up one of his instruments in the belly of his patient" ("The Anatomy of Metaphor," in *The Social Use of Metaphor: Essays on the Anthropology of Rhetoric,* ed. J. David Sapir and J. Christopher Crocker [Philadelphia: University of Pennsylvania Press, 1977], 32).

8. Claude Lévi-Strauss first posited metaphor as culturally determined, in *The Savage Mind* (Chicago: University of Chicago Press, 1966). See also James W. Fernandez, "The Mission of Metaphor in Expressive Culture," *Current Anthropology* 15 (1974): 119–45; Stanley Brandes, *Metaphors of Masculinity: Sex and Status in Andalusian Folklore* (Philadelphia: University of Pennsylvania Press, 1980), 8, 9.

See also William Bascom, who posited one of folklore's functions as that of validating culture, justifying its rituals and institutions; "The Four Functions of Folklore," in *The Study of Folklore,* ed. Alan Dundes (Englewood Cliffs, N.J.: Prentice-Hall, 1965), 292.

9. Others have experienced this pull of tradition in their crafts. Before his death, Ott Moore (a flat-splint basketmaker in Adams County, Ohio) still wove the bottom of his baskets on the floor, as he'd learned from his mother, in spite of the difficulty of working on his elbows and knees; interview with the author, August 1980. In making the top portion of a churn,

the potter Lanier Meaders explained that he made the top, then cut it off and set it aside for use later, a habit he got into watching his father forty years ago. "His left arm [was] crippled . . . and he couldn't reach the bottom. But mine's not broke, and it's long enough to reach the bottom, but I just got in the habit of doing it. And I don't see any reason to change now" (Rinzler and Sayers, *The Meaders Family*, 137).

For interesting commentary on the pull tradition still has in the dominant culture today, see, for example, Alan Dundes, ed., *Every Man His Way: Readings in Cultural Anthropology* (Englewood Cliffs, N.J.: Prentice-Hall, 1968), especially the section "The Anthropologist Looks at His Own Culture," 381–438; Jan Brunvand, *The Study of American Folklore*, 2d ed. (New York: Norton, 1978); Barre Toelken, *The Dynamics of Folklore* (Boston: Houghton Mifflin, 1979); Richard M. Dorson, ed., *Handbook of American Folklore* (Bloomington: Indiana University Press, 1983); Elaine Katz, *Folklore for the Time of Your Life* (Birmingham: Oxmoor House, 1978).

10. Kenneth L. Ames, *Beyond Necessity: Art in the Folk Tradition* (Winterthur, Del.: Norton for the Winterthur Museum, 1977), 27–31.

11. Clifford Geertz, *The Interpretation of Cultures* (New York: Basic, 1973), 30.

12. Robert Penn Warren, in his foreword to *Local Color,* by Ferris, xi.

13. For an excellent, provocative book on the interplay of life cycle, aging, and creativity, see Mary Hufford, Marjorie Hunt, and Steven Zeitlin, *The Grand Generation: Memory, Mastery, Legacy* (Seattle: University of Washington Press for the Smithsonian Institution Traveling Exhibition Service and Office of Folklife Programs, 1987).

See, for example, a description of the positive side of aging showcased in the exhibit "Older Cleveland Folk Artists," *Ohio Humanities* 7 (Spring 1984): 2.

For further information on folk artists and aging, see two paper presentations: Simon J. Bronner, "Folk Art and Aging in Historical Perspective"; and C. Kurt Dewhurst and Marsha MacDowell, "Teaching Old Folks Old Arts: The Place of Folk Arts in Programs for the Elderly" (Papers presented at the annual meeting of the American Folklore Society, Cincinnati, October 1985).

For those wishing to pursue the topic of aging, useful anthropological works are, for example, Barbara Myerhoff, *Number Our Days* (New York: Dutton, 1978); and David I. Kertzer and Jennie Keith, eds., *Age and Anthropological Theory* (Ithaca, N.Y.: Cornell University Press, 1984).

14. Archie Green, "Marcus Daly Enters Heaven," *Speculator* 1 (Winter 1984): 29, 31–32.

15. Alan Jabbour discussed "cultural custodianship" in *Folklife Center News* 7 (July–September 1984): 2–3.

"Chaque fois qu'un vieillard meurt en Afrique, c'est la bibliothèque d'Alexandrie que brule," was cited by the French ethnocinematographer Jean Rouch at a session on urgent anthropology, Ninth International Congress of Anthropological and Ethnographic Sciences, Chicago, 5 September 1973; quoted in Rinzler and Sayers, *The Meaders Family*, 17–18.

Works Consulted

Allen, Barbara, and Lynwood Montell. *From Memory to History: Using Oral Sources in Local Historical Research.* Nashville: American Association for State and Local History, 1981.

Alvey, R. Gerald. *Dulcimer Maker: The Craft of Homer Ledford.* Lexington: University Press of Kentucky, 1984.

Ames, Kenneth L. *Beyond Necessity: Art in the Folk Tradition.* Winterthur, Del.: Norton for the Henry Francis du Pont Winterthur Museum, 1977.

Armstrong, Robert Plant. *The Affecting Presence.* Urbana: University of Illinois Press, 1971.

Bascom, William. "The Four Functions of Folklore." In *The Study of Folklore,* edited by Alan Dundes, 279–98. Englewood Cliffs, N.J.: Prentice-Hall, 1965.

Baum, Willa K. *Transcribing and Editing Oral History.* Nashville: American Association for State and Local History, 1977.

Bauman, Richard. *Story, Performance, and Event: Contextual Studies of Oral Narrative.* Cambridge, England: Cambridge University Press, 1986.

Bealer, Alex W. *The Art of Blacksmithing.* New York: Funk and Wagnalls, 1969.

Berger, John. *Ways of Seeing.* London: Penguin, 1972.

Brandes, Stanley. *Metaphors of Masculinity: Sex and Status in Andalusian Folklore.* Philadelphia: University of Pennsylvania Press, 1980.

Britton, Nathaniel Lord, and Addison Brown. *An Illustrated Flora of the Northern United States, Canada, and the British Possessions.* Vols. 1–3. New York: Scribner's, 1913. Reprint. *An Illustrated Flora of the Northern United States and Canada.* Vols. 1–3. New York: Dover, 1970.

Brockman, C. Frank. *Trees of North America.* New York: Western, 1968.

Bronner, Simon J. *Chain Carvers: Old Men Crafting Meaning.* Lexington: University Press of Kentucky, 1985.

———. "Folk Art and Aging in Historical Perspective." Paper presented at the annual meeting of the American Folklore Society, Cincinnati, October 1985.

———. *Grasping Things: Folk Material Culture and Mass Society in America.* Lexington: University Press of Kentucky, 1986.

Brown, James Seay, Jr. *Up Before Daylight: Life Histories from the Alabama Writers Project.* University: University of Alabama Press, 1982.

Brown, Jim. "Zen and the Art of Basketry." Student paper, Western Kentucky University, 1977.

Brunvand, Jan. *The Study of American Folklore.* 2d ed. New York: Norton, 1978.

Carman, J. Ernest. *The Geologic Interpretation of Scenic Features in Ohio.* Ohio Geological Survey Reprint Series 3. Columbus: Ohio Geological Survey, 1972.

Carpenter, Inta Gale. *"Introspective Accounts of the Field Experience: A Bibliographic Essay." Folklore Forum* 11 (Winter 1978): 191–219.

Cogswell, Roby. "Folk Arts, Outside Markets, and Exploitation of the Folk in Kentucky's Lincoln Trail District." Paper presented at the annual meeting of the Great Lakes American Studies Association, Oxford, Ohio, 9 April 1983.

Crampton, Charles. *The Junior Basketmaker.* 16th ed. Leicester, England: Dryad Press, 1972.

Crawford, Jean. *Jugtown Pottery: History and Design.* Winston-Salem, N.C.: Blair, 1964.

Davis, Gerald L. "Afro-American Coil Basketry in Charleston County, South Carolina: Affective Characteristics of an Artistic Craft in a Social Context." In *American Folklife,* edited by Don Yoder, 151–84. Austin: University of Texas Press, 1976.

Dewhurst, C. Kurt, and Marsha MacDowell. "Teaching Old Folks Old Arts: The Place of Folk Arts in Programs for the Elderly." Paper presented at the annual meeting of the American Folklore Society, Cincinnati, October 1985.

Dorson, Richard M. *Buying the Wind.* Chicago: University of Chicago Press, 1964.

———. Introduction to *Folklore and Folklife,* edited by Richard M. Dorson, 1–50. Chicago: University of Chicago Press, 1975.

———, ed. *Handbook of American Folklore.* Bloomington: Indiana University Press, 1983.

Dragoo, Don. "Mounds for the Dead: An Analysis of the Adena Culture." *Annuals of the Carnegie Museum* 37 (1963).

Dundes, Alan, ed. *Every Man His Way: Readings in Cultural Anthropology.* Englewood Cliffs, N.J.: Prentice-Hall, 1968.

Edgerton, Robert B., and L. L. Langness. *Methods and Styles in the Study of Culture.* San Francisco: Chandler and Sharp, 1974.

Falconer, John. "Agricultural Changes." In *Ohio in the Twentieth Century,* compiled by Harlow Lindley, 120–34. Vol. 6 of *The History of the State of Ohio,* edited by Carl Wittke. Columbus: Ohio State Archaeological and Historical Society, 1942.

Farrer, Claire. "Play and Inter-Ethnic Communication: A Practical Ethnography of the Mescalero Apache." Ph.D. dissertation, University of Texas, 1977.

Fernandez, James W. "The Mission of Metaphor in Expressive Culture." *Current Anthropology* 15 (1974): 119–45.

Ferris, William. *Local Color: A Sense of Place in Folk Art.* Edited by Brenda McCallum. New York: McGraw-Hill, 1982.

Fess, Simeon D. *Ohio: A Four-Volume Reference Library.* Chicago: Lewis, 1937.

Fine, Elizabeth C. *The Folklore Text: From Performance to Print.* Bloomington: Indiana University Press, 1984.

Geertz, Clifford. *The Interpretation of Cultures.* New York: Basic, 1973.

Georges, Robert A., and Michael Owen Jones. *People Studying People: The Human Element in Fieldwork.* Berkeley and Los Angeles: University of California Press, 1980.

Glassie, Henry. "William Houck, Maker of Pounded Ash Pack-Baskets." *Keystone Folklore Quarterly* 12 (Spring 1967): 23–54.

———. *Passing the Time in Ballymenone: Culture and History of an Ulster Community.* Philadelphia: University of Pennsylvania Press, 1982.

Glazer, Nathan. "The Universalisation of Ethnicity." *Encounter* 44 (February 1975): 8–17.

Gordon, Francis. "Early History of Hocking County." M.A. thesis, Ohio State University, 1940.

Gordon, Milton. *Assimilation in American Life: The Role of Race, Religion, and National Origins.* New York: Oxford University Press, 1964.

Green, Archie. *Only a Miner.* Urbana: University of Illinois Press, 1972.

———. "Marcus Daly Enters Heaven." *Speculator* 1 (Winter 1984): 26–33.

Greenfield, Vernie. *Making Do or Making Art: A Study of American Recycling.* Ann Arbor, Mich.: UMI Research Press, 1985.

Hall, Debbie. "Preparing Timber for Basketmaking." Student paper, Western Kentucky University, 1977.

Harvey, Virginia. *Techniques of Basketry.* New York: Van Nostrand Reinhold, 1974.

Harzoff, Elizabeth. "The Long-Distance Basket Trade." Student paper, Western Kentucky University, 1977.

Havighurst, Walter. *Ohio: A Bicentennial History.* New York: Norton, 1976.

Hawkes, Terence. *Metaphor.* London: Methuen, 1972.

Herskovits, Melville. *Cultural Relativism: Perspectives in Cultural Pluralism.* New York: Random House, 1972.

Heseltine, Alastair. *Baskets and Basketmaking.* Aylesbury, England: Shire, 1982.

History of Hocking Valley, Ohio. Chicago: Interstate, 1883.

Hitchings, Bradley. "Finding Folk Art with a Future." *Business Week,* 10 June 1985, 126–30.

Howard, Michael C. *Contemporary Cultural Anthropology.* Boston: Little, Brown, 1986.

Howe, Henry. *Historical Collections of Ohio.* Vol. 1. Cincinnati: Krehbiel, 1888, 1908.

Hufford, Mary, Marjorie Hunt, and Steven Zeitlin. *The Grand Generation: Memory, Mastery, Legacy.* Seattle: University of Washington Press for the Smithsonian Institution Traveling Exhibition Service and Office of Folklife Programs, 1987.

Hunt, Marjorie. "'Born into the Stone': Carvers at the Washington Cathedral." In *Folklife Annual,* edited by Alan Jabbour and James Hardin, 120–41. Washington, D.C.: Library of Congress, 1985.

Irwin, John Rice. *Baskets and Basket Makers in Southern Appalachia.* Exton, Pa.: Schiffer, 1982.

———. *Alex Stewart: Portrait of a Pioneer.* West Chester, Pa.: Schiffer, 1985.

Ives, Edward D. "Common-Man Biography: Some Notes by the Way." In *Folklore Today,* edited by Linda Dégh, Henry Glassie, and Felix Oinas, 251–64. Bloomington: Indiana University Press, 1976.

———. *The Tape-Recorded Interview: A Manual for Field Workers in Folklore and Oral History.* Rev. ed. Knoxville: University of Tennessee Press, 1980.

Jabbour, Alan. "Director's Column." *Folklife Center News* 7 (July–September 1984): 2–3.

James, George Wharton. *Indian Basketry.* 1909. Reprint. New York: Dover, 1972.

Jefferson, Gail. "Transcript Notation." In *Structures of Social Action: Studies in Conversation Analysis,* edited by J. Maxwell Atkinson and John Heritage, ix–xvi. Cambridge, England: Cambridge University Press, 1984.

Jones, Loyal. *Minstrel of the Appalachians: The Story of Bascom Lamar Lunsford.* Boone, N.C.: Appalachian Consortium Press, 1984.

Jones, Michael Owen. *The Hand Made Object and Its Maker.* Berkeley and Los Angeles: University of California Press, 1975.

Jordan, Philip D. *Ohio Comes of Age: 1873–1900.* Vol. 5 of *The History of the State of Ohio,* edited by Carl Wittke. Columbus: Ohio Archaeological and Historical Society, 1943.

Joyce, Rosemary O. "Dwight Stump, Traditional Basketweaver of Southeastern Ohio." Paper presented at the annual meeting of the American Folklore Society, Salt Lake City, 12 October 1978.

———. *The Art of Basketmaking.* Washington, D.C.: American Folklife Center, 1982.

———. *A Woman's Place: The Life History of a Rural Ohio Grandmother.* Columbus: Ohio State University Press, 1983.

———. "Toward an Analysis of Personal Narrative." *Papers in Comparative Studies* 2 (1983): 119–35.

———. "'Fame Don't Make the Sun Any Cooler': Traditional Artists and the Marketplace." In *Folk Art and Art Worlds,* edited by John Michael Vlach and Simon J. Bronner, 225–41. Ann Arbor, Mich.: UMI Research Press, 1986.

———. "To Market, to Market, to *Sell* Some Folk Art: Introduction." *New York Folklore* 12 (Winter–Spring 1986): 43–47.

Katz, Elaine. *Folklore for the Time of Your Life.* Birmingham: Oxmoor House, 1978.

Kertzer, David I., and Jennie Keith, eds. *Age and Anthropological Theory.* Ithaca, N.Y.: Cornell University Press, 1984.

Kingsbury, John M. *Poisonous Plants of the United States and Canada.* Englewood Cliffs, N.J.: Prentice-Hall, 1964.

Kluckhohn, Clyde. "The Personal Document in Anthropological Science." In *The Use of Personal Documents in History, Anthropology, and Sociology,* edited by Louis Gottschalk, Clyde Kluckhohn, and Robert Angell, 77–173. New York: Social Science Research Council, 1945.

Knepper, George W. *An Ohio Portrait.* Columbus: Ohio Historical Society, 1976.

Korn, Michael. "Report on Basketry in the Mammoth Cave Area in South-Central Kentucky." Student paper, Western Kentucky University, 1977.

Langness, L. L., and Gelya Frank. *Lives: An Anthropological Approach to Biography*. Novato, Calif.: Chandler and Sharp, 1981.

Lasansky, Jeannette. *Willow, Oak, and Rye: Basket Traditions in Pennsylvania*. University Park: Pennsylvania State University Press, 1979.

Law, Rachel Nash, and Cynthia W. Taylor. "Handing Down the Basket: Appalachian White Oak Basketry." Manuscript.

Lévi-Strauss, Claude. *The Savage Mind*. Chicago: University of Chicago Press, 1966.

Ludden, Keith. "Ten-Cent Coffee and Twenty-Cent Baskets: Local Basket Trade in the Mammoth Cave Area." Student paper, Western Kentucky University, 1977.

Marshall, Howard Wight. "Mr. Westfall's Baskets: Traditional Craftmanship in Northcentral Missouri." *Mid-South Folklore* 2 (Summer 1974): 43–60. Reprinted in *Readings in American Folklore,* edited by Jan Harold Brunvand, 168–91. New York: Norton, 1979.

Martin-Perdue, Nancy J. "Case Study: On Eaton's Trail: A Genealogical Study of Virginia Basket Makers." In *Traditional Craftsmanship in America: A Diagnostic Report,* edited by Charles Camp, 79–100. Washington, D.C.: National Council for the Traditional Arts, 1983.

Metcalf, Eugene W. "Black Art, Folk Art, and Social Control." *Winterthur Portfolio* (1983): 271–89.

———. "The Politics of the Past and the Myth of American Folk Art History." In *Folk Art and Art Worlds,* edited by John Michael Vlach and Simon J. Bronner, 27–50. Ann Arbor, Mich.: UMI Research Press, 1986.

Meyer, Joseph E. *The Herbalist*. N.p.: N.p., 1918.

Montell, Lynwood. *The Saga of Coe Ridge*. Knoxville: University of Tennessee Press, 1970.

Mullen, Patrick, and Timothy Lloyd. *Work and Identity: Tradition Among Lake Erie Commercial Fishermen*. Urbana: University of Illinois Press, 1989.

Myerhoff, Barbara. *Number Our Days*. New York: Dutton, 1978.

Nelson, Kelleigh. "What? Where? Which? . . . Just Ask the Water Witch." *Country Living,* September 1987, 18–20.

Ohio Department of Development, Community Development Division. *Ohio Appalachian Development Plan*. Columbus: Department of Economic and Community Development, 1974.

———. *Profiles of Change, Ohio Appalachia: 1965–1984*. Columbus: Department of Economic and Community Development, 1985.

Ohio Writers Program, Works Progress Administration. *The Ohio Guide*. New York: Oxford University Press, 1940.

"Older Cleveland Folk Artists." *Ohio Humanities* 7 (Spring 1984): 2.

Ostrofsky, Martin. "Aesthetics of Basket Making in the Mammoth Cave Area of Kentucky." Student paper, Western Kentucky University, 1977.

Payton, Lyndell. "The Process of Basketmaking: A Personal Interview with Mr. George Childress." Student paper, Western Kentucky University, 1977.

Peterson, Roger Troy, and Margaret McKinney. *A Field Guide to Wild-*

flowers of Northeastern and North-Central North America. Boston: Houghton Mifflin, 1968.

Preston, Dennis. "'Ritin' Fowklower Daun 'Rong': Folklorists' Failure in Phonology." *Journal of American Folklore* 95 (July–September 1982): 304–26.

Prufer, Olaf. *The McGraw Site: A Study in Hopewellian Dynamics.* Cleveland: Cleveland Museum of Natural History, 1964.

Randall, Emilius O., and Daniel J. Ryan. *History of Ohio: The Rise and Progress of an American State.* Vol. 5. New York: Century History, 1912.

Rinzler, Ralph, and Robert Sayers. *The Meaders Family, North Georgia Potters.* Washington, D.C.: Smithsonian Institution Press, 1980.

Roseboom, Eugene H. *The Civil War Era: 1850–1873.* Vol. 4 of *The History of the State of Ohio,* edited by Carl Wittke. Columbus: Ohio State Archaeological and Historical Society, 1944.

Roseboom, Eugene H., and Francis P. Weisenburger. *A History of Ohio.* Columbus: Ohio Historical Society, 1976.

Rosengarten, Theodore. *Tombee: Portrait of a Cotton Planter.* New York: Morrow, 1986.

Rossbach, Ed. *Baskets as Textile Arts.* New York: Van Nostrand Reinhold, 1973.

Sapir, J. David. "The Anatomy of Metaphor." In *The Social Use of Metaphor: Essays on the Anthropology of Rhetoric,* edited by J. David Sapir and J. Christopher Crocker, 3–32. Philadelphia: University of Pennsylvania Press, 1977.

Shulimson, Judith. "The Quilt as a Visual Metaphor." Paper presented at the annual meeting of the American Folklore Society, Minneapolis, 17 October 1982.

Shuman, Amy. *Story Telling Rights: The Uses of Oral and Written Texts by Urban Adolescents.* Cambridge, England: Cambridge University Press, 1986.

Smith, Thomas H. *The Mapping of Ohio.* Kent, Ohio: Kent State University Press, 1977.

Soday, Frank, and Mark Seeman. "The Russell Brown Mounds: Three Hopewell Mounds in Ross County." *Mid-Continental Journal of Archaeology* 5 (1980): 73–116.

Stephenson, Sue. *Basketry in the Southern Appalachian Mountains.* New York: Van Nostrand Reinhold, 1977.

Teleki, Gloria Roth. *Baskets of Rural America.* New York: Dutton, 1975.

———. *Collecting Traditional American Basketry.* New York: Dutton, 1979.

Teske, Robert. "'Crafts Assistance Programs' and Traditional Crafts." *New York Folklore* 12 (Winter–Spring 1986): 75–83.

Toelken, Barre. *The Dynamics of Folklore.* Boston: Houghton Mifflin, 1979.

Vlach, John Michael. *Charleston Blacksmith: The Work of Philip Simmons.* Athens: University of Georgia Press, 1981.

———. "Commentary." *New York Folklore* 12 (Winter–Spring 1986): 88–89.

Vlach, John Michael, and Simon J. Bronner, eds. *Folk Art and Art Worlds.* Ann Arbor, Mich.: UMI Research Press, 1986.

Vogt, Evan Zartman, and Ray Hyman. *Water Witching, U.S.A.* Chicago: University of Chicago Press, 1959.

Warren, Robert P. "Foreword." In *Local Color: A Sense of Place in Folk Art,* by William Ferris, edited by Brenda McCallum, ix–xi. New York: McGraw-Hill, 1982.

Weed, John M. "Business—As Usual." In *Ohio in the Twentieth Century,* compiled by Harlow Lindley, 159–97. Vol. 6 of *The History of the State of Ohio,* edited by Carl Wittke. Columbus: Ohio Archaeological and Historical Society, 1942.

Whisnant, David. *All That Is Native and Fine: The Politics of Culture in an American Region.* Chapel Hill: University of North Carolina Press, 1983.

Whisnant, Susan S. "Traditional Craftsmanship in America: A Bibliography of Published Sources." In *Traditional Craftsmanship in America: A Diagnostic Report,* edited by Charles Camp, 105–27. Washington, D.C.: National Council for the Traditional Arts, 1983.

Wigginton, Eliot. *Foxfire.* Vols. 1–9. Garden City, N.Y.: Doubleday, Anchor Press, 1972–86.

Wright, Dorothy. *The Complete Book of Baskets and Basketry.* Newton Abbott, England: David and Charles, 1983.

Young, Kathryn Galloway. *Tale Worlds and Story Realms.* Dordrecht, The Netherlands: Martinus Nijhoff, 1987.

Index